T0214223

Lecture Notes in Computer Science

Lecture Notes in Artificial Intelligence   13779

Founding Editor

Jörg Siekmann

Series Editors

Randy Goebel, *University of Alberta, Edmonton, Canada*
Wolfgang Wahlster, *DFKI, Berlin, Germany*
Zhi-Hua Zhou, *Nanjing University, Nanjing, China*

The series Lecture Notes in Artificial Intelligence (LNAI) was established in 1988 as a topical subseries of LNCS devoted to artificial intelligence.

The series publishes state-of-the-art research results at a high level. As with the LNCS mother series, the mission of the series is to serve the international R & D community by providing an invaluable service, mainly focused on the publication of conference and workshop proceedings and postproceedings.

Stephen H. Muggleton ·
Alireza Tamaddoni-Nezhad

Editors

Inductive Logic Programming

31st International Conference, ILP 2022
Windsor Great Park, UK, September 28–30, 2022
Proceedings

 Springer

Editors
Stephen H. Muggleton
Imperial College London
London, UK

Alireza Tamaddoni-Nezhad
University of Surrey
Guildford, UK

ISSN 0302-9743 ISSN 1611-3349 (electronic)
Lecture Notes in Artificial Intelligence
ISBN 978-3-031-55629-6 ISBN 978-3-031-55630-2 (eBook)
https://doi.org/10.1007/978-3-031-55630-2

LNCS Sublibrary: SL7 – Artificial Intelligence

This Springer imprint is published by the registered company Springer Nature Switzerland AG
The registered company address is: Gewerbestrasse 11, 6330 Cham, Switzerland

Paper in this product is recyclable.

Preface

The 31st International Conference on Inductive Logic Programming (ILP 2022) was held at Cumberland Lodge, Windsor Great Park, UK, from 28 to 30 September 2022. Inductive Logic Programming (ILP) is a subfield of machine learning, focusing on learning logical representations from relational data. The ILP conference series, started in 1991, is the premier international forum for learning from structured or semi-structured relational data, multi-relational learning and data mining. Originally focusing on the induction of logic programs, over the years it has expanded its research horizon significantly, welcoming contributions to all aspects of learning in logic, statistical relational learning, graph and tree mining, learning in other (non-propositional) logic-based knowledge representation frameworks, and exploring intersections with statistical learning and other probabilistic approaches.

The ILP 2022 conference was part of the 2nd International Joint Conference on Learning & Reasoning (IJCLR 2022) and was co-located with the 16th International Workshop on Neural-Symbolic Learning and Reasoning (NeSy 2022), the 11th International Workshop on Approaches and Applications of Inductive Programming (AAIP 2022), and the 3rd International Workshop on Human-Like Computing (HLC 2022). IJCLR 2022 aimed to bring together researchers and practitioners working on various aspects of learning & reasoning, via presentation of cutting-edge research on topics of special interest to the participating conferences/workshops. In addition to each event's individual programs, held in parallel, IJCLR 2022 aimed to promote collaboration and cross-fertilization between different approaches and methodologies for integrating learning & reasoning, via joint plenary keynotes/invited talks, joint journal paper sessions, poster sessions and panel discussions.

The format of the proceedings for the 31st International Conference on Inductive Logic Programming (ILP 2022) follows a similar format to that of previous conferences and is particularly close to that used in ILP 2019 and ILP 2021. The ILP 2022 call for papers solicited several types of submissions, including regular conference papers, late-breaking abstracts, recently published papers and journal track papers submitted to the Machine Learning Journal Special Issue on Learning & Reasoning. This volume contains ten accepted regular conference papers selected from twenty-six in-area submissions considered for ILP 2022. Each paper was reviewed by three reviewers from the ILP 2022 Program Committee, and accepted papers were presented at the conference. In addition, the best theory and the best application ILP paper prizes were awarded to eligible papers with the highest average reviewers' scores. Apart from the regular papers from the ILP conference track, this volume also includes one accepted paper from the AAIP 2022 workshop that was highly relevant to ILP and was also presented at a joint ILP/AAIP session.

The papers in the proceedings represent the diversity and vitality in current ILP research, including statistical relational learning, transfer learning, scientific reasoning, learning temporal models, synthesis and planning, and argumentation and language. In addition to the many technical paper presentations, the plenary keynotes/invited talks at IJCLR 2022 were given by a distinguished group of AI researchers. The ILP invited talk was given by Véronique Ventos, Head of Research and Co-founder of NukkAI.

We would like to express our gratitude to the members of the IJCLR 2022 Steering Committee, the ILP 2022 Program Committee, the reviewers, and all the authors who contributed to the IJCLR/ILP 2022 conference. We gratefully acknowledge the contributions from the IJCLR/ILP 2022 sponsors, particularly Springer, Machine Learning Journal, and Google DeepMind. Finally, we would like to thank the many individuals involved in the preparation of the conference, including the website and physical and virtual organisation of the conference. These individuals include Lun Ai, Céline Hocquette, Nikos Katzouris, Ernesto Jiménez-Ruiz and Stassa Patsantzis. Special thanks are also due to Bridget Gundry who supported various aspects of the conference, including the registration and local arrangements.

March 2023   Stephen H. Muggleton
                                                             Alireza Tamaddoni-Nezhad

Organization

Program Chairs

Stephen Muggleton   Imperial College London, UK
Alireza Tamaddoni-Nezhad University of Surrey, UK

Program Committee

Lun Ai	Imperial College London, UK
Alexander Artikis	NCSR "Demokritos", Greece
Michael Bain	University of New South Wales, Australia
Krysia Broda	Imperial College London, UK
William Cohen	Google AI, USA
Andrew Cropper	University of Oxford, UK
James Cussens	University of Bristol, UK
Wang-Zhou Dai	Nanjing University, China
Richard Evans	DeepMind, UK
Céline Hocquette	University of Oxford, UK
Katsumi Inoue	National Institute of Informatics, Japan
Dimitar Kazakov	University of York, UK
Nikos Katzouris	National Center for Scientific Research, Greece
Ross King	Chalmers University of Technology, Sweden
Nada Lavrač	Jožef Stefan Institute, Slovenia
Francesca Lisi	Università degli Studi di Bari Aldo Moro, Italy
Sriraam Natarajan	University of Texas at Dallas, USA
Aline Paes	Federal Fluminense University (UFF), Brazil
Stassa Patsantzis	Imperial College London, UK
Fabrizio Riguzzi	University of Ferrara, Italy
Celine Rouveirol	Université Paris 13, France
Alessandra Russo	Imperial College London, UK
Ashwin Srinivasan	Birla Institute of Technology & Science, India
Ute Schmid	University of Bamberg, Germany
Mikkel Schmidt	Technical University of Denmark, Denmark
Gerson Zaverucha	Federal University of Rio de Janeiro, Brazil
Filip Zelezny	Czech Technical University, Czech Republic

Organization

Contents

Learning the Parameters of Probabilistic Answer Set Programs

Damiano Azzolini[1](✉), Elena Bellodi[2], and Fabrizio Riguzzi[3]

[1] Dipartimento di Scienze dell'Ambiente e della Prevenzione, Università di Ferrara,
Ferrara, Italy
`damiano.azzolini@unife.it`
[2] Dipartimento di Ingegneria, Università di Ferrara, Ferrara, Italy
`elena.bellodi@unfe.it`
[3] Dipartimento di Matematica e Informatica, Università di Ferrara, Ferrara, Italy
`fabrizio.riguzzi@unife.it`

Abstract. Probabilistic Answer Set Programming (PASP) is a powerful formalism that allows to model uncertain scenarios with answer set programs. One of the possible semantics for PASP is the credal semantics, where a query is associated with a probability interval rather than a sharp probability value. In this paper, we extend the learning from interpretations task, usually considered for Probabilistic Logic Programming, to PASP: the goal is, given a set of (partial) interpretations, to learn the parameters of a PASP program such that the product of the lower bounds of the probability intervals of the interpretations is maximized. Experimental results show that the execution time of the algorithm is heavily dependent on the number of parameters rather than on the number of interpretations.

Keywords: Probabilistic Answer Set Programming · Parameter Learning · Statistical Relational Artificial Intelligence

1 Introduction

Probabilistic Answer Set Programming (PASP) [8,20] extends the capabilities of Answer Set Programming (ASP) [5] by introducing uncertain data representable with probabilistic facts. In traditional semantics for Probabilistic Logic Programming (PLP) [23], such as the Distribution Semantics [25], usually each world has a total well-founded model and thus a single answer set [29]. In the case of PASP, it is not guaranteed that every world has a unique answer set. Thus, there are two layers that must be considered: the worlds, identified by the choices made for the probabilistic facts, and the answer sets for every world. To handle this, we adopt here the credal semantics [6], that associates every query with a lower and upper probability bound, according to the number of models where the query is satisfied for a given world.

Parameter learning is a central topic in the field of Statistical Relational Artificial Intelligence (StarAI) [22]. Given a set of examples, the goal is to find a probability assignment to probabilistic facts such that the likelihood of the examples is maximized. There are two main types of parameter learning tasks: learning

S. H. Muggleton and A. Tamaddoni-Nezhad (Eds.): ILP 2022, LNAI 13779, pp. 1–14, 2024.
https://doi.org/10.1007/978-3-031-55630-2_1

from interpretations and learning from entailment. Both have been extensively studied in the context of PLP [4,16,26] but none of these algorithms works for PASP under the credal semantics.

In this paper, we adapt the learning from interpretations setting described in [16] and propose the first algorithm to perform parameter learning (learning the probabilities of probabilistic facts) in PASP: given a set of interpretations and a PASP program with unknown parameters, the goal is to set the values of the parameters such that the products of the lower probabilities of the interpretations is maximized.

The paper is structured as follows: in Sect. 2 we review some background concepts, in Sect. 3 we introduce our algorithm for parameter learning, that is tested in Sect. 4. Section 5 discusses some related work and Sect. 6 concludes the paper.

2   Background

We assume the reader is familiar with the basic concepts of Logic Programming, such as atoms, literal, clauses, etc. For a book on the topic see [19].

2.1   Answer Set Programming

In addition to the basic elements of Logic Programming, ASP also allows the definition of aggregate atoms [1] with the syntax $g_0 \circ_0 \#f\{e_1; \ldots; e_n\} \circ_1 g_1$ where g_0 and g_1 can be either constants or variables, f is an aggregate function symbol, and $\circ_0$ and $\circ_1$ are arithmetic comparison operators (that may be omitted). Every e_i has the structure $t_1, \ldots, t_l : E$ where E is a conjunction of literals and every t_i is a term with variables appearing in E. There are several aggregate function symbols, such as *count* or *sum*.

A *disjunctive rule*, or simply *rule* for short, is a rule with multiple heads, i.e.,

$$\underbrace{h_1; \ldots; h_m}_{\text{head}} \leftarrow \underbrace{b_1, \ldots, b_n}_{\text{body}}.$$

where each h_i is an atom and each b_i is a literal. While describing actual code, $\leftarrow$ is usually replaced with :-. The meaning is: "if all the literals in the body are true, then one of the heads h_i is true". We consider here only rules where variables in the head also appear in a positive literal in the body: these are called *safe* rules. An *integrity constraint* is a rule with no atoms in the head, a *fact* is a rule with only one atom in the head and no literals in the body. An answer set program is a set of rules. A rule is called *ground* when it does not contain variables. If a rule is not ground, we can ground it through a process called *grounding* that consists in replacing all the variables with constants in the program in all possible ways.

To illustrate the semantics of answer set programs, we need to introduce some additional concepts. The Herbrand base (B_P) of an answer set program

P is the set of all ground atoms that can be constructed using the symbols in the program. An *interpretation* I for P is such that $I \subseteq B_P$ and it satisfies a ground rule if at least one head atom is true in it when every literal in the body is true in it. An interpretation that satisfies all the groundings of all the rules of P is named *model*. Given a ground program P_g and an interpretation I, if we remove from P_g the rules in which a literal in the body is false in I we obtain the *reduct* [12] of P_g with respect to I. Finally, an *answer set* I for a program P is a minimal model (in terms of set inclusion) of the reduct of P_g with respect to I. With $AS(P)$ we denote the set of all the answer sets of P.

Consider the following example:

```
0{noise}1.
0{tired}1.
angry ; relaxed:- tired.
angry:- noise.
```

This program has 5 answer sets: $\{\}$, $\{$relaxed,tired$\}$, $\{$angry,tired$\}$, $\{$angry, noise$\}$, $\{$angry,noise,tired$\}$. The cautious consequences, i.e., the set of atoms that are present in every answer set, form an empty set, and the solutions projected [14] on the noise/0 and tired/0 atoms are $\{\}$, $\{$noise$\}$, $\{$tired$\}$ and $\{$noise,tired$\}$.

2.2 Probabilistic Logic Programming

Following the ProbLog [11] syntax, Probabilistic Logic Programming [10,23] allows the definition of *probabilistic facts* of the form

$$\Pi :: f$$

where f is an atom and $\Pi \in]0,1]$ is its probability. Intuitively, f is true with probability Π and it is false with probability $1 - \Pi$. If we consider the Distribution Semantics [25], an *atomic choice* indicates whether a grounding for a probabilistic fact f, denoted with $f\theta$ is selected or not. A set of atomic choices is called *composite choice* and if it contains an atomic choice for every grounding of every probabilistic fact is called *total composite choice* or *selection*. The probability of a composite choice κ is computed as:

$$P(\kappa) = \underbrace{\prod_{(f_i,\theta,1)\in\kappa} \Pi_i}_{\text{selected}} \cdot \underbrace{\prod_{(f_i,\theta,0)\in\kappa} (1 - \Pi_i)}_{\text{not selected}} \tag{1}$$

where with $(f_i, \theta, 1)$ we indicate that the grounding θ of f_i is selected and with $(f_i, \theta, 0)$ that it is not. We consider here only consistent sets of atomic choices, i.e., if $(f_i, \theta, 0) \in \kappa$ then $(f_i, \theta, 1) \notin \kappa$ and vice versa. A selection identifies a logic program called *world* composed by the rules of the program and the selected probabilistic facts. The probability of a world, $P(w)$, is given by the probability of the correspondent selection. The probabilities of all the worlds sum up to 1.

A query is a conjunction of ground literals, and its probability can be computed with the formula:

$$P(q) = \sum_{w \models q} P(w) \tag{2}$$

For example, if we consider the program

```
0.2::noise.
0.6::tired.
angry:- noise.
angry:- tired.
```

there are 2 probabilistic facts, noise and tired that identify $2^2 = 4$ worlds: w_1 where both probabilistic facts are false, with $P(w) = (1 - 0.2) \cdot (1 - 0.6) = 0.32$, w_2 where noise is true and tired is false, with $P(w_2) = 0.2 \cdot (1 - 0.6) = 0.08$, w_3 where noise is false and tired is true, with $P(w_3) = (1 - 0.2) \cdot 0.6 = 0.48$, and w_4 where both noise and tired are true, with $P(w_4) = 0.2 \cdot 0.6 = 0.12$. Note that $P(w_1) + P(w_2) + P(w_3) + P(w_4) = 0.32 + 0.08 + 0.48 + 0.12 = 1$. If we are interested in the probability of the query $q = $ angry, $P(q) = P(w_2) + P(w_3) + P(w_4) = 0.08 + 0.48 + 0.12 = 0.68$. For this example, every world has a unique answer set. However, if we consider an ASP program extended with probabilistic facts, this usually does not hold, and other semantics must be adopted.

2.3   Credal Semantics

As previously discussed, with the Distribution Semantics we can manage only programs with a unique answer set for every world. If this does not hold, we need to consider an alternative semantics, such as the credal semantics [6]. Under this semantics, a query q has a lower probability $\underline{P}(q)$ and an upper probability $\overline{P}(q)$, and thus is associated with a probability interval. A world contributes to the lower probability if the query is true in every answer set and contributes to the upper probability if the query is true in at least one answer set. Thus $\overline{P}(q) \geq \underline{P}(q)$. In formulas:

$$\overline{P}(q) = \underbrace{\sum_{w_i | \exists m \in AS(w_i),\ m \models q} P(w_i)}_{\text{query true in at least one answer set}} \tag{3}$$

$$\underline{P}(q) = \underbrace{\sum_{w_i | |AS(w_i)| > 0 \wedge \forall m \in AS(w_i),\ m \models q} P(w_i)}_{\text{query true in every answer set}} \tag{4}$$

Note that the credal semantics [6] is defined only for programs where all the worlds have at least one answer set. In fact, if a world w had no answer sets, $P(w)$ would neither contribute to the probability of the query nor to the probability of the negation of the query. If this happened, $\underline{P}(q) + \overline{P}(\neg q) < 1$, and there would be a loss of probability mass (with $\neg q$ we indicate the query $not\ q$, adopting negation as failure).

Example 1 *(Smokers)*. Consider the following example, adapted from [16].

```
smokes(Y) ; not_smokes(Y):- smokes(X), friend(X,Y).

:- #count{Y,X:smokes(X),friend(X,Y)} = F,
   #count{Y,X:smokes(X),friend(X,Y),smokes(Y)} = SF,
   10*SF < 4*F.

smokes(a).
smokes(c).
smokes(e).
```

The first disjunctive rule states that a person can either smoke or not smoke if he/she is a friend with a person that smokes. The constraint imposes that at least in the 40% of the pairs person-friend the friend smokes. Finally, we know for certain that a, c, and e smoke. Suppose that there are the following 5 probabilistic facts

```
0.5::friend(a,b).
0.5::friend(b,c).
0.5::friend(c,e).
0.5::friend(b,d).
0.5::friend(d,e).
```

With these values, the probability of the query smokes(b) lies in the range $[0.25, 0.5]$.

Also conditional queries are described by a lower and an upper probability bound: the upper conditional probability for a query q given evidence e is given by [7]

$$\overline{P}(q \mid e) = \frac{\overline{P}(q, e)}{\overline{P}(q, e) + \underline{P}(\neg q, e)} \tag{5}$$

If $\overline{P}(q, e) + \underline{P}(\neg q, e) = 0$ and $\overline{P}(\neg q, e) > 0$, $\overline{P}(q \mid e) = 0$. This value is undefined if both $\overline{P}(q, e)$ and $\overline{P}(\neg q, e)$ are 0.

Similarly, the formula for the lower conditional probability is

$$\underline{P}(q \mid e) = \frac{\underline{P}(q, e) \cdot}{\underline{P}(q, e) + \overline{P}(\neg q, e)} \tag{6}$$

If $\underline{P}(q, e) + \overline{P}(\neg q, e) = 0$ and $\overline{P}(q, e) > 0$, $\underline{P}(q \mid e) = 1$. As before, this value is undefined if both $\overline{P}(q, e)$ and $\overline{P}(\neg q, e)$ are 0.

3   Parameter Learning in PASP

To learn the parameters of PASP programs, we adapt the learning from interpretations settings described in [16].

A partial interpretation $I = \langle I^+, I^- \rangle$ is such that I^+ is the set of atoms that should be considered true and I^- is the set of atoms that should be considered false. A partial interpretation specifies the truth value of only some atoms. In [16], the authors define the probability of an interpretation I, $P(I)$, as the probability of the query $q_I = \bigwedge_{i^+ \in I^+} i^+ \bigwedge_{i^- \in I^-} not\ i^-$. We call q_I *interpretation query*.

Here we consider probabilistic answer set programs under the credal semantics so the probability of an interpretation is associated with a probability interval rather than a sharp probability value, since a world may have more than one answer set. Given a PASP program $\mathcal{P}(\Pi)$, where Π is the set of parameters that can be tuned, the lower probability of an interpretation I, $\underline{P}(I \mid \mathcal{P}(\Pi))$ is the sum of the probabilities of the worlds $w \in \mathcal{P}(\Pi)$ where all the literals of the interpretation query q_I are true (i.e., the interpretation query is true) in *all* the answer sets of w. Similarly, the upper probability of an interpretation I, $\overline{P}(I \mid \mathcal{P}(\Pi))$, is the sum of the probabilities of the worlds $w \in \mathcal{P}(\Pi)$ where the interpretation query q_I is true in *at least one* answer set of w. In formulas:

$$\overline{P}(I \mid \mathcal{P}(\Pi)) = \sum_{w \in \mathcal{P}(\Pi) \mid \exists m \in AS(w),\ m \models I} P(w) \tag{7}$$

$$\underline{P}(I \mid \mathcal{P}(\Pi)) = \sum_{w \in \mathcal{P}(\Pi) \mid \forall m \in AS(w),\ m \models I} P(w) \tag{8}$$

For example, if we consider the program shown in Example 1 with the probabilities of all the probabilistic facts set to 0.5, the partial interpretation $I = \langle \{\text{smokes(b)}, \text{smokes(c)}\}, \{\text{smokes(d)}\} \rangle$ has lower probability 0.125 and upper probability 0.5. This is computed by asking the query
smokes(b),smokes(c), not smokes(d).

To compute the parameters of a PASP program with partial interpretations, we adapt the algorithm presented in [16]. Here we consider a PASP program and a set of *ground* probabilistic facts of the form $\Pi :: f$ whose probabilities can be learned.

Definition 1 (Parameter Learning in probabilistic answer set programs). *Given a PASP $\mathcal{P}(\Pi)$ with a set of ground probabilistic facts f_i whose probabilities Π_i can be learned, and a set of (partial) interpretations $\mathcal{I}$, the goal is to find a probability assignment to the probabilistic facts such that the product of the lower probabilities of the partial interpretations is maximized, i.e., solve:*

$$\Pi^* = \arg\max_{\Pi} \underline{P}(\mathcal{I} \mid \mathcal{P}(\Pi)) = \arg\max_{\Pi} \prod_{I \in \mathcal{I}} \underline{P}(I \mid \mathcal{P}(\Pi)) \tag{9}$$

This is equivalent to maximize the sum of the log likelihood of the interpretations:

$$\Pi^* = \arg\max_{\Pi} \log(\underline{P}(\mathcal{I} \mid \mathcal{P}(\Pi))) = \arg\max_{\Pi} \sum_{I \in \mathcal{I}} \log(\underline{P}(I \mid \mathcal{P}(\Pi))) \tag{10}$$

To solve the parameter learning problem, we consider a scenario with partial observability, i.e., some atoms may be not observed, and adopt the Expectation

Maximization (EM) algorithm. The EM process consists in finding the expected value of the probabilistic facts given the interpretations and then updating the probability values accordingly. Since we consider ground probabilistic facts, in the expectation step we need to compute, for each probabilistic fact f_j,

$$\underline{\mathrm{E}}[f_{jk}] = \sum_{i=1}^{|\mathcal{I}|} \underline{\mathrm{P}}(f_{jk} \mid I_i) \tag{11}$$

where in f_{ik} $k \in \{0,1\}$ indicates whether it is true or false. In the maximization step each parameter Π_i is updated as

$$\Pi_j = \frac{\underline{\mathrm{E}}[f_{j1}]}{\underline{\mathrm{E}}[f_{j0}] + \underline{\mathrm{E}}[f_{j1}]} = \frac{\sum_{i=1}^{|\mathcal{I}|} \underline{\mathrm{P}}(f_j = \top \mid I_i)}{\sum_{i=1}^{|\mathcal{I}|} \underline{\mathrm{P}}(f_j = \bot \mid I_i) + \underline{\mathrm{P}}(f_j = \top \mid I_i)} \tag{12}$$

The whole pipeline is described in Algorithm 1. Function LEARNPA-RAMETERSPASP works as follows: first, we create two data structures (*LLComputations* and *CondComputations*) to store the computations made during the main loop of line 6. Both data structures, initially empty, will contain the worlds and the probabilities for the ones involved in the computation of the lower probability of the interpretations and of the probabilistic facts. The stored values depend on the probabilities of the parameters: in this way, we can call only once the ASP solver to compute the worlds, and simply update their probabilities when the parameters of the program change. Before entering the EM cycle, we first compute the log likelihood of all the examples using function COMPUTEL-OGLIKELIHOOD. Then, iteratively, as long as the log likelihood does not converge, in the expectation step (line 8) we generate the query for the current interpretation with the function GENERATEINTERPRETATIONQUERY and then compute the conditional probability for every probabilistic fact f_i, both negated ($\bot$, with the query *not* f_i) and not negated ($\top$, with the query f_i), given the current interpretation. The computation of the conditional probability is either performed by calling the solver (function COMPUTECONDITIONALPROBABILITY, needed only for the first iteration) or by retrieving the values from the *CondComputations* data structure. In the maximization step (line 23) we update the parameters of the probabilistic facts according to Eq. 12 and update the values for the stored computations (line 26). The algorithm can be straightforwardly adapted to find the parameters that maximize the upper probability (that may not coincide).

To compute the lower (and upper) probability of a query (function COM-PUTELOWERPROBABILITY [2]), we first translate every ground probabilistic fact $\Pi :: f$ into an ASP rule 0{f}1. The probability is stored in a data structure. First, we check whether there are some probabilistic facts that must always be true by computing the cautious consequences of the ASP program plus the probabilistic facts converted as previously described. These facts constitute the *minimal set of probabilistic facts* (that may be empty). This is possible because every world has at least one answer set. Then, we add every element of this set to the initial program as a constraint, i.e., if an atom a is in this set, we add the constraint :- not a. Finally, to obtain the probability interval of a query, we consider the program composed of the ASP program plus the converted probabilistic facts, the inserted constraints, and two additional rules of the form `query:- q` and `not_query:- not q`, and project the solutions on the probabilistic facts and the `query` and `not_query` atoms. We then analyse all the solutions and identify every world, evaluate the probability, and update the lower (and upper) probability bound according to the number of associated answer sets. In case of conditional queries with evidence `e` (function COMPUTECONDITIONAL-PROBABILITY), the process remains almost the same, but we add two additional rules, `evidence:- e` and `not_evidence:- not e` and project the solutions also on the `evidence` and `not_evidence` atoms. This process avoids the generations of all the answer sets for every world, as happens in [28], but is still exponential in the number of worlds.

4   Experiments

We ran several experiments on a computer with Intel® Xeon® E5-2630v3 running at 2.40 GHz. For all the experiments, 60% of the dataset is used as a training set and the remaining 40% is used as a test set[1]. The initial value for all the facts whose probabilities can be learned is set to 0.5 and ϵ of Algorithm 1 is set to 10^{-5}. We used clingo as ASP solver [13] and Python as programming language.

The first dataset (*smoke*) contains programs with the structure shown in Example 1. We ran the experiments by increasing both the number of smokers and the number of interpretations. The interpretations are generated by running the ASP version of the program (with the probabilistic facts converted as previously described) and extracting the `smoke/1` and `friend/2` atoms (or their negation if they are not present) from a random answer set. The number of atoms of every interpretation randomly ranges between 1 and the total number of atoms of the selected answer set. In a first experiment, we fix the number of parameters to 5 (*smoke5*) and increase the number of interpretations. Results are shown in Fig. 1a, where the execution time seems to scale almost linearly by increasing the number of interpretations. We then analyse how the number of parameters influences the execution time. Results are shown in Fig. 2b, where the execution time increases exponentially by increasing the number of parameters.

The second dataset (*shop*, adapted from [24]) encodes a scenario where some person can buy some products. There are 4 instances of this dataset, with 4 (*shop4*), 8 (*shop8*), 10 (*shop10*), and 12 (*shop12*) people each. There is a disjunctive rule for each person. The dataset *shop4* has the following structure:

```
shops(a).  shops(b).
shops(c).  shops(d).
bought(spaghetti,a) ; bought(steak,a)  :- shops(a).
bought(spaghetti,b) ; bought(beans,b)  :- shops(b).
bought(tomato,c)  ; bought(onions,c)  :- shops(c).
```

---

[1] Source code and datasets available at https://github.com/damianoazzolini/pasta.

Algorithm 1. Function LEARNPARAMETERSPASP: learning the parameters of a PASP program $\mathcal{P}(\Pi)$ from interpretations $\mathcal{I}$.

```
1: function LEARNPARAMETERSPASP(P(Π), I)
2:     LL₀ ← −∞
3:     LLComputations ← ∅
4:     CondComputations ← ∅
5:     LL₁ ← COMPUTELOGLIKELIHOOD(P(Π), I, LLComputations)
6:     while LL₁ − LL₀ > ε do
7:         LL₀ ← LL₁
8:         for all fᵢ ∈ P(Π) do                               ▷ Expectation.
9:             lp⊤_fᵢ ← 0, lp⊥_fᵢ ← 0
10:            for all I ∈ I do
11:                if (I, fᵢ) ∈ CondComputations then    ▷ Computation steps already stored.
12:                    lp⊥_fᵢ ← lp⊥_fqi + CondComputations[I, fᵢ].f
13:                    lp⊤_fᵢ ← lp⊤_fᵢ + CondComputations[I, fᵢ].t
14:                else
15:                    evidence ← GENERATEINTERPRETATIONQUERY(I)
16:                    lp⊥′_fᵢ ← COMPUTECONDITIONALPROBABILITY(not fᵢ, evidence)
17:                    lp⊥_fᵢ ← lp⊥_fᵢ + lp⊥′_fᵢ
18:                    lp⊤′_fᵢ ← COMPUTECONDITIONALPROBABILITY(fᵢ, evidence)
19:                    lp⊤_fᵢ ← lp⊤_fᵢ + lp⊤′_fᵢ
20:                end if
21:            end for
22:        end for
23:        for all fᵢ ∈ P(Π) do                               ▷ Maximization.
24:            Πᵢ ← lp⊤_fᵢ / (lp⊤_fᵢ + lp⊥_fᵢ)
25:        end for
26:        UPDATECONDCOMPUTATIONS(Π, I, CondComputations)
27:        LL₁ ← COMPUTELOGLIKELIHOOD(P(Π), I)
28:    end while
29: end function
30: function COMPUTELOGLIKELIHOOD(P(Π), I, LLComputations)
31:     LogP_int ← 0
32:     for all I ∈ I do
33:         if I ∈ LLComputations then              ▷ Computation steps already stored.
34:             LogP_int ← LogP_int + LLComputations[I]
35:         else
36:             LP ← COMPUTELOWERPROBABILITY(I | P(Π))
37:             LogP_int ← LogP_int + log(LP)
38:             LLComputations[I] ← log(LP)
39:         end if
40:     end for
41:     return LogP_int
42: end function
```

```
bought(steak,d) ; bought(onions,d) :- shops(d).

cs(C):-
    #count{X : bought(spaghetti,X)} = C0,
    #count{X : bought(onions,X)} = C1,
    C = C0 + C1.
ce(C):- #count{X,Y : bought(Y,X)} = C.

:- cs(S), ce(C), 10*S < 4*C.
```

The `shops/1` facts are probabilistic, and their probabilities must be learned. The constraint states that at least 40% of the buying actions involve spaghetti or onions. The dataset *shop8* has four additional disjunctive rules with 3 possible heads, the dataset *shop10* has 2 additional rules with respect to *shop8* with 4 possible heads, the dataset *shop12* has 2 additional rules with respect to *shop10* with 5 possible heads. The generation of the interpretations follows the same pattern used for the *smoke* dataset. However, we consider only the first $n/2$ disjunctive rules during this process, where n is the size of the instance. Figure 1a and 1b show that, by increasing the number of involved people and the number of interpretations, the overhead of execution time becomes substantial. It is interesting to note that, even if *shop4* has one less parameter than *smoke5*, the computations time are comparable: this may be due to an increasing number of answer sets that must be computed for every interpretation for the *shop4* instance. For this dataset, we also tested how the log likelihood varies during the learning process by fixing the interpretations to 125. Figure 2a shows that after a few iterations the log likelihood has almost reached its maximum value. *shop8* and *shop10* seem to be faster than *shop4* and *shop12* (whose plots are almost identical, even thus *shop4* requires some more iterations to fully converge with the given ϵ). Finally, we plotted the number of iterations needed to converge for the *shop4* and *shop8* instances up to 800 interpretations. Figure 3 shows that *shop4* seems to require more iterations to converge. This is may be due to the structure of the program, since it has less parameters to tweak. Overall, the main limitation of the algorithm is that, by increasing the number of parameters and probabilistic facts, the execution time increase exponentially, since the inference task is exponential in the number of parameters. This may seem unavoidable given the expressiveness of the ASP syntax. By limiting the possible types of rules, it will be maybe possible to leverage knowledge compilation [9] to represent the program and the answer sets in more compact forms where inference can be performed faster. This is a possible direction for a future work.

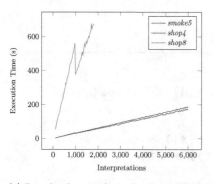

(a) Results for *smoke5*, *shop4*, and *shop8*.

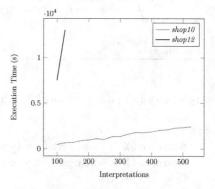

(b) Results for *shop10* and *shop12*.

Fig. 1. Variation of the execution time by increasing the number of interpretations.

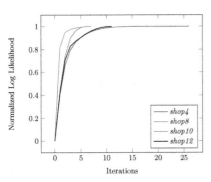

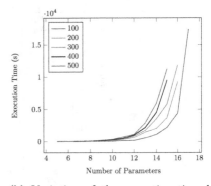

(a) Variation of the (normalized) log likelihood during learning for the *shop* experiment.

(b) Variation of the execution time by increasing the number of parameters for a different number of interpretations for the *smoke* experiment.

Fig. 2. Results for the *shop* and *smoke* experiments.

5 Related Work

Most of the related work involves parameter learning in PLP. One of the first approaches to learn the parameters of a probabilistic logic program can be found in [25], where the authors propose a learning algorithm based on Expectation Maximization that starts from a set of positive and negative examples (ground atoms). This has been later extended in [26]. LeProbLog [15] is another approach to learn the parameters of a probabilistic logic program that starts from a series of examples annotated with a probability and uses gradient descent. In this setting, the goal is to learn the parameters such that the probabilities of the examples are as close as possible to the ones provided. EMBLEM [4] is another algorithm that adopts EM to learn the parameters of logic programs with annotated disjunction [30]. LFI-ProbLog [16] is one of the first algorithms to perform parameter learning given a set of interpretations, and it has been already discussed in this paper. The authors of [17] propose an algorithm to learn the parameters of an extended PRISM [25] program, i.e., a probabilistic logic program that also allows continuous random variables, and the authors of [3] introduce an algorithm to learn the parameters of some facts in the programs given some constraints involving their probabilities. In [27] the authors propose SMProbLog, a framework that extends the system (and language) ProbLog [11] and the Distribution Semantics to manage worlds with multiple models. With their system, it is possible to compute the probability of a query (that is a sharp value) by dividing the probability of every world by the number of models. Differently from them, we adopt the credal semantics and associate a probability range rather than a probability value to a query. Moreover, they use the ProbLog syntax while we support the ASP syntax, so all the possible types of rules and constraints described in the previous sections. Few systems allow parameter

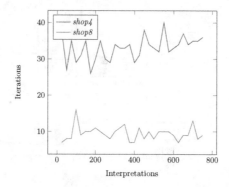

Fig. 3. Number of iterations until convergence for the *shop4* and *shop8* instances.

learning in ASP: LP^{MLN} [18] is an extension to ASP that allows the representation of weighted rules that also include an algorithm for parameter learning, but it does not adopt the credal semantics. PrASP [21] is similar and also does not use the credal semantics. Some recent work also combine probabilistic ASP with neural networks, such as NeurASP [31], but with a different semantics.

6   Conclusions

In this paper, we proposed the first algorithm to perform learning from interpretations in Probabilistic Answer Set Programming under the credal semantics. The goal is, given a set of interpretations, to maximize the product of the lower probabilities of the interpretations by tweaking the parameters of the program. We tested the algorithm on two different datasets and showed how the algorithm scales by increasing the number of interpretations and parameters. As future work we plan to develop approximate algorithms for the inference part to scale this approach on real world datasets.

Acknowledgment. This research was partly supported by TAILOR, a project funded by EU Horizon 2020 research and innovation programme under GA No. 952215. Damiano Azzolini was supported by IndAM - GNCS Project with code CUP_E55F22000270001.

References

1. Alviano, M., Faber, W.: Aggregates in answer set programming. KI-Künstliche Intelligenz **32**(2), 119–124 (2018). https://doi.org/10.1007/s13218-018-0545-9
2. Azzolini, D., Bellodi, E., Riguzzi, F.: Statistical statements in probabilistic logic programming. In: Inclezan, G.G.D., Maratea, M. (eds.) 16th International Conference on Logic Programming and Nonmonotonic Reasoning (LPNMR 2022) (2022)
3. Azzolini, D., Riguzzi, F.: Optimizing probabilities in probabilistic logic programs. Theory Pract. Logic Program. **21**(5), 543–556 (2021). https://doi.org/10.1017/S1471068421000260

4. Bellodi, E., Riguzzi, F.: Expectation maximization over binary decision diagrams for probabilistic logic programs. Intell. Data Anal. **17**(2), 343–363 (2013). https://doi.org/10.3233/IDA-130582
5. Brewka, G., Eiter, T., Truszczyński, M.: Answer set programming at a glance. Commun. ACM **54**(12), 92–103 (2011). https://doi.org/10.1145/2043174.2043195
6. Cozman, F.G., Mauá, D.D.: The structure and complexity of credal semantics. In: Hommersom, A., Abdallah, S.A. (eds.) PLP 2016. CEUR Workshop Proceedings, vol. 1661, pp. 3–14. CEUR-WS.org (2016)
7. Cozman, F.G., Mauá, D.D.: On the semantics and complexity of probabilistic logic programs. J. Artif. Intell. Res. **60**, 221–262 (2017). https://doi.org/10.1613/jair.5482
8. Cozman, F.G., Mauá, D.D.: The joy of probabilistic answer set programming: semantics, complexity, expressivity, inference. Int. J. Approx. Reason. **125**, 218–239 (2020). https://doi.org/10.1016/j.ijar.2020.07.004
9. Darwiche, A., Marquis, P.: A knowledge compilation map. J. Artif. Intell. Res. **17**, 229–264 (2002). https://doi.org/10.1613/jair.989
10. De Raedt, L., Kersting, K.: Probabilistic inductive logic programming. In: De Raedt, L., Frasconi, P., Kersting, K., Muggleton, S. (eds.) Probabilistic Inductive Logic Programming. LNCS (LNAI), vol. 4911, pp. 1–27. Springer, Heidelberg (2008). https://doi.org/10.1007/978-3-540-78652-8_1
11. De Raedt, L., Kimmig, A., Toivonen, H.: Problog: a probabilistic prolog and its application in link discovery. In: Veloso, M.M. (ed.) IJCAI, pp. 2462–2467 (2007)
12. Faber, W., Leone, N., Pfeifer, G.: Recursive aggregates in disjunctive logic programs: semantics and complexity. In: Alferes, J.J., Leite, J. (eds.) JELIA 2004. LNCS (LNAI), vol. 3229, pp. 200–212. Springer, Heidelberg (2004). https://doi.org/10.1007/978-3-540-30227-8_19
13. Gebser, M., Kaminski, R., Kaufmann, B., Schaub, T.: Multi-shot asp solving with clingo. Theory Pract. Logic Program. **19**(1), 27–82 (2019). https://doi.org/10.1017/S1471068418000054
14. Gebser, M., Kaufmann, B., Schaub, T.: Solution enumeration for projected Boolean search problems. In: van Hoeve, W.-J., Hooker, J.N. (eds.) CPAIOR 2009. LNCS, vol. 5547, pp. 71–86. Springer, Heidelberg (2009). https://doi.org/10.1007/978-3-642-01929-6_7
15. Gutmann, B., Kimmig, A., Kersting, K., De Raedt, L.: Parameter learning in probabilistic databases: a least squares approach. In: Daelemans, W., Goethals, B., Morik, K. (eds.) ECML PKDD 2008. LNCS (LNAI), vol. 5211, pp. 473–488. Springer, Heidelberg (2008). https://doi.org/10.1007/978-3-540-87479-9_49
16. Gutmann, B., Thon, I., De Raedt, L.: Learning the parameters of probabilistic logic programs from interpretations. In: Gunopulos, D., Hofmann, T., Malerba, D., Vazirgiannis, M. (eds.) ECML PKDD 2011. LNCS (LNAI), vol. 6911, pp. 581–596. Springer, Heidelberg (2011). https://doi.org/10.1007/978-3-642-23780-5_47
17. Islam, M.A., Ramakrishnan, C., Ramakrishnan, I.: Parameter learning in PRISM programs with continuous random variables. arXiv:1203.4287 (2012). https://doi.org/10.48550/ARXIV.1203.4287
18. Lee, J., Wang, Y.: Weight learning in a probabilistic extension of answer set programs. In: Thielscher, M., Toni, F., Wolter, F. (eds.) Principles of Knowledge Representation and Reasoning: Proceedings of the Sixteenth International Conference, KR 2018, Tempe, Arizona, 30 October–2 November 2018, pp. 22–31. AAAI Press (2018)
19. Lloyd, J.W.: Foundations of Logic Programming, 2nd edn. Springer, Heidelberg (1987). https://doi.org/10.1007/978-3-642-96826-6

20. Mauá, D.D., Cozman, F.G.: Complexity results for probabilistic answer set programming. Int. J. Approx. Reason. **118**, 133–154 (2020). https://doi.org/10.1016/j.ijar.2019.12.003

21. Nickles, M.: A tool for probabilistic reasoning based on logic programming and first-order theories under stable model semantics. In: Michael, L., Kakas, A. (eds.) JELIA 2016. LNCS (LNAI), vol. 10021, pp. 369–384. Springer, Cham (2016). https://doi.org/10.1007/978-3-319-48758-8_24

22. Raedt, L.D., Kersting, K., Natarajan, S., Poole, D.: Statistical relational artificial intelligence: logic, probability, and computation. Synth. Lect. Artif. Intell. Mach. Learn. **10**(2), 1–189 (2016)

23. Riguzzi, F.: Foundations of Probabilistic Logic Programming: Languages, semantics, inference and learning. River Publishers, Gistrup, Denmark (2018)

24. Riguzzi, F., Di Mauro, N.: Applying the information bottleneck to statistical relational learning. Mach. Learn. **86**(1), 89–114 (2012). https://doi.org/10.1007/s10994-011-5247-6

25. Sato, T.: A statistical learning method for logic programs with distribution semantics. In: Sterling, L. (ed.) ICLP 1995, pp. 715–729. MIT Press, Cambridge (1995). https://doi.org/10.7551/mitpress/4298.003.0069

26. Sato, T., Kameya, Y.: Parameter learning of logic programs for symbolic-statistical modeling. J. Artif. Intell. Res. **15**, 391–454 (2001)

27. Totis, P., Kimmig, A., Raedt, L.D.: Smproblog: stable model semantics in problog and its applications in argumentation. arXiv:2110.01990 (2021). https://doi.org/10.48550/ARXIV.2110.01990

28. Tuckey, D., Russo, A., Broda, K.: Pasocs: a parallel approximate solver for probabilistic logic programs under the credal semantics. arXiv:2105.10908 (2021). https://doi.org/10.48550/ARXIV.2105.10908

29. Van Gelder, A., Ross, K.A., Schlipf, J.S.: The well-founded semantics for general logic programs. J. ACM **38**(3), 620–650 (1991)

30. Vennekens, J., Verbaeten, S., Bruynooghe, M.: Logic programs with annotated disjunctions. In: Demoen, B., Lifschitz, V. (eds.) ICLP 2004. LNCS, vol. 3132, pp. 431–445. Springer, Heidelberg (2004). https://doi.org/10.1007/978-3-540-27775-0_30

31. Yang, Z., Ishay, A., Lee, J.: NeurASP: embracing neural networks into answer set programming. In: Bessiere, C. (ed.) Proceedings of the Twenty-Ninth International Joint Conference on Artificial Intelligence, IJCAI 2020, pp. 1755–1762. ijcai.org (2020). https://doi.org/10.24963/ijcai.2020/243

Navigable Atom-Rule Interactions in PSL Models Enhanced by Rule Verbalizations, with an Application to Etymological Inference

Verena Blaschke[(✉)] [iD], Thora Daneyko [iD], Jekaterina Kaparina [iD],
Zhuge Gao [iD], and Johannes Dellert [iD]

Seminar für Sprachwissenschaft, Eberhard Karls Universität, Tübingen, Germany
{verena.blaschke,johannes.dellert}@uni-tuebingen.de

Abstract. Adding to the budding landscape of advanced analysis tools for Probabilistic Soft Logic (PSL), we present a graphical explorer for grounded PSL models. It exposes the structure of the model from the perspective of any single atom, listing the ground rules in which it occurs. The other atoms in these rules serve as links for navigation through the resulting rule-atom graph (RAG). As additional diagnostic criteria, each associated rule is further classified as exerting upward or downward pressure on the atom's value, and as active or inactive depending on its importance for the MAP estimate.

Our RAG viewer further includes a general infrastructure for making PSL results explainable by stating the reasoning patterns in terms of domain language. For this purpose, we provide a Java interface for "talking" predicates and rules which can generate verbalized explanations of the atom interactions effected by each rule. If the model's rules are structured similarly to the way the domain is conceptualized by users, they will receive an intuitive explanation of the result in natural language.

As an example application, we present the current state of the loanword detection component of EtInEn, our upcoming software for machine-assisted etymological theory development.

Keywords: PSL · Explainable reasoning · Visual model inspection

1 Introduction

Probabilistic Soft Logic (PSL) [1] is a popular templating language for a tractable class of graphical models which has already been applied to a wide range of domains, but poses some challenges in terms of understanding and debugging inference behavior. In this paper, we describe and publicly release additional tooling which we found necessary in order to address these challenges while developing a range of complex PSL models for tasks in historical linguistics.

We first describe our strategies for analyzing MAP states of PSL programs (Sect. 2), then introduce our approach to explaining inference behavior through

© The Author(s), under exclusive license to Springer Nature Switzerland AG 2024
S. H. Muggleton and A. Tamaddoni-Nezhad (Eds.): ILP 2022, LNAI 13779, pp. 15–24, 2024.
https://doi.org/10.1007/978-3-031-55630-2_2

rule verbalization (Sect. 3), outline the main features of our implementation (Sect. 4), and finally illustrate the application within our domain (Sect. 5).

2 Analyzing PSL Programs as Rule-Atom Graphs

A grounded PSL program consists of rules which define constraints and loss potentials on combinations of probabilistic atoms. Logical rules are disjunctions of literals whose value is defined via the strong disjunction of Łukasiewicz logic, whereas arithmetic rules directly express constraints on weighted sums of atom values. PSL facilitates the definition of large models by providing a first-order templating language where atoms are expressed as predicate symbols with arguments, and variables can be used to specify the combinations of atoms that can instantiate a rule template. The rules which make up the model are then produced by grounding the templates against a universe of ground atoms.

This flexibility comes at the cost of making the behavior of PSL models difficult to understand, to debug and to analyze. The grounding process makes the link between specification and model quite indirect, and MAP inference on the grounded model is much less reducible to individual reasoning steps than in classical programming paradigms, because messages will be propagated through many atoms in sometimes very complex ways to arrive at the MAP state.

While debugging for query-based probabilistic logic paradigms can rely on provenance graphs [8], a grounded PSL program is inspected most naturally via its **rule-atom graph (RAG)**. The RAG is a bipartite graph where each ground rule instance corresponds to a **rule node**, each ground atom in the universe is represented by an **atom node**, and the node for each rule is connected to the nodes for each of the atoms which occur in it.

VMI-PSL [6], a recent PSL debugging and analysis tool, can be seen as operating on the RAG, focusing on individual rules and their groundings as the primary points of interest. Whereas VMI-PSL mainly supports a debugging paradigm where rules are analyzed in terms of the number of groundings as well as aggregate measures of (dis)satisfaction, our tool focuses the analysis on the perspective of the individual ground atom whose value in a MAP state might be unexpected or undesired. Adopting this view of the structure of a PSL problem leads us to two diagnostic criteria which, to our knowledge, have only been discussed implicitly in the literature, and for which no tools have been available.

2.1 Upward and Downward Pressure

The inference goal in a feasible grounded instance of a PSL program can be expressed as minimizing the distance to satisfaction of its rules. Framed in terms of the rule-atom graph, this can be seen as applying pressure to the rule nodes, which in turn results in upward or downward pressures on the values of various atoms when being distributed throughout the graph. A MAP state for the PSL problem can thus be interpreted as a state of equilibrium between these pressures in the RAG, at which the weighted sum of hinge-loss potentials cannot be minimized any further by modifying the values assigned to atoms.

One of the interesting properties of PSL is that each rule-atom link can be classified as exerting upward or downward pressure on the value of the atom. For example, if a grounding of the following example rule from the PSL documentation is unsatisfied, it exerts upward pressure on the value of Knows(P1,P2), but downward pressure on the values of Lives(P1,L) and Lives(P2,L):

20: Lives(P1,L) & Lives(P2,L) & (P1 != P2) -> Knows(P1,P2) ^2

This makes associated groundings of this rule relevant if we are interested in finding out why some grounding of Knows(P1,P2) receives a higher value than expected, but irrelevant if we are interested in the pressures pushing up the value of some grounding of Lives(P1,L). To connect this perspective to the underlying mathematical structures, we can use the inequality representation of logical rules which forms the basis of the corresponding hinge-loss potential:

$$1 - \sum_{i \in I^+} y_i - \sum_{i \in I^-} (1 - y_i) \leq 0$$

A rule exerts upward pressure on exactly those atoms which correspond to variables y_i where $i \in I^+$, and downward pressure on those atoms corresponding to y_i where $i \in I^-$. In arithmetic rules, the direction of the pressure arises trivially from the sign of the atom's weight and the direction of the inequality.

2.2   Active and Inactive Rules

As in VMI-PSL, the distance to satisfaction of ground rules plays a central role in our debugging paradigm. We see ground rules which are unsatisfied in a MAP state as a key means to detect the places where the rule system is under pressure, i.e. where competing evidence might exist. In addition to making rule nodes sortable by distance to satisfaction, we also analyse their relevance.

If a ground rule has a distance to satisfaction of ≥ 0, this means that the rule is contributing to the value of the associated atoms, in the sense that if the corresponding potential were not part of the hinge-loss function, the function could be minimized further and the current estimate would cease to be a MAP state. In contrast, a negative distance to satisfaction implies that the value of the associated atoms in the MAP state would not be any different if the rule did not exist, making it irrelevant for understanding why the MAP state is optimal.

This difference can be framed in terms of rule activity. As a minor complication, the values assigned to atoms by MAP inference in the PSL reference implementation are not very precise. Rounding errors often lead to minor distances to satisfaction that cannot actually be interpreted as meaning that the rule is not satisfied. This leads us to a more robust counterfactual definition of activity: a ground rule is **active** at some state if its distance to satisfaction would reach some ϵ (by default, $\epsilon = 0.01$) if we changed the value of the context atom by 2ϵ in the potentially pressure-inducing direction, and **inactive** otherwise.

We have found rule activity to be a very useful diagnostic criterion for detecting problems in complex rule systems. If many groundings of some rule turn out to be inactive, this might indicate that its reasoning pattern is already covered by (a combination of) other rules, or that the rule needs to be tightened in some way in order to increase its influence on the results.

3   Verbalization of Atoms and Rules

In addition to its role as a debugging tool for complex PSL models, our second goal for the RAG viewer is the ability to communicate the system's reasoning back to the user. Unlike in some scenarios where the user will be content with a rough explanation in terms of the information that was used to infer a value [4], we want to generate explanations directed at a domain expert user who wants to be able to fully understand the system's reasoning, which is closer to the concept of explanation in symbolic expert systems [7].

Using terminology from the field of recommender systems [5], the rule-atom graph already provides an explicit model of the relationships between knowledge objects, and the decisive input values for a context atom are the ones which are connected to it though active rule nodes. An explanation could thus be provided by a direct visualization of the rule-atom graph where rule nodes are annotated by our diagnostic criteria, but as Kouki et al. [4] find for their PSL-based application, users prefer textual explanations over visualizations.

As an additional advantage, textual explanations make it easier to provide further inference and domain knowledge. Since PSL rule templates are powerful enough to translate common domain-specific reasoning patterns rather directly, the roles of many rules in the overall model can be grasped quite intuitively by a domain expert. For explainable inference, this leads to the idea of exposing the RAG, but verbalizing the mechanics of each ground rule in terms of domain-specific natural language.

In practice, we begin each explanation with an introductory sentence summarizing the reasoning pattern expressed by the rule. For our example rule, this could be: "If there is evidence that two people live at the same address, this makes it more likely that they know each other." A second sentence then fills in the specifics of the grounding. Since in our paradigm, the ground rules always occur from the perspective of some context atom, a ground rule is verbalized in different ways depending on which atom is currently being inspected.

Consider a grounding of our example rule where P1 = "Bob", P2 = "Alice", and L = "18" ("house number 18"). The shape of the second sentence depends on the role of the context atom within the rule. If the context atom is in the consequent of a logical rule (e.g. Knows("Alice","Bob")), the explanation will typically correspond directly to the intuition expressed by the rule: "We are certain that Bob lives in house number 18, and Alice probably lives in house number 18 as well, therefore Bob and Alice probably know each other." If the context atom occurs in the antecedent of a logical rule (e.g. Lives("Alice","18")), we explain that the values of the other atoms prevent it from taking a higher/lower value: "We are certain that Bob lives in house number 18, but there is some reason to doubt that Alice and Bob know each other, therefore we cannot be certain that Alice also lives in house number 18."

Special treatment is given to several boundary cases where a relevant atom takes an extreme value (0 or 1), e.g. by expressing that the rule is trivially satisfied, and providing verbalizations of the associated atoms in parentheses.

4   Implementation

4.1   Infrastructure

Our implementation[1] is built on a custom abstraction layer which we implemented in pure Java on top of the PSL reference implementation. This layer is publicly released as a Java package[2] which, among other features, provides an API for defining and administering PSL problems in Java (e.g. in order to generate problem instances programmatically), and to extract rule-atom graphs from the underlying PSL implementation. Our RAG viewer is implemented as a JavaFX component which allows to analyse the output of any PSL problem defined via our abstraction layer. In addition to providing a more reactive interface, this also means that unlike web-based services like VMI-PSL, our viewer runs locally without any server availability or data security issues.

4.2   Design of the RAG Viewer

The main functionality of the viewer can be described as an atom browser where for each atom, the reasoning leading to its value in the PSL output is laid out on a separate page. Each page contains representations of all the ground rules which had an influence on the atom's belief value, and these representations contain hyperlinks which allow to navigate to the other atoms tied together by that rule instance. The associated ground rules and constraints are divided into two blocks depending on the direction of pressure they exert on the context atom, and sorted by their weighted distance to satisfaction at the current MAP estimate, where inactive rules are greyed out. A sidebar provides the option to filter a list of all ground atoms by their argument constants, as well as sorting the matching atoms by their values in the MAP state.

4.3   Interface for Verbalizations

Our infrastructure also provides an interface and various helper methods for defining application-specific atom and rule verbalizations. A **talking atom** can express the associated predicate and its arguments as a noun phrase or full sentence. The value of the atom in the current solution can additionally be expressed as an adverb ("perhaps", "probably", "very likely") or, in some contexts, as a

---

[1] https://github.com/verenablaschke/psl-ragviewer.
[2] https://github.com/jdellert/psl-infrastructure.

full phrase ("reaches a high level of certainty"). The interface for what we call a **talking rule** requires the model developer to write a method that, given the atom groundings and values, produces an explanation of the pressure exerted on the context atom. Good verbalizations will be highly dependent on the rule and the domain, but generic implementations are supported by template methods for the format and the different scenarios discussed in the previous section.[3]

5   Application Example

We illustrate the concepts introduced in the previous sections in the context of our application of PSL within the framework of EtInEn, our forthcoming software suite for machine-assisted historical linguistics. Historical linguists try to explain the origin and development of attested languages by forming theories about their common ancestors. Language families arise from repeated language splits followed by divergence of the descendant languages. In addition to this tree-shaped process, languages will often copy material from languages that they are in contact with, a process that is called **borrowing**. On the level of the lexicon, this will result in **loanwords** entering the language. Layers of loanwords often provide important hints about the nature of (pre)historic cultural contacts.

5.1   Etymological Reasoning

Establishing an **etymology** means to trace the origin of a word into the past, thereby explaining which other words (most often in other languages) are related to the word by common descent. This entails the important step of deciding for **homologues** (words that are etymologically related) whether they are a result of inheritance or borrowing. Many different sources of evidence need to be brought to bear in order to find loanwords. Our example model derives judgments from two types of patterns. The first is to project homologue set membership upwards in the family tree, detecting situations where the homologue set being used for a concept in some language is different from the one reconstructed for the parent language, e.g. in a situation where a single language uses a word from a different family branch or family. The second type of evidence, which helps to detect loanwords within a homologue set, is based on deviations from the expectation that the phonetic similarity of words will roughly mirror language relatedness.

5.2   Expressing Etymologies in PSL

The following predicates are used to express the input data and the etymologies: In order to create the universe for a specific problem, the language tree and the directional language contacts are translated into Xinh and Xloa observations as well as the corresponding Einh and Eloa targets. Attested words have observed

---

`Einh(X,Y)`	belief that the etymology of X is inheritance from Y
`Eloa(X,Y)`	belief that the etymology of X is borrowing from Y
`Eunk(X)`	belief that the etymology of X is unknown (outside scope of data)
`Fhom(X,H)`	belief that the word X belongs to the homologue set H
`Fsim(X,Y)`	phonetic similarity of the words X and Y
`Xinh(X,Y)`	possibility of inheritance (language of Y is parent of that of X)
`Xloa(X,Y)`	possibility of borrowing (language of Y influenced that of X)

`Fhom` and `Fsim` values, potentially derived by specialized algorithms, the remaining atoms are targets and will be inferred in conjunction with the values of the `Einh(X,Y)` and `Eloa(X,Y)` items that constitute the model output.

5.3   The Etymological Inference Model

The constraints mainly ensure symmetry and a certain degree of transitivity, and that homologue judgments and etymologies for each word form distributions:

```
Eloa(X,Y) + Eloa(Y,X) <= 1 .
Einh(X,+Y) + Eloa(X,+Z) + Eunk(X) = 1 .
Einh(X,Y) & Fhom(Y,H) -> Fhom(X,H).
Eloa(X,Y) & Fhom(Y,H) -> Fhom(X,H).
Fhom(X,+H) = 1.
Fsim(X,Y) = Fsim(Y,X) .
Fsim(X,Y) & Fsim(Y,Z) & (X != Y) & (X != Z) & (Y != Z) -> Fsim(X,Z) .
```

`Eloa` and `Eunk` atoms carry negative priors, the remaining rules are:

```
a. 2.0: Einh(X,Z) & Einh(Y,Z) & (X != Y) -> Fsim(X,Y)
b. 1.0: Fsim(X,Y) & Einh(X,W) & Einh(Y,Z) & (W != Z) -> Fsim(W,Z)
c. 1.0: Eloa(X,Y) & Fsim(X,Z) & (Y != Z) & (X != Z) -> Fsim(X,Y)
d. 0.6: Fhom(X,H) & Xinh(X,Z) -> Fhom(Z,H)
e. 0.2: Fhom(Z,H) & Xinh(X,Z) -> Fhom(X,H)
f. 0.4: Fhom(X,H) & Fhom(Y,H) & Xinh(X,Y) -> Einh(X,Y)
g. 1.0: Fhom(X,H) & ~ Fhom(Y,H) & Xinh(X,Y) & Xloa(X,Z) -> Eloa(X,Z)
```

To state the intuitions behind each of these rules in the given order, there is a very strong preference for two words which are inherited from the same word to be phonetically similar *(a)*, and sources of similar words should be similar as well *(b)*. A borrowed word should be more similar to its source than to any other word *(c)*. Evidence of homologue set presence is propagated along parent-child links, with the child-to-parent direction being dominant *(d, e)*. If parent and child share a homologue set, that suggests inheritance *(f)*. In contrast, if there is any reason to doubt the presence of a homologue set in the parent, an available loanword etymology becomes much more likely *(g)* (Fig. 1).

5.4   Exploring an Example Instance

In our example, we want to infer that English *take* is a Norse loan (i.e. from Proto-North-Germanic) based on its equivalents in seven modern Germanic languages. Our Germanic tree consists of the West Germanic branch with three children (German, Dutch, and Old English with the attested child English) and the North Germanic branch with children West Scandinavian (Icelandic and Norwegian), Swedish, and Danish. This tree is extended into a network by contact

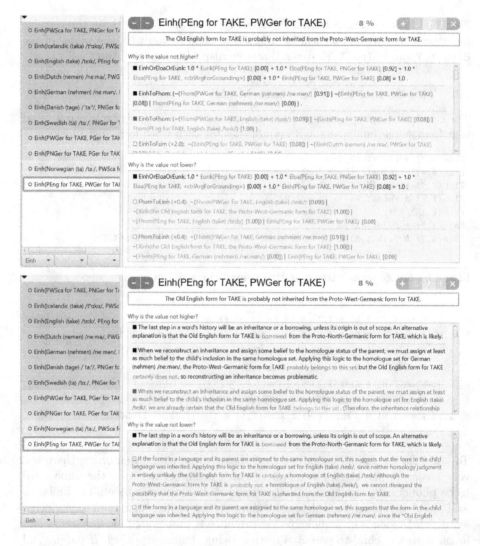

Fig. 1. Our tool explains why the Old English word for TAKE is probably not inherited from Proto-West-Germanic. Users can toggle between the internal representation of the ground rules and the verbalized explanations. Inactive rules have been greyed out.

links from German to every modern North Germanic language except Icelandic, from Danish to Norwegian, and from Proto-North-Germanic to Old English.

The input data consist of the following equivalents of TAKE: German *nehmen*, Dutch *nemen*, English *take*, Danish *tage*, Norwegian *ta*, Swedish *ta*, Icelandic *taka*. The `Fsim` and `Fhom` values for these forms are derived by applying the IWSA algorithm [2] to the phonetic data from the NorthEuraLex database [3].

Inference is successful. Below, we show two screenshots of our RAG browser displaying an explanation for an etymological reasoning step. A linguist user who wants do understand the output will navigate through the relevant atoms by following the links inside the verbalizations.

6 Conclusion

In addition to the functionality described in this paper, several experimental features that will be of interest to other PSL users are still in development. They include the ability to perform conditional inferences after fixing the values of selected atoms, and support for persisting RAGs in files for post-hoc inspection.

We also plan to extend the user interface by the possibility to switch to a rule-focused view in order to receive an overview of all groundings, but enhanced by our diagnostic criteria, such as activity status at the MAP state.

On the application side, our loanword detection module is being expanded by additional sources of evidence, such as the general tendency for words for concepts from certain cultural or technological spheres to be borrowed jointly. In the finished EtInEn architecture where soundlaws and reconstructions will be modeled, the very important criterion of deviation from sound laws is going to contribute to loanword inference as well.

Acknowledgements. This work has been funded by the European Research Council (ERC) under the European Union's Horizon 2020 research and innovation programme (CrossLingference, grant agreement no. 834050) as well as the Institutional Strategy of the University of Tübingen (Deutsche Forschungsgemeinschaft, ZUK 63) and a RiSC grant by the MWK Baden-Württemberg.

References

1. Bach, S.H., Broecheler, M., Huang, B., Getoor, L.: Hinge-loss Markov random fields and Probabilistic Soft Logic. J. ML Res. **18**(109), 1–67 (2017)
2. Dellert, J.: Combining information-weighted sequence alignment and sound correspondence models for improved cognate detection. In: Proceedings of COLING 2018, pp. 3123–3133. Association for Computational Linguistics (2018)
3. Dellert, J., Daneyko, T., Münch, A., Ladygina, A., Buch, A., Clarius, N., et al.: NorthEuraLex: a wide-coverage lexical database of northern Eurasia. Lang. Resour. Eval. **1**(54), 273–301 (2020). https://doi.org/10.1007/s10579-019-09480-6
4. Kouki, P., Schaffer, J., Pujara, J., O'Donovan, J., Getoor, L.: Personalized explanations for hybrid recommender systems. In: Proceedings of IUI 2019, pp. 379–390 (2019). https://doi.org/10.1145/3301275.3302306

5. Nunes, I., Jannach, D.: A systematic review and taxonomy of explanations in decision support and recommender systems. User Model. User-Adap. Inter. **27**, 393–444 (2017). https://doi.org/10.1007/s11257-017-9195-0
6. Rodden, A., Salh, T., Augustine, E., Getoor, L.: VMI-PSL: visual model inspector for probabilistic soft logic. In: Proceedings of RecSys 2020, pp. 604–606 (2020). https://doi.org/10.1145/3383313.3411530
7. Southwick, R.W.: Explaining reasoning: an overview of explanation in knowledge-based systems. Knowl. Eng. Rev. **6**(1), 1–19 (1991). https://doi.org/10.1017/S0269888900005555
8. Wang, S., Lyu, H., Zhang, J., Wu, C., Chen, X., Zhou, W., et al.: Provenance for probabilistic logic programs. In: Proceedings of EDBT 2020 (2020). https://doi.org/10.5441/002/edbt.2020.14

A Program-Synthesis Challenge
for ARC-Like Tasks

Aditya Challa[1]([✉]), Ashwin Srinivasan[1], Michael Bain[2], and Gautam Shroff[3]

[1] Department of CSIS and APPCAIR, BITS Pilani, Goa Campus, Sancoale, India
`adityac@goa.bits-pilani.ac.in`
[2] School of CSE, University of New South Wales, Sydney, Australia
[3] TCS Research, New Delhi, India

Abstract. We propose a program synthesis challenge inspired by the Abstraction and Reasoning Corpus (ARC) [3]. The ARC is intended as a touchstone for human intelligence. It consists of 400 tasks, each with very small numbers (3–5) of 'input-output' image pairs. It is known that the tasks are 'human-solvable' in the sense that, for any of the tasks, there exists a human-authored description that transforms input images in the task to the corresponding output images. Besides the 'small data problem', other features of ARC make it hard to use as a yardstick for machine learning. The solutions are not provided, nor is it known if they are unique. The use of some basic prior knowledge is acknowledged, but no definitions are available. The solutions are known also to apply to images that may be significantly different to those provided, but those images are not described. Inspired by ARC, but motivated to address some of these issues, in this paper we propose the Inductive Program Synthesis Challenge for ARC-like tasks (IPARC). The IPARC challenge is much more controlled, focusing on the inductive synthesis of structured programs. We specify for the challenge a set of 'ARC-like' tasks characterised by: training and test example sets drawn from a clearly-defined set of 'ARC-like' input-output image pairs; a set of image transformation functions from the image-processing field of Mathematical Morphology (MM); and target programs known to solve the tasks by transforming input to output images. The IPARC tasks rely on a result known as the 'Structured Program Theorem' that identifies a small set of rules as sufficient for construction of a wide class of programs. Tasks in the IPARC challenge are intended for machine learning methods of program synthesis able to address instances of these rules. In principle, Inductive Logic Programming (ILP) has the techniques needed to identify the constructs implied by the Structured Program Theorem. But, in practice, is there an ILP implementation that can achieve this? The purpose of the IPARC challenge is to determine if this is the case.

Keywords: Program synthesis · IPARC · ILP

A. Srinivasan—AS is currently visiting the Centre for Health Informatics, Macquarie University and the School of CSE, UNSW.

S. H. Muggleton and A. Tamaddoni-Nezhad (Eds.): ILP 2022, LNAI 13779, pp. 25–39, 2024.
https://doi.org/10.1007/978-3-031-55630-2_3

1 Introduction

Perhaps the earliest demonstration of inductive program synthesis using images was by Evans [4]. ANALOGY solved tasks of the kind shown in Fig. 1. Computation in ANALOGY proceeded in two stages: a representation stage, that detected objects and extracted represented them using pre-defined basic functions and relations. The second stage then proceeded to find an appropriate program. The first step in the program-synthesis process was to find automatically one or more rules–in ANALOGY, LISP programs–that describe (in Evans' words): "how the objects of figure A are removed, added to, or altered in their properties and their relations to other objects to generate B". Generalisations of the rules are then constructed to ensure that C is transformed to exactly one of the alternatives 1–5. If multiple programs are possible, then ANALOGY used a notion of *generalisation strength* to select one[1].

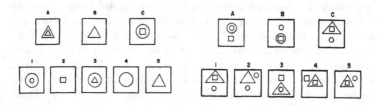

Fig. 1. Examples for program-synthesis from [4]. Images are all line-drawings, and the tasks considered were all of the kind "if A:B then which one of the following is true: (a) C:1; (b) C:2; ···; (e) C:5".

Now, nearly six decades later, a significantly more complex and wider variety of visual tasks, with some overlapping motivations to those of Evans' paper, has been proposed in the Abstraction and Reasoning Corpus (ARC [3]). The ARC consists of 400 tasks of the kind shown in Fig. 2.

The tasks in the ARC are not especially envisaged as being exclusively for program synthesis. What is known is the tasks are 'human-solvable' in the sense that, for any of the tasks, there exists a human-authored procedure that transforms input images in the task to the corresponding output images. But, as noted by Francois Chollet in his description of the ARC:

> Crucially, to the best of our knowledge, ARC does not appear to be approachable by any existing machine learning technique (including Deep Learning), due to its focus on broad generalization and few-shot learning, as well as the fact that the evaluation set only features tasks that do not appear in the training set. For a researcher setting out to solve it, ARC is perhaps best understood as a program synthesis benchmark.

---

[1] In general, such analogical tasks can be 'ill-posed', in that multiple solutions might exist for all training examples but only one of these is correct for unseen test cases, with the criteria as to which to choose being impossible to 'logically' deduce from the training examples alone.

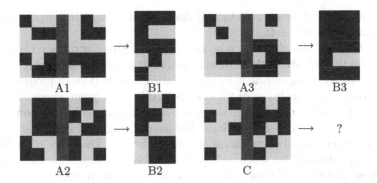

Fig. 2. An example task from the ARC (taken from https://samacquaviva.com/LARC/explore/). The task to be solved is of the form "if A1:B1 and A2:B2 and A3:B3 then C: ?".

However, there are several aspects that pose a challenge when considering the ARC as a benchmark for program synthesis. The human-authored solutions are not provided, nor is it known if they are unique. The use of some basic prior knowledge is acknowledged, but no definitions are available. The solutions are known also to apply to images that may be significantly different to those provided, but those images are not described. Two different routes have been sought to address these limitations. The authors of [1] re-interpret the ARC tasks in terms of language. Solutions are 'natural programs' in the form of instructions in a natural language. A natural program for a task is first obtained from a human participant. This natural language description is then tested by a second participant. A natural program is considered successful if it can be used by the second participant to solve the task. The intent is that a collection of successful natural programs will allow the identification of prior knowledge that can subsequently be used as prior knowledge for inductive program synthesis by machine. Separately, a Kaggle competition[2] focussed on automated techniques for solving the ARC without reference to any prior knowledge, but providing the usual machine-learning artefacts of training- and test-data; and allowing the possibility that solutions may not be unique.

Inspired by ARC, but in a more controlled setting, we propose the Inductive Program Synthesis Challenge for ARC-like tasks (IPARC). We are particularly interested in the identification of structured programs. For the challenge, we define a set of 'ARC-like' tasks characterised by: (a) *Data*, consisting of training- and test-sets for constructing and testing programs, with images drawn from a clearly defined set (which we call 'ARC-like' images); (b) *Basic functions*, drawn from four different categories of image-transformation operations (mathematical morphology operations, re-colouring, re-sizing, and endomorphisms), that we show are sufficient for constructing a transformation between any single pair of input-output ARC-like images; and (c) *Target programs*, known to solve the

---

[2] https://www.kaggle.com/c/abstraction-and-reasoning-challenge.

tasks in the sense of being able to transform input images to output image in both training- and test-sets.

The tasks in the IPARC rely on a result from structured program-construction that identifies three rules of grammar (encoding sequence, selection and iteration) as being sufficient for representing a wide class of programs. It is possible to view any instance of these rules within a program as constituting a 'subprogram', with a meaning given by a mathematical (sub-)function defined using some pre-defined basic functions. The overall computation of the program is then a (mathematical) composition of (sub-)functions. The tasks in the IPARC challenge are intended for machine learning methods of program-synthesis that can address instances of these three rules. It is useful to clarify immediately what is not being claimed in this paper. Given the open-ended nature of ARC, we do not claim solving tasks in the IPARC is necessary or sufficient to solve tasks in the ARC. However, it seems plausible that a machine-learning approach equipped with techniques for addressing the IPARC would be able to re-use those techniques to good effect to address tasks in the ARC.

There are good reasons to consider ILP as being well-suited to address tasks in the IPARC: (a) Sequences, selection and iteration can all be represented as logic- (or functional-)programs; (b) Basic functions can be provided as background knowledge to an ILP system; (3) Identification of sub-functions corresponds to the invention of new predicates by an ILP system; and (4) Identification of iteration can be achieved through the construction of recursive statements by an ILP system. In principle therefore, the tasks in the IPARC challenge should be solvable by an ILP system. But, in practice is there a single ILP system or approach that can effectively construct structured programs? The purpose of the IPARC challenge is to determine if this is the case.

The rest of the paper is organised as follows. Section 2 provides an introduction to the area of morphological filters that form a significant component of the background knowledge for the tasks we propose later. Section 3.3 describes a set basic functions for ARC-like tasks. Section 4 describes the 'IPARC' challenge that contains 3 categories of tasks aimed at testing the capabilities of current ILP systems to both invent new functions and synthesise complete programs. Section 5 concludes the paper.

2   Mathematical Morphology (MM)

Mathematical Morphology (MM) is field developed during the 1960s [9] for the purpose of analysis of petrographic samples. However, it has evolved into a strong image processing framework based on non-linear operators. In this section, we review three important operators from MM for binary images relevant to this paper. For details regarding other operators and theory of MM refer to [7,8]. Before describing the operators we make some remarks:

- All MM operators in this paper operate with *two* images—one is considered to be the input image and the other, referred to as the *structuring element* (s.e.), is used to "probe" the input to generate the output;

- Note that a binary image can be written as a function $f : \mathbb{Z}^2 \to \{0, 1\}$. Hence, each pixel within the image can be "addressed" using pairs of integers. The set of pixels which take the value 1 are referred to as *foreground* and the set of pixels which take the value 0 are referred to as *background*;
- The structuring element (s.e.) is defined with an origin $(0, 0)$, usually identified with a $\bigcirc$ at the pixel. The other pixels are accordingly addressed using integers. For instance, the pixel to the left of the origin is given the address of $(-1, 0)$, and so on.
- Also, observe that each binary image can be equivalently represented as a set by considering the set of pixels with value 1. We will use binary images and sets interchangeably in this paper. Thus, union of two images refers to the union of sets equivalent to the image, and intersection of two images refers to the intersection of sets equivalent to the image. Note that these are only valid when the images are of same size;
- It is useful to think of MM operators as belonging to the class of functions $\mathcal{I} \times \mathcal{F} \times \mathcal{B} \to \mathcal{I}$. Here $\mathcal{I}$ is a set of images, $\mathcal{F}$ is a set of Boolean functions, and $\mathcal{B}$ is a set of s.e.'s. Any particular MM operator usually involves a specific Boolean function $F \in \mathcal{F}$ and a specific s.e. $B \in \mathcal{B}$. The resulting operator is then $\mu_{F,B} : \mathcal{I} \to \mathcal{I}$. When one or the other or both of F, B is obvious from the context, it is dropped from the suffix of the operator.

For reasons of space, we direct the reader to the IPARC website for informal descriptions of some commonly used MM operators.

3   Program Synthesis for ARC-Like Tasks

3.1   ARC-Like Images and Tasks

We first develop an abstract characterisation of what we will call ARC-like' images (the corresponding tasks being ARC-like tasks). Let $I_{m,n}^k$ denote a particular image, where (m, n) denotes the size of the grid and k denotes the set of possible colours each pixel can take. This image can be decomposed as follows:

$$I_{m,n}^k = \langle I_{m,n}^{(1)}, I_{m,n}^{(2)}, \cdots, I_{m,n}^{(k)} \rangle \tag{1}$$

where $I_{m,n}^{(i)}$ denotes a binary image (only possible values are $0, 1$) of colour i. Let

$$\mathcal{L}_{m,n}^k = \{I_{m,n}^k \mid m, n \text{ fixed and each pixel has value 1 in} \tag{2}$$
$$\text{at most one of } \langle I_{m,n}^{(j)} \rangle_{j=1}^k \}$$

We distinguish $\mathcal{L}_{m,n}^k$ from:

$$\tilde{\mathcal{L}}_{m,n}^k = \{I_{m,n}^k \mid m, n \text{ fixed where each of} \tag{3}$$
$$\langle I_{m,n}^{(j)} \rangle_{j=1}^k \text{ can be any binary image.}\}$$

That is, the set $\tilde{\mathcal{L}}$ contains images which can have multiple colours associated with any pixel. We will denote the set of 'ARC-like' images as $\mathcal{L} = \bigcup_{m,n} \mathcal{L}_{m,n}^k$.

An 'ARC-like' task T is a finite set $\{(i, o) : i, o \in \mathcal{L}\}$. Usually, $|T|$ will be some small number, like three. In this paper, program-synthesis for an ARC-like task T will mean constructing a sequence of functional compositions that identifies a many-to-one mapping $f : \mathcal{I} \to \mathcal{I}$ s.t. for every $(i, o) \in T$, $f(i) = o$. Additionally, we will require the function f to be "general enough" to be correct on additional sets of input images *not* used in the construction of f.

3.2   Functional Categories for ARC-Like Tasks

Given colours $1 \ldots k$ recall that all the input/output images in an ARC-like task belong to the space $\mathcal{L} = \bigcup_{m,n} \mathcal{L}_{m,n}^k$, where $\mathcal{L}_{m,n}^k$ is the set of all colour-images of a (fixed) size m, n. Also, for a fixed m, n let $\mathcal{I}_{m,n}^{(j)}$ denote the set of $m \times n$ binary images of colour j. In this paper, we propose functions in the following basic categories for solving ARC-like tasks:

Structure. Functions in this category are concerned with changing the structure of the image. We provide definitions for the following kinds of functions:

1. For each colour $j = 1 \ldots k$, colour-specific MM-operators are functions of the form $\phi^{(j)} : \mathcal{I}_{m,n}^{(j)} \to \mathcal{I}_{m,n}^{(j)}$ [3]
2. An overall structuring operation is a function $\phi : \mathcal{L}_{m,n}^k \to \tilde{\mathcal{L}}_{m,n}^k$ defined as follows:

$$\phi(\langle I_{m,n}^{(1)}, \cdots, I_{m,n}^{(k)} \rangle) = \langle \tilde{I}_{m,n}^{(1)}, \cdots, \tilde{I}_{m,n}^{(k)} \rangle$$

where $\tilde{I}_{m,n}^{(j)} = \phi^{(j)}(I_{m,n}^{(j)})$. Note that the l.h.s. is the same as $\phi(I_{m,n}^k)$ and is an element of $\tilde{\mathcal{L}}_{m,n}^k$. That is, a ϕ operation can assign more than one colour to a pixel.

Colour. Functions in this category either resolve conflicting assignments of colours to the same pixel, or perform consistent re-colourings. For some m, n this category contains functions of the form $\gamma : \tilde{\mathcal{L}}_{m,n}^k \to \mathcal{L}_{m,n}^k$.

Size. One or more re-sizing functions of the form $\psi : \mathcal{L}_{m_1,n_1}^k \to \mathcal{L}_{m_2,n_2}^k$. These change the size of the grids of an image I_{m_1,n_1}^k to I_{m_2,n_2}^k where $(m_1, n_1) \neq (m_2, n_2)$ [4].

It is useful also to distinguish an overall structure-and-colour operation $\Phi : \mathcal{L}_{m,n}^k \to \mathcal{L}_{m,n}^k$ defined as:

$$\Phi(I_{m,n}^k) = \gamma(\phi(I_{m,n}^k))$$

$\Phi(\cdot)$ transforms an image in the manner shown in Fig. 3.

We define one further category of operations based on $\Phi(\cdot)$:

---

[3] Correctly, the function is $\phi_{F_j, B_j}^{(j)}$, where F_j is the Boolean function used by the MM operator, and B_j is the set of s.e's used by the operator.

[4] That is, either $m_1 \neq m_2$ or $n_1 \neq n_2$.

$$\tilde{I}_{m,n}^k \quad = \left\langle \tilde{I}_{m,n}^{(1)}\ \tilde{I}_{m,n}^{(2)} \quad \tilde{I}_{m,n}^{(3)} \quad \cdots \quad \tilde{I}_{m,n}^{(k)} \right\rangle$$

$$\uparrow \qquad\qquad \uparrow \quad\ \uparrow \quad\ \uparrow \qquad\qquad \uparrow$$

$$\boxed{\text{Color Change}}$$

$$\Phi \quad := \qquad\qquad \uparrow \quad\ \uparrow \quad\ \uparrow \qquad\qquad \uparrow$$

$$\phi^{(1)} \quad \phi^{(2)} \quad \phi^{(3)} \qquad\qquad \phi^{(k)}$$

$$I_{m,n}^k \quad = \left\langle I_{m,n}^{(1)}\ I_{m,n}^{(2)} \quad I_{m,n}^{(3)} \quad \cdots \quad I_{m,n}^{(k)} \right\rangle$$

Fig. 3. Illustrating the Φ operator

Endomorphisms. Two specific endomorphic functions are defined on $\mathcal{L}_{m,n}^k$:

$$\oplus(I_{m,n}^k) = I_{m,n}^k \cup \Phi(I_{m,n}^k)$$

and

$$\otimes(I_{m,n}^k) = I_{m,n}^k \cap \Phi(I_{m,n}^k)$$

where,

$$\begin{aligned}
I_{m,n}^k \cup \phi(I_{m,n}^k) &= \langle I_{m,n}^{(1)} \cup \tilde{I}_{m,n}^{(1)}, I_{m,n}^{(2)} \cup \tilde{I}_{m,n}^{(2)}, \cdots, I_{m,n}^{(k)} \cup \tilde{I}_{m,n}^{(k)} \rangle \\
I_{m,n}^k \cap \phi(I_{m,n}^k) &= \langle I_{m,n}^{(1)} \cap \tilde{I}_{m,n}^{(1)}, I_{m,n}^{(2)} \cap \tilde{I}_{m,n}^{(2)}, \cdots, I_{m,n}^{(k)} \cap \tilde{I}_{m,n}^{(k)} \rangle
\end{aligned} \tag{4}$$

Although not explicitly defined as such, we will take each of Structure, Colour, Size and Endomorphisms to be sets of functions, and denote $\Sigma = Structure \cup Colour \cup Size \cup Endomorphisms$. We claim that these sets are *sufficient* for a restricted form of ARC-like tasks. Specifically, we have the following proposition.

Proposition 1. *If $I_{m_1,n_1}^k, \tilde{I}_{m_2,n_2}^k$ are from $\bigcup \mathcal{L}_{m,n}^k$ and I_{m_1,n_1}^k is non-empty, then there exists a sequence of functions $\langle f_1, f_2, \ldots, f_N \rangle$ s.t. each $f_i \in \Sigma$ and $\tilde{I}_{m_2,n_2}^k = f_N(f_{N-1} \cdots (f_1(I_{m_1,n_1}^k)) \cdots)$.*

Proof. See Appendix A.

We will use $\tilde{I} =_\Sigma f(I)$ to denote that given an input-output pair $(I, \tilde{I})$, $\tilde{I}$ is obtained by the composition f of some functions from Σ applied to I.

The result in Proposition 1 is useful in that it identifies the kinds of functions needed for ARC-like tasks. But the result does not immediately tell us what the $\langle f_i \rangle_1^N$ are, because: (a) Other than Φ, $\oplus$, and $\otimes$, all other functions remain unspecified. These are the $\phi_{m,n}^{(j)}$-functions in Structure, the γ-functions in Colour and the ψ-functions in Size; (b) Even if all the functions were specified, the proof does not provide a constructive method to identify the sequence; and (c) Even if an appropriate sequence for an image-pair was found, this may still not be sufficient for solving an ARC-like task T. We would like a function sequence to be 'general enough' to apply to all image-pairs in T. We will have more to say on this shortly.

We have minimally to address each of these problems when identifying a solution for ARC-like tasks.

3.3   ILP-Based Program Synthesis for ARC-Like Tasks

Before we consider the use of ILP for solving ARC-like tasks it is useful to clarify what exactly we will mean by a program and the computation it performs. In this paper, we will adopt the position taken in the Structured Program Theorem (or the Böhm-Jacopini Theorem [2]), according to which structured programs can be constructed solely by combining subprograms containing sequence, selection, or iteration. We will further assume each subprogram can be mathematically represented by a function, which we will call a sub-function, and that a program's computation given some input is equivalent to the application of the composition of the sub-functions to the input.

We turn now to an ILP formulation of identifying such compositions. A first-cut at an ILP formulation is just this:

Given: the set of basic functions B as background knowledge, and examples E of input-output images,
  Find: a program H s.t. $B \wedge H \models E$.

For ARC-like tasks, we will assume the basic functions will include well understood image-manipulation functions from the sets Structure, Colour, Size, and Endomorphisms categories. Also, we restrict ourselves to the standard MM operators of *Dilation* and *Erosion* with different structuring elements to model the Structure operators. The structuring elements to be used are those shown in Fig. 4. The set of functions Σ_1 consists of: (1) *Dilation* and *Erosion* with eight different structuring elements as shown in Fig. 4; (2) *Colour* and *Size* operations as described above; and (3) *Endomorphisms* as described above. The functions in Σ_1 are available at: https://ac20.github.io/IPARC/Challenge/.

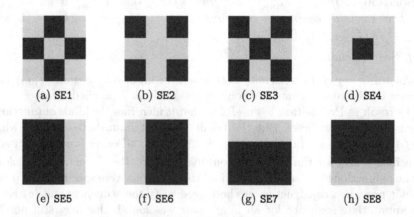

Fig. 4. The eight structuring elements (s.e.'s) used in this paper, where yellow pixels denote value 1 and purple denotes 0. Each s.e. is a 3×3 grid. Functions in Σ_1 comprise the `Dilation` and `Erosion` operators with any of these structuring elements, along with Color, Size and Endomorphism operators (see text for details).

Even though Σ_1 is a restriction of Σ, it remains challenging as we note with the following proposition.

Proposition 2. *Given the set of functions Σ_1 there exists an ARC-like task T that contains elements $(I_1, \tilde{I}_1)$, $(I_2, \tilde{I}_2)$, s.t. $\tilde{I}_1 =_{\Sigma_1} f(I_1)$, and $\tilde{I}_2 =_{\Sigma_1} g(I_2)$ but there is no h s.t. $\tilde{I}_1 =_{\Sigma_1} h(I_1)$ and $\tilde{I}_2 =_{\Sigma_1} h(I_2)$.*

Proof. See Appendix A.

That is, there may not be any single composition sequence of functions from Σ_1 that can solve all examples in an ARC-like task.[5] It follows that solving a given set of ARC-like tasks may require enlargement of the set of functions Σ_1. Here we will restrict ourselves to enlarging the existing set of functions Σ_1 by constructing new functions that re-use elements of Σ_1 within the constructs described by the Structured Program Theorem, namely sequence, selection and iteration. Specifically, we will require that the new functions of these kinds should be constructed automatically by the program-synthesis engine (in ILP terminology, we require Σ_1 to be augmented by predicate-invention only). In turn, this means that the background knowledge B in the ILP formulation of the program-synthesis task will need to be augmented with definitions for sequence, selection and iteration to allow inference; and perhaps also meta-information that can help learn these control structures from data. The former is straightforward, the latter is less obvious.

Remark: Note that all problems in IPARC can be solved using Σ_1^+ (Σ with predicate-invention), even though not all (i,o) pairs from $\mathcal{L}$ would have a solution in Σ_1^+. (From proposition 1, we have Σ is sufficient to obtain a solution to an arbitrary (i,o) pair.)

4   IPARC

The Inductive Program Synthesis Challenge for ARC-like Tasks, or IPARC, is intended to assess the current state of readiness of ILP systems to address challenges posed by the synthesis of structured programs. Specifically, we structure tasks in the IPARC in the following way: (A) Tasks that require simple sequence of steps; (B) Tasks that augment techniques in (A) with techniques for synthesis of sub-programs; and (C) Tasks that augment techniques in (B) with techniques for constructing full programs from sub-programs.

Below we describe the categories of tasks in the IPARC and provide examples in each category. Within each category, we distinguish between "easy" and "hard" variants.[6] In all cases, programs that solve the tasks are generated automatically. The programs serve two purposes: they serve as potential 'target programs' for the program-synthesis engines; and they can be used as generators of

---

[5] This is consistent with the Böhm-Jacopini result, which says that more than just sequence will be needed.

[6] For reasons of space, a complete listing of tasks in each category is not provided. Instead, we describe the requirements in each category, and provide some illustrative examples. A complete listing will be available at the IPARC website.

data. The latter may prove useful for approaches that require more data than are provided.

Remark 1. *Assuming that the length of sequence of operators is l and number of options for each operator is d, the size of this set is $\mathcal{O}(d^l)$. So, the complexity increases exponentially with the length. For IPARC tasks, we seek to have the length between 4–8. For instance, the Structure functions we have chosen to strictly alternate between Dilation and Erosion, starting with Dilation, and each operator has a choice of eight structuring elements (illustrated in Fig. 4). Hence d in this case is 8. So, the size of the search space is of the order 2^{24}.*

4.1   Category A: Warm-Up

Category A tasks consist simply of learning generalisations by functional compositions of relations in Σ_1. The tasks are in two sub-categories: (a) **Easy.** Solutions of tasks consist of programs that require relations from the categories of Structure and Endomorphisms; and (b) **Hard.** Solutions of tasks consist of programs that require relations from the entire set in Σ_1.

In principle, all programs in Category A can be obtained by a generate-and-test approach, with some simple generalisation over parameters used by the background relations. However the size of the search-space (see Remark 1) may preclude such a brute-force approach. Figure 5 illustrates a simple program from category A.

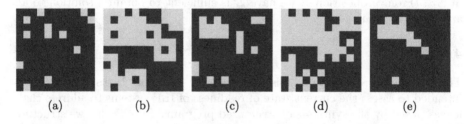

| (a) | (b) | (c) | (d) | (e) |

Fig. 5. Example images from a program used to generate data in Category A, where (a) shows a sample input image, (b) shows the image obtained after operating on (a) with Dilation_SE4, (c) shows the image after operating on (b) with Erosion_SE5, (d) shows the image after operating on (c) with Dilation_SE1, and (e) shows the image after operating on (d) with Erosion_SE3

4.2   Category B: Learning Sub-programs

Proposition 2 suggests that in general, an ability to invent new functions may be needed to construct programs that explain multiple instances in an ARC-like task. Here we consider a simpler but nevertheless still useful variant of the general predicate-invention problem. All the tasks we consider here are solvable as in Category A, but inventing one or more new functions defined in terms of functions already in Σ_1 will allow a more compact definitions across tasks, due to reuse of definitions. Within this restricted setting, we propose tasks that require the invention of predicates corresponding to subsets of functions in Σ_1.

For all tasks in this category, systems are given a set of ARC-like tasks $\{T_1, T_2, \ldots, T_N\}$. Let $H_1, H_2, \ldots, H_N$ be individual programs obtained independently for each task using background relations in Σ_1. The tasks involve automatically augmenting Σ_1 to $\Sigma_1^+ \supset \Sigma_1$ and obtaining programs $H_1', H_2', \ldots, H_N'$ such that $(|\Sigma_1 \cup H_i \cup H_2 \cdots \cup H_N|) > (|\Sigma_1^+ \cup H_1' \cup H_2' \cdots \cup H_N'|)$, where $|\cdot|$ denotes some measure of size.

Augmentations correspond to sub-programs, and in an ILP setting corresponds to invention of the new predicates. We propose tasks that benefit from the following kinds of predicate-invention:

(a) Invention of Sequence. The predicate to be invented can be seen as to be of the kind used in the inter-construction operation of inverse resolution [6]. It may be helpful to think of this form of predicate-invention as 'slot-filling' in the value of NewP in the following higher-order statement (the syntax is Prolog-ish; X, Y are images):

```
newp(X,Y,NewP):- NewP(X,Y).
```

New predicate definitions are therefore similar to the programs obtained in Category A, except they may only represent some sub-computation. As with Category A, we will distinguish between Easy and Hard variants, where specifications of these sub-categories will be available on the IPARC website.

(b) Invention of Selection. Here predicate-invention is used to represent conditionals. As above, it may be helpful to see this to mean slot-filling the values of Q, NewP1, and NewP2 in the following Prolog-like higher-order statement:[7]

```
if_else(X,Y,Q,NewP1,NewP2):- (Q(X) -> NewP1(X,Y); NewP2(X,Y)).
```

In all tasks, we will assume Q to be restricted to one of the Hit-or-Miss relations in Σ_1. We again propose to distinguish between Easy and Hard variants; we refer the reader to the IPARC website for details.

(c) Invention of Iteration. We will restrict iteration to bounded repetition. corresponding to slot-filling K and NewP in:

```
repeat_k(X,Y,K,NewP):-
  (K > 0 -> (NewP(X,Y1), K1 is K - 1, repeat_k(Y1,Y,K1,NewP));
Y=X).
```

Again, some tasks will involve the invention of more complex iterators than others.

In each case, the benefit of predicate-invention has to be decided automatically, based on: (a) the repeated occurrence on some subset of tasks provided;

---

[7] A->B;C is to be read as "if A then B else C"; X, Y are images, Q is a variable, standing for any Boolean function of X from Σ_1, NewP1 and NewP2 are invented predicates.

and (b) the trade-off of increasing the size of Σ_1 with the addition of new functions and the decrease in overall size of the programs for all tasks. Figure 6 shows example of **Selection** predicate-invention.

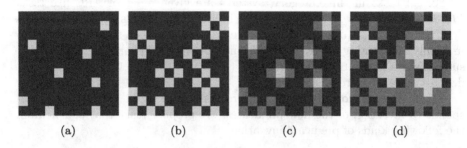

(a)   (b)   (c)   (d)

Fig. 6. Example of Selection predicate-invention in Category B. (a) indicates the input image. (b) is obtained using the `Dilation_SE3` operator on (a). (c) indicates the pixels selected using `Hit_Or_Miss_SE3`. Recall that `Hit_Or_Miss` selects those pixels which fit a particular pattern and is used to simulate the Conditional `Q`. (d) shows the final image where pixels identified by the conditional are transformed using `Dilation_SE1` and the rest of the pixels are transformed using `Dilation_SE2`. That is, we have `NewP1` = `Dilation_SE1` and `NewP2` = `Dilation_SE2`

4.3   Category C: Learning Programs from Traces

This category is concerned with the connecting sub-programs using a sequence of examples describing a computation trace. This requires us to generalise the definition of ARC-like tasks to include data in a manner akin to inductive program synthesis by demonstration (PBD [5]). Instead of a task containing a set pairs of input-output images, it is now a set of sequences of images. Each sequence represents a computation by the program from an input-image to an output-image.[8] Given a set of tasks $\{T_1, T_2, \ldots, T_N\}$, the requirement is to find a program that correctly derives all the intermediate input-output pairs of images. Suppose the computation for task T_j is represented by the sequence of images $\langle I_{j,1}, I_{j,2}, \ldots, I_{j,n_k} \rangle$. Then each pair $(I_{j,k}, I_{j,k+1})$ in this sequence can be seen as a specification for a Category B task. Several (sub-)programs may synthesised could solve this task. In principle, a complete solution for a set of tasks in Category C can be found by identifying and combining alternative sub-programs for all such image-pairs, possibly with some generalisation. Again, the combinations possible may preclude such a brute-force approach. Tasks within the category C would provide snapshots after each sub-program (belonging to Category A or B) similar to the one provided in Figs. 5 and 6.

---

[8] This is clearly more information than provided in Categories A and B, and, in that sense, Category C tasks can be seen as providing more constraints on the program-synthesis problem.

Website for the Dataset
The dataset and the generating procedures will be hosted on https://github.com/ac20/IPARC_ChallengeV2.

5 Concluding Remarks

Inductive program synthesis, especially using small data sets exemplifying visual analogy problems has a surprisingly long history in Computer Science. The Abstraction and Reasoning Corpus (ARC) continues this long tradition. The ARC presents a formidable challenge to the use of machine learning techniques for program synthesis: it is abstract, dealing with apparently arbitrary visual patterns; the data are extremely limited; it requires some core background knowledge, which may be necessary but not sufficient. Finally, the programs are required to be applicable on data which may look substantially different. No significant details are available on either the background knowledge or the new data, and all that is known is that all tasks in the ARC have been solved manually (but the solutions are not known). While the ARC represents a laudable goal to achieve, we have used it as inspiration for the Inductive Program Synthesis Challenge for ARC-like Tasks (IPARC). The IPARC presents a controlled setting directly concerned with the automated synthesis of programs. We propose a definition of 'ARC-like' images, identify a set of 'ARC-like' tasks, and provide background knowledge, with the following properties: (a) All images in the ARC are also in the set of ARC-like images; (b) The tasks are concerned with identifying constructs known to be sufficient for a large class of structured programs; and (c) The background knowledge is provably sufficient for any specific pair of images in the data provided for each ARC-like task. We provide training- and test-data sets for all tasks, and also present programs that correctly transform input-images to output-images (although these may not be the only solutions).

We note here that the background knowledge proposed for solving IPARC tasks may not immediately useful for ARC tasks. For example, consider the case that there exists a unique program in Σ_1^+, (that is, functions in Σ_1 and augmented with predicates invented for specific compositions, selection and iteration) that solves every training example of an ARC task. An IPARC solver will find this program, but this program may still fail for the test example(s) in the ARC task, with the 'true' solution program being outside Σ_1^+, which uses the hitherto unspecified and possibly unknown set of 'core knowledge' primitives that ARC tasks are based on. This does not of course invalidate the utility of an ILP engine capable of starting with some set background primitives and enlarging that set to construct programs automatically from examples.

Despite its restricted setting, tasks in the IPARC are still non-trivial. They require the identification of sub-programs consisting of sequences of functional transformations, conditionals and iteration. In principle, techniques have been proposed and demonstrated within ILP systems for addressing each of these requirements. But these have been over nearly 4 decades of conceptual development in the use of domain-knowledge, predicate-invention, and learning recursive programs. What about in practice? That is, are there any current ILP systems that can address the type of problems posed in the IPARC? We invite ILP practitioners to participate in the IPARC and showcase the program-synthesis capabilities of their ILP system.

Acknowledgements. AS is a Visiting Professor at Macquarie University, Sydney. He is also the Class of 1981 Chair Professor at BITS Pilani, Goa, the Head of the Anuradha and Prashant Palakurthi Centre for AI Research (APPCAIR) at BITS Pilani, and a Research Associate at TCS Research.

A   Proofs

We prove Proposition 1 by using the following two lemmas.

Lemma 1. *Given any $m_1 \neq m_2$ and $n_1 \neq n_2$, there exists a sequence of ψ transitions which take an image from $\mathcal{L}_{m_1,n_1}$ and returns an image from $\mathcal{L}_{m_2,n_2}$.*

Lemma 2. *Given any two images $I^k_{m,n}, \tilde{I}^k_{m,n} \in \mathcal{L}^k_{m,n}$, one can find a sequence of transitions within ϕ operators which takes in as input $I^k_{m,n}$ and returns $\tilde{I}^k_{m,n}$.*

From Lemmas 1 and 2, it is clear that there exists a sequence of transitions which takes in as input $I^k_{m_1,n_1}$ and returns $\tilde{I}^k_{m_2,n_2}$. We first prove Lemma 1

Proof (Proof of Lemma 1). The proof follows from the observation that one can find an integer p such that $pm_1 \geq m_2$ and $pn_1 \geq n_2$. Thus, consider the resizing operator $\psi^{1,p}$ which copies the image $I^k_{m_1,n_1}$ on a grid of size $p \times p$, followed by $\psi_{(0,0),(m_2,n_2)}(.)$ which crops the image with corners $(0,0)$ and (m_2, n_2). This achieves the desired result.

Proof (Proof of Lemma 2). Observe the following - Given any two binary images (of same shape) I_1, I_2, with I_1 as non-zero, we have that,

$$\delta_{I_2} \epsilon_{I_1}(I_1) = I_2 \tag{5}$$

Case A: If all of $I^{(i)}_{m,n}$ (refer Fig. 3.2) are non-empty, we have that there exists a transition $\phi^{(i)}$ which takes $I^{(i)}_{m,n}$ to output $\tilde{I}^{(i)}_{m,n}$.

Case B: Let $I^{(i_0)}_{m,n}$ be empty for some colour i_0. Since $I^k_{m,n}$ is non-empty, there exists an i' such that $I^{(i')}_{m,n}$ is non-empty. We define the operator ϕ as follows - $\phi^{(i)} = id$, where id denotes the identity map, and the colour change c maps colour i' to i_0. Then the proof is as in Case A.

Proof (Proof of Proposition 2). The proof of Proposition 2 follows from the following observation - Any given transition in Σ_1 either

- Takes an element from $\mathcal{L}^k_{m,n}$ to itself, or
- Takes an element from $\mathcal{L}^k_{m,n}$ to $\tilde{\mathcal{L}}^k_{m,n}$, or

– Takes an element from $\mathcal{L}^k_{m,n}$ to $\mathcal{L}^k_{m',n'}$ where $m' \neq m$ and $n' \neq n$.

Thus, given any I_1, I_2 and f we have that the shape of $(\tilde{I}_1) =_\Sigma f(I_1)$ should be the same as $(\tilde{I}_2) =_\Sigma f(I_2)$.

However, it is possible for an ARC-like task to have different shapes for $(\tilde{I}_1)$ and $(\tilde{I}_2)$. An example of this is shown below (Fig. 7).

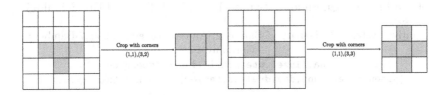

Fig. 7. Example of ARC-like task with different output shapes

References

1. Acquaviva, S., et al.: Communicating natural programs to humans and machines. arXiv preprint arXiv:2106.07824 (2021)
2. Böhm, C., Jacopini, G.: Flow diagrams, turing machines and languages with only two formation rules. Commun. ACM **9**(5), 366–371 (1966)
3. Chollet, F.: On the measure of intelligence. CoRR abs/1911.01547 (2019). http://arxiv.org/abs/1911.01547
4. Evans, T.G.: A heuristic program to solve geometric-analogy problems. In: Fischler, M.A., Firschein, O. (eds.) Readings in Computer Vision, pp. 444–455. Morgan Kaufmann, San Francisco (1987). https://doi.org/10.1016/B978-0-08-051581-6.50046-5. https://www.sciencedirect.com/science/article/pii/B9780080515816500465
5. Lau, T.A., Domingos, P.M., Weld, D.S.: Learning programs from traces using version space algebra. In: Gennari, J.H., Porter, B.W., Gil, Y. (eds.) Proceedings of the 2nd International Conference on Knowledge Capture (K-CAP 2003), 23–25 October 2003, Sanibel Island, FL, USA, pp. 36–43. ACM (2003). https://doi.org/10.1145/945645.945654
6. Muggleton, S.H., Raedt, L.D.: Inductive logic programming: theory and methods. J. Log. Program. **19/20**, 629–679 (1994). https://doi.org/10.1016/0743-1066(94)90035-3
7. Najman, L., Talbot, H.: Mathematical Morphology: from theory to applications, 520 p. ISTE-Wiley (2010). ISBN 9781848212152. https://hal-upec-upem.archives-ouvertes.fr/hal-00622479. https://doi.org/10.1002/9781118600788
8. Soille, P.: Morphological Image Analysis. Springer, Heidelberg (2004). https://doi.org/10.1007/978-3-662-05088-0
9. Soille, P., Serra, J. (eds.): Mathematical Morphology and Its Applications to Image Processing. Springer, Dordrecht (1994). https://doi.org/10.1007/978-94-011-1040-2

Explaining with Attribute-Based and Relational Near Misses: An Interpretable Approach to Distinguishing Facial Expressions of Pain and Disgust

Bettina Finzel[✉][iD], Simon P. Kuhn, David E. Tafler, and Ute Schmid[iD]

Cognitive Systems, University of Bamberg, An der Weberei 5, 96047 Bamberg, Germany
{bettina.finzel,ute.schmid}@uni-bamberg.de,
{simon-peter.kuhn,david-elias.tafler}@stud.uni-bamberg.de

Abstract. Explaining concepts by contrasting examples is an efficient and convenient way of giving insights into the reasons behind a classification decision. This is of particular interest in decision-critical domains, such as medical diagnostics. One particular challenging use case is to distinguish facial expressions of pain and other states, such as disgust, due to high similarity of manifestation. In this paper, we present an approach for generating contrastive explanations to explain facial expressions of pain and disgust shown in video sequences. We implement and compare two approaches for contrastive explanation generation. The first approach explains a specific pain instance in contrast to the most similar disgust instance(s) based on the occurrence of facial expressions (attributes). The second approach takes into account which temporal relations hold between intervals of facial expressions within a sequence (relations). The input to our explanation generation approach is the output of an interpretable rule-based classifier for pain and disgust. We utilize two different similarity metrics to determine near misses and far misses as contrasting instances. Our results show that near miss explanations are shorter than far miss explanations, independent from the applied similarity metric. The outcome of our evaluation indicates that pain and disgust can be distinguished with the help of temporal relations. We currently plan experiments to evaluate how the explanations help in teaching concepts and how they could be enhanced by further modalities and interaction.

Keywords: Contrastive Explanations · Near Miss Explanations · Similarity Metrics · Inductive Logic Programming · Affective Computing

The work presented in this paper was funded partially by grant FKZ 01IS18056 B, BMBF ML-3 (TraMeExCo) and partially by grant DFG (German Research Foundation) 405630557 (PainFaceReader). We would like to thank Mark Gromowski who helped us with preparing the used data set.

S. H. Muggleton and A. Tamaddoni-Nezhad (Eds.): ILP 2022, LNAI 13779, pp. 40–51, 2024.
https://doi.org/10.1007/978-3-031-55630-2_4

1 Introduction

Reliable pain analysis is an open challenge in clinical diagnosis [18]. Pain is a highly individual experience influenced by multiple factors, e.g., the state of health [13]. If not expressed verbally, pain is often displayed through facial expressions and can be recognized by analyzing those [8,25,37]. While individuals who are fully conscious are usually able to communicate their level of pain to the medical staff, patients with limited communication skills, e.g., sedated patients in intensive care units or patients with neurodegenerative disorders such as dementia are often not able to express themselves properly [1,32]. Furthermore, pain can be easily confused with emotions such as disgust due to the similarity in facial expressions [26], which makes pain assessment and treatment a complex task. The quality of pain assessment highly depends on the health care management. Medical staff is often not experienced enough or trained sufficiently to recognize pain in individual patients [39]. Pain assessment methods supported by technology that analyze facial expressions are therefore important tools to tackle this challenge in the future [27].

One possibility to help medical staff in their decision making processes is to provide support based on artificial intelligence (AI) systems. Especially in image-based medical diagnostics, machine learning algorithms can be applied to segment images or to propose a classification [12]. However, for reasons of accountability and traceability of a diagnostic outcome, experts have to justify their decision based on the observations they made. This applies as well to machine learning models that are used as decision-support for critical tasks, such as choosing the right dose of medication to treat pain [1]. However, machine learned decision models are often black boxes. That is, it is not transparent on what information the system's decision has been based on. With respect to transparency of algorithmic decisions, explainable artificial intelligence (XAI) is an important research field which aims at (1) making obscure and complex machine learning models transparent, or (2) using interpretable and inherently comprehensible machine learning approaches [2,20,33,36]. In both cases, the human expert gets an explanation that gives insights into why a certain decision was made by the learned model.

To make explanations efficient, they have to be tailored to the specific needs of stakeholders and situational demands [28]. Mostly, explanations are given to justify why a certain example has been classified in a specific way. Such, so called *local* explanations, are especially helpful to confirm or broaden an expert's opinion. In contrast, it might be helpful for domain experts to gain insight into the complex decision space underlying a medical concept, that is, get a more *global* explanation for the patterns observed in the patient's data. Such global explanations are mostly given in the form of general and comprehensible rules which can be communicated independent of a specific example [30]. With respect to diagnosis it is more often of interest to justify the decision for a particular case in terms of local explanations. A specific type of local explanations are contrastive explanations [10]. As pointed out by research on how humans explain phenomenons [28], contrastive explanations are an efficient means to highlight which attributes should be present or absent in an example's data to classify it in one way rather than another ("Why class P rather than class Q?"). For instance, it may be highlighted what characterizes pain in contrast to disgust, e.g., the nose is *not* wrinkled and the lids are tightened [34,35].

We hypothesize that it might not be enough to assign an example to a class based on the occurrence or absence of attributes. For instance, due to the similarity of facial expressions of pain and disgust, they might be only discernible if temporal relations between different muscle movements are taken into account [37,40], e.g., lowering the brows *overlaps* with closing the eyes in case of an expression of pain in contrast to disgust. In the context of relational domains, it has been pointed out that crucial differences are most suitably demonstrated in the form of near misses [41]. This involves the selection of appropriate contrastive examples for a concept (near misses) that differ only in small significant characteristics from a target example. Near misses research follows mainly two directions [6]: near miss *generation* [16,17,31] and near miss *selection* [19]. While methods that generate near misses, usually do this by adapting the target example, near miss selection strategies search the input space in order to find contrastive examples that are most similar to the target example.

In this work we present and compare two approaches that produce contrastive explanations for a pain versus disgust classification task by *selecting* near misses: one approach that takes only *attributes* into consideration and another one that takes *temporal relations* into account. Both approaches have been applied to a real-world data set containing video sequences of facial expressions of pain and disgust. The data set has been obtained from a carefully designed psychological experiment, where facial expressions of pain have been induced through *transcranial magnetic stimulation* [22] in human participants in contrast to expressions of disgust. Recording the participants resulted in a data set of pain and disgust video sequences, where each facial expression in a sequence was labelled as an action unit (AU) in accordance to the well-established Facial Action Coding System (FACS) [11]. The experiment has been reported in detail in [22].

We apply Inductive Logic Programming (ILP) to obtain an interpretable classification model for each group of video sequences (pain and disgust). For this purpose all video sequences with their annotations have been translated into examples represented as Horn clauses. We train a model for our attribute-based approach (taking into account only the occurrences of AUs) and for our relational approach (where examples are enriched by temporal relations between AUs according to the Allen calculus [5]). Correctly classified examples are considered for near miss explanations. In both settings, we determine the near misses by ranking contrastive examples according to two different similarity measures. We apply the Jaccard- and the Overlap-coefficient [7,21] due to their efficiency in comparing sets. In order to enable set-based similarity computation, we utilize loss-free propositionalisation to the Horn clauses [24]. We hypothesize that near miss explanations yield shorter and more relevant explanations in contrast to less similar examples (far misses) due to the bigger intersection with target examples. We further hypothesize that temporal relations help to distinguish pain from disgust, where attribute-based methods do not suffice. We therefore evaluate the quality of explanations generated by both approaches with respect to contrasting pain with disgust. We compare the length of explanations as an indicator for information aggregation and discuss the separability of pain and disgust by temporal relations.

The paper is organized as follows: in Sect. 2 we first give an overview of existing works on near miss explanations. Afterwards we describe both our similarity-based near miss selection approaches, one for attribute-based and one for relational input in Sect. 3. In Sect. 4 we present the results of our evaluation. In Sect. 5 we conclude with a discussion and summary of our findings, and outline future prospects for the utilization and extension of our work.

2 Contrastive Explanations with Near Misses

According to Gentner's and Markman's seminal work about structure mapping in analogy and similarity, differences help humans to distinguish between multiple concepts, especially if the concepts are similar [15]. Therefore, contrastive explanations can help making sense of a classifier's decision based on differences between examples that do not belong to the same concept. As motivated in the introduction, contrastive explanations can be generated based on *near misses*. Near misses are defined as being *the examples most similar* to a given example, which do *not* belong to the same class as the given example due to few significant differences [41]. The differences obtained can be seen as representative characteristics of an example of a class in contrast to the near misses. Contrastive explanations can be derived with the help of near misses in two particular ways [6]. One approach is, to create an artificial example by making a smallest possible change to the example that is explained (near miss generation), so that it gets classified as an example of another class. The second approach is, to select the most similar example from an opposite class and contrast it with the example that is explained (near miss selection).

Hammond et al. [17] propose a generative approach for the use case of interface sketching, where interfaces are automatically created based on sketches of shapes, like arrows and boxes, provided by users. To facilitate the process, the authors' approach generates near misses for the given descriptions as suggestions to the users. Although this work is implemented based on Winston's seminal work on near misses [41], it heavily depends on pre-defined constraints, which might not always be feasible. Another method that was introduced by Gurevich et al. [16] applies a random sequence of at most 10 different so-called modification operators to positive examples (images of objects belonging to a target concept) in order to generate negative examples, the near misses. This approach can be applied in domains, where modification operators can be easily defined, such as functions over physical properties. Another approach to generating near miss explanations was published lately by Rabold et al. [31]. Their method explains a target example by modifying the rule(s) that apply to it taken from a set of rules learned with Inductive Logic Programming. Each target rule can be adapted by pre-defined rewriting procedures such that it covers a set of near misses, but not the target example. The grounding of the adapted rule serves then as a contrastive explanation.

For some domains it can be tedious or even impossible to pre-define constraints or modification operators and policies. State-of-the-art concept learning often uses feature selection mechanisms to generalize on most relevant features from the feature space, e.g., with the help of statistical methods [23]. However, such techniques may not find the smallest possible subset of relevant features of a concept and are often not designed for explaining classification results. A recently published approach *selects* a set of near miss examples based on similarity metrics, Euclidean, Manhattan and Cosine distance in particular, for the task of image classification and explanation [19]. Even though their method looks promising, it cannot be applied to relational data due to the metric feature space.

In this paper, we present an approach that is based on Winston's definition of a near miss, proposing near miss *selection* for relational data. This way, we want to circumvent the need for constraints and modification operators, since defining them may not be a trivial task in medical use cases, such as pain assessment. To select suitable examples from a contrastive class, we rank the set of contrastive examples based on their similarity to a target example. In order to keep the computational cost of the ranking algorithm low, we propositionalize the relational input and apply two set-based similarity metrics to the examples: the Jaccard- and the Overlap-coefficient. To evaluate whether our proposed approach is useful for explaining pain in contrast to disgust, we apply the similarity-based method for attributes (AUs) and for relations (temporal relations between AUs). Since, according to Winston, contrastive explanations should describe only significant differences, we compare the length of near miss and far miss explanations for both approaches. In the following section we introduce how we produce explanations for interpretable video sequence classification and present our near miss selection approaches.

3   An Interpretable Approach to Explain Facial Expressions of Pain Versus Disgust

Similar to Rabold et al. we learn a model, a set of rules, for a target class (either pain or disgust) with Inductive Logic Programming (ILP). ILP supports relational explanations in contrast to visual explanations that may not express more than just the presence or absence of features [4,19]. ILP is suitable for inducing rules from data sets that are limited in size [9] and due to its inherent transparency it is applicable to decision-critical domains, e.g., medicine [35], where comprehensibility of results and accountability play a key role. Explanations generated based on ILP can be tailored to the information need of medical staff, e.g., with verbalized global and local explanations as recently presented in Finzel et al. [14]. The following subsections introduce our similarity-based method for ILP to explain facial expressions of pain in contrast to disgust.

3.1 Learning from Symbolic Representations of Video Sequences

The input, internal program structure and output of an ILP classifier is represented in expressive first-order logic, in Prolog. The symbolic representation in the form of predicates and implications makes ILP a comprehensible approach, related to logical reasoning processes in humans. The foundations of ILP have already been introduced by Stephen Muggleton in 1991 [29]. Since then, ILP has been applied to various problems of relational learning [9].

In ILP clauses must conform to *Horn clauses* and can be written in the form of an implication rule as

$$A_0 \leftarrow A_1 \land \ldots \land A_n, \text{where } n \geq 0.$$

A_0 is called the *head* of the rule and the conjunction of elements $\bigwedge_{i=1}^n A_i$ is called the *body* of the rule. In Prolog programs that contain predicates and no propositions, each element A_i has the form $p(a_1, \ldots, a_m)$, consisting of a predicate p that takes arguments a_i. An argument is either a constant, a variable or a complex term itself (a predicate with arguments).

Prolog programs consist basically of *facts* (Horn clauses without a body) and may further contain *rules*. While facts state *unconditionally* true relations, e.g.,"a penguin is a bird", rules state what is *conditionally* true, like "birds can fly" (unless they are penguins). In Prolog, implication $\leftarrow$ is denoted by ":-".

Having introduced the basic terminology and syntax, we now define ILP's learning task. ILP learns a set of Horn clauses, also called a *theory*, from a set of positive examples E^+ that belong to the target concept and a set of negative examples E^- that do not belong to the target concept, given background knowledge B about all examples. The goal is to learn a theory T such that, given B, T covers all and no negative examples by fulfilling the following conditions:

- $\forall e \in E^+: B \cup T \models e$ (T is *complete*)
- $\forall e \in E^-: B \cup T \not\models e$ (T is *consistent*)

To learn a theory based on the symbolic representations of pain and disgust video sequences, we applied the ILP framework *Aleph* [38]. Its default algorithm performs four steps. First, an example is selected from E^+. Then, a most specific clause is constructed based on B respectively. In the third step, Aleph searches a clause that is more general than the most specific clause, and finally, all the examples that are covered by the more general clause are removed from the set of remaining positive candidate examples.

Figure 1 illustrates the symbolic representations of video sequences in the form of background knowledge and an exemplary learned rule in Prolog from which local and global explanations can be derived. Part A depicts the occurrence of AUs in terms of intervals along the time line of a pain video sequence (AU 4 = *brow lowerer*, AU 6 = *cheek raiser*, AU 7 = *lid tightener*, AU 43 = *eyes closed*, according to [11]). Based on the Allen calculus [5], which defines an algebra for formal representation and reasoning on time intervals, temporal relations are extracted. For example, AU 7 starts with AU 6 (obviously, the start time of

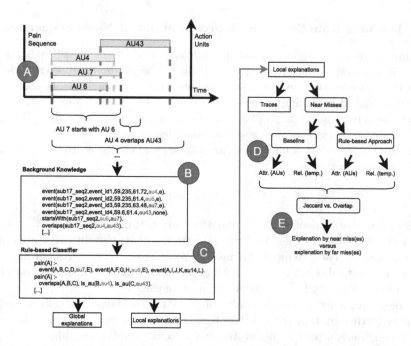

Fig. 1. An overview of our approach, showing an illustration of a video sequence of pain (A), an excerpt from the background knowledge in Prolog (B), a subset of the learned rules (C), the implementation (D) and the evaluation setting (E)

both AUs is the same) and AU 4 overlaps with AU 43. The given sequence is transformed into Prolog predicates, the background knowledge (part B). AUs are represented as events here, where each event has a sequence identifier as a first argument, followed by an event identifier, a start and an end timestamp as well as an indicator for the intensity of the emotion or pain (if applicable for the AU, ranging from a to e). Furthermore temporal relations between AUs are added to the background knowledge and denoted by predicates that contain a sequence identifier and the constants for the AUs respectively.

In a next step (part C), a rule-based model is induced from positive and negative examples and the background knowledge. Our implementation learns rules either on attributes or temporal relations. In the attribute-based approach a rule like the first one, was learned. It consists of event predicates and AUs have been included as constants (letters in lower case). The second rule was learned in the relational setting. It consists of temporal relation predicates and additional predicates to denote AUs. The first rule indicates that persons show pain in a video sequence if AU 7, AU 6 and AU 4 occur. The second rule applies to all pain sequences, where AU 4 overlaps AU 43.

The rule-based classifier can be used to produce global as well as local explanations. A global explanation can be obtained by transforming rules into verbal statements. For local explanations, a rule can be used to query each covered pain example. Therefor variables in a rule (letters in upper case) get grounded with the values from an example's background knowledge. This process is called *tracing*. The computed traces can be considered as being local explanations for the classification of examples [14], yet, they are not contrastive. Ideally, a rule separates examples well and its traces may suffice as explanations. However, where data is very similar, the decision boundary gets thin, meaning that false classifications may occur more often. Contrastive explanations may better describe its borders. The following subsection presents for both our approaches (attribute-based vs. relational), how we produce and evaluate contrastive explanations based on near misses (part D and E, Fig. 1).

3.2   Selecting Attribute-Based and Relational Near Misses Based on Similarity Metrics

In order to explain what characterizes a pain video sequence in contrast to a disgust video sequence of human facial expressions, we train two ILP models. The first is trained solely on the basis of attributes (AU events). To check, whether including temporal information is beneficial in terms of separating classes, we train another model for relations (temporal relations) between AUs. With the help of the learned models, we produce traces of all examples that we want to contrast. This way, we aim to ensure, that the characteristics, that are highly relevant to separate the different classes, are contained in the explanations.

Both approaches work with finding the most similar example(s) of the opposite class (disgust sequence(s)) first and computing the differences between the target example and the near miss(es) afterwards. The examples have a complex structure and can be represented as graphs. However, computing the similarity between graphs is not trivial. We therefore decided to reduce the problem to computing the similarity between sets. We apply two different similarity metrics: the Jaccard index and the Overlap coefficient (see part E of Fig. 1).

The Jaccard index [21], shown in Eq. 1, is a similarity measure, where the size of the intersection of two sets, A and B, is divided by the size of the union of both sets. The Overlap coefficient divides the size of the intersection of two sets by the size of the smaller set [7]. This measure is shown in Eq. 2.

$$\frac{|A \cap B|}{|A \cup B|} \tag{1}$$

$$\frac{|A \cap B|}{min(|A|,|B|)} \tag{2}$$

In order to represent the examples from the data sets as sets, we propositionalize each example's trace. For the attributes, we propositionalize the AU events, such that a feature is composed of an AU, its intensity and an index that indicates the number of occurrence (so that graphs in which an AU occurs multiple times are not reduced to sets that are similar to those of graphs, where the same AU occurs less times). The features for the relations consist of time relation between two AUs and an index that indicates the occurrence as well.

4 Evaluation

We evaluated which metric yields desirably less near misses for the attributes and relations and whether the explanation length decreases with increasing similarity, by comparing the length of explanations produced by *near* misses versus *far* misses (see Table 1). We compared our results to a baseline that takes the whole background knowledge per example into account for contrasting instead of just taking the traces. We further examine the separability of the trained classifiers.

The attribute-based classifiers trained on the TMS data set [22] reached an accuracy of 100% for pain, covering 37 positive examples, and an acc. of 100% for disgust, covering 93 pos. examples. The relational classifiers reached an acc. of 100% for pain, covering 37 pos. examples, and an acc. of more than 60,76% for disgust, covering 42 pos. examples.

Table 1. Results for the avg. number of near misses $\bar{n}_{NM}$ per target example and per approach as well as the avg. explanation length for near misses $\bar{L}_{NM}$ and far misses $\bar{L}_{FM}$ in comparison to a baseline for each similarity metric (Jaccard vs. Overlap)

	Jaccard			Overlaps		
	$\bar{n}_{NM}$	$\bar{L}_{NM}$	$\bar{L}_{FM}$	$\bar{n}_{NM}$	$\bar{L}_{NM}$	$\bar{L}_{FM}$
Attributes (baseline)	**1,09**	**7,92**	18,92	2,36	8,69	12,33
Relations (baseline)	**1,19**	**50,68**	99,88	3,06	69,76	57,49
Attributes (our approach)	**1,75**	**4,52**	6,72	3,58	4,65	6,21

The results in Table 1 show that near misses (most similar examples) yield considerably shorter contrastive explanations than far misses (least similar examples) for all settings. Although the average number of near misses is lower for the attribute-based baseline compared to our attribute-based approach, the explanation length computed on traces of trained classifiers is much lower for learned attributes compared to whole sequences. For our relational approach, no near misses could be found, since the classifiers learned for pain and disgust had no intersecting features; thus no similarity could be measured. All in all, the Jaccard coefficient produced less near misses and shorter explanations than the Overlap coefficient (highlighted in bold font).

5 Discussion and Conclusion

We presented two interpretable approaches to distinguish facial expressions of pain and disgust with the help of attribute-based and relational near misses. We computed contrastive explanations based on near miss selection, since, for the given real-world data set, we could not ensure that artificially produced near misses would yield valid real-world examples. To find near misses, we applied the Jaccard and the Overlap coefficient. Our results show that near miss explanations are shorter than far miss explanations and thus yield more efficient contrastive explanations. We found that contrastive explanations are more concise for Jaccard compared to the Overlap coefficient. Furthermore, comparing propositionalized traces gained from the rule-based classifiers, produce much shorter explanations compared to a baseline approach, where examples are considered as a whole, which is not surprising, but an additional validation of our method. For the approach of relational near misses the intersection between examples was empty, which is not a weakness of our approach, but rather indicates the separability of pain and disgust with the help of temporal relations.

One limitation of the presented results is however, that the explanations learned for pain versus disgust may not apply in general. Facial expression data bases are usually small, since the effort of labelling the video sequences is big. Only the data is used for analysis, where multiple FACS experts came to the same label decision. A particular challenge lies in the diversity of the data and in the similarity between emotional states [26]. High quality data bases for facial expressions of pain are rather sparse (e.g., [3]) and often do not contain further emotions for contrasting. We therefore plan to examine a new data set that is currently curated by psychologists but not published yet.

The two approaches presented in this paper complement existing work on contrastive explanation with near misses by providing an interpretable solution using ILP without the necessity to define contraints or modification operators. We introduced a method for near miss selection based on two computationally simple similarity metrics and applied it to efficiently explain pain versus disgust. We currently plan experiments to evaluate how the explanations help in teaching concepts and how the framework could be enhanced by further similarity measures and modalities, such as visuals and interaction [4,14]. The ultimate goal is, to provide actionable and flexible explainability in the medical domain.

References

1. Achterberg, W.P., Erdal, A., Husebo, B.S., Kunz, M., Lautenbacher, S.: Are chronic pain patients with dementia being undermedicated? J. Pain Res. **14**, 431 (2021)
2. Arrieta et al., A.B.: Explainable artificial intelligence (xai): Concepts, taxonomies, opportunities and challenges toward responsible ai. arXiv preprint arXiv:1910.10045 (2019)
3. Lucey, P., et al.: Painful data: The UNBC-McMaster shoulder pain expression archive database. In: FG, pp. 57–64. IEEE (2011)
4. Bach, S., et al.: On pixel-wise explanations for non-linear classifier decisions by layer-wise relevance propagation. PloS One **10**(7), e0130140 (2015)
5. Allen, J.F.: Towards a general theory of action and time. Artif. Intell. **23**(2), 123–154 (1984)
6. Barnwell, J.A.: Using near misses to teach concepts to a human intelligence system. Ph.D. thesis, Massachusetts Institute of Technology (2018)
7. Bradley, E.L.: Overlapping coefficient. Am. Cancer Soc. (2006). https://doi.org/10.1002/0471667196.ess1900.pub2

8. Chen, Z., Ansari, R., Wilkie, D.: Automated pain detection from facial expressions using facs: a review. arXiv preprint arXiv:1811.07988 (2018)

9. Cropper, A., Dumancic, S., Muggleton, S.H.: Turning 30: new ideas in inductive logic programming. In: Bessiere, C. (ed.) Proc. of the Twenty-Ninth Int. Joint Conference on Artificial Intelligence, IJCAI 2020, pp. 4833–4839. ijcai.org (2020). https://doi.org/10.24963/ijcai.2020/673

10. Dhurandhar, A., et al.: Explanations based on the missing: towards contrastive explanations with pertinent negatives. In: Advances in Neural Information Processing Systems, pp. 592–603 (2018)

11. Ekman, P., Friesen, W.V.: Measuring facial movement. Environ. Psychol. Nonverbal Behav. **1**(1), 56–75 (1976). https://doi.org/10.1007/BF01115465

12. Erickson, B.J., Korfiatis, P., Akkus, Z., Kline, T.L.: Machine learning for medical imaging. Radiographics **37**(2), 505–515 (2017)

13. Fillingim, R.B.: Individual differences in pain: understanding the mosaic that makes pain personal. Pain **158**(1), 11–18 (2017)

14. Finzel, B., Tafler, D.E., Thaler, A.M., Schmid, U.: Multimodal explanations for user-centric medical decision support systems. In: Doyle, T.E., et al. (eds.) Proc. of the AAAI 2021 Fall Symposium on Human Partnership with Medical AI: Design, Operationalization, and Ethics (AAAI-HUMAN 2021), November 4–6, 2021, vol. 3068. CEUR-WS.org (2021), ceur-ws.org/Vol-3068/short2.pdf

15. Gentner, D., Markman, A.B.: Structure mapping in analogy and similarity. Am. Psychol. **52**(1), 45 (1997)

16. Gurevich, N., Markovitch, S., Rivlin, E.: Active learning with near misses. In: Proc. of the National Conference on Artificial Intelligence, vol. 21, p. 362. Menlo Park, CA; Cambridge, MA; London; AAAI Press; MIT Press; 1999 (2006)

17. Hammond, T., Davis, R.: Interactive learning of structural shape descriptions from automatically generated near-miss examples. In: Proc. of the 11th Int. Conference on Intelligent User Interfaces, pp. 210–217 (2006)

18. Hassan, T., et al.: Automatic detection of pain from facial expressions: a survey. IEEE Trans. Pattern Anal. Mach. Intell. **43**(6), 1815–1831 (2019)

19. Herchenbach, M., Müller, D., Scheele, S., Schmid, U.: Explaining image classifications with near misses, near hits and prototypes: Supporting domain experts in understanding decision boundaries. In: Proc. of Pattern Recognition and Artificial Intelligence: Third Int. Conference, ICPRAI 2022, Paris, France, June 1–3, 2022, Part II, pp. 419–430. Springer, Heidelberg (2022). https://doi.org/10.1007/978-3-031-09282-4_35

20. Holzinger, A., Biemann, C., Pattichis, C.S., Kell, D.B.: What do we need to build explainable ai systems for the medical domain? arXiv:1712.09923 (2017)

21. Jaccard, P.: Distribution de la flore alpine dans le bassin des dranses et dans quelques régions voisines. Bulletin de la Socit Vaudoise des Sciences Naturelles **37**, 241–272 (1901)

22. Karmann, A.J., Maihöfner, C., Lautenbacher, S., Sperling, W., Kornhuber, J., Kunz, M.: The role of prefrontal inhibition in regulating facial expressions of pain: a repetitive transcranial magnetic stimulation study. J. Pain **17**(3), 383–391 (2016)

23. Kira, K., Rendell, L.A.: A practical approach to feature selection. In: Sleeman, D., Edwards, P. (eds.) Machine Learning Proceedings 1992, pp. 249–256. Morgan Kaufmann, San Francisco (CA) (1992). https://doi.org/10.1016/B978-1-55860-247-2.50037-1

24. Kuhn, S.P.: Identifying near misses for relational concepts with graph matching - explaining classifier decisions of facial expressions (2019)

25. Kunz, M., Meixner, D., Lautenbacher, S.: Facial muscle movements encoding pain- a systematic review. Pain **160**(3), 535–549 (2019). https://doi.org/10.1097/j.pain. 0000000000001424
26. Kunz, M., Peter, J., Huster, S., Lautenbacher, S.: Pain and disgust: the facial signaling of two aversive bodily experiences. PloS One **8**(12) (2013)
27. Lautenbacher, S., et al.: Automatic coding of facial expressions of pain: Are we there yet? Pain Research & Management 2022 (2022)
28. Miller, T.: Explanation in artificial intelligence: insights from the social sciences. arXiv:1706.07269 [cs], June 2017. arxiv.org/abs/1706.07269
29. Muggleton, S.: Inductive logic programming. N. Gener. Comput. **8**(4), 295–318 (1991). https://doi.org/10.1007/BF03037089
30. Muggleton, S.H., Schmid, U., Zeller, C., Tamaddoni-Nezhad, A., Besold, T.: Ultra- strong machine learning: comprehensibility of programs learned with ilp. Mach. Learn. **107**(7), 1119–1140 (2018)
31. Rabold, J., Siebers, M., Schmid, U.: Generating contrastive explanations for induc- tive logic programming based on a near miss approach. Mach. Learn. **111**(5), 1799– 1820 (2022)
32. Rieger, I., Finzel, B., Seuß, D., Wittenberg, T., Schmid, U.: Make pain estima- tion transparent: a roadmap to fuse bayesian deep learning and inductive logic programming. In: IEEE EMBS (2019)
33. Rudin, C.: Stop explaining black box machine learning models for high stakes decisions and use interpretable models instead. Nature Mach. Intell. **1**(5), 206–215 (2019)
34. Schmid, U.: Inductive programming as approach to comprehensible machine learn- ing. In: DKB/KIK@ KI, pp. 4–12 (2018)
35. Schmid, U., Finzel, B.: Mutual explanations for cooperative decision making in medicine. KI - Künstliche Intelligenz (2020)
36. Schwalbe, G., Finzel, B.: A comprehensive taxonomy for explainable artificial intelligence: A systematic survey of surveys on methods and concepts. CoRR abs/2105.07190 (2021). arxiv.org/abs/2105.07190
37. Siebers, M., Schmid, U., Seuß, D., Kunz, M., Lautenbacher, S.: Characterizing facial expressions by grammars of action unit sequences-a first investigation using abl. Inf. Sci. **329**, 866–875 (2016)
38. Srinivasan, A.: The Aleph Manual. www.cs.ox.ac.uk/activities/machinelearning/ Aleph/
39. Tsai, I.P., Jeong, S.Y.S., Hunter, S.: Pain assessment and management for older patients with dementia in hospitals: an integrative literature review. Pain Manage. Nursing **19**(1), 54–71 (2018). https://www.sciencedirect.com/science/article/pii/ S152490421730022X
40. Wang, Z., Wang, S., Ji, Q.: Capturing complex spatio-temporal relations among facial muscles for facial expression recognition. In: Proceedings of the IEEE Con- ference on Computer Vision and Pattern Recognition, pp. 3422–3429 (2013)
41. Winston, P.H.: Learning structural descriptions from examples. In: Winston, P. (ed.) The Psychology of Computer Vision, pp. 157–210. McGraw-Hil, New York (1975)

Learning Automata-Based Complex Event Patterns in Answer Set Programming

Nikos Katzouris[✉] and Georgios Paliouras

Institute of Informatics and Telecommunications, National Center for Scientific Research (NCSR) "Demokritos", Athens, Greece
{nkatz,gpaliourg}@iit.demokritos.gr

Abstract. Complex Event Recognition and Forecasting (CER/F) techniques attempt to detect, or even forecast ahead of time, event occurrences in streaming input using predefined event patterns. Such patterns are not always known in advance, or they frequently change over time, making machine learning techniques, capable of extracting such patterns from data, highly desirable in CER/F. Since many CER/F systems use symbolic automata to represent such patterns, we propose a family of such automata where the transition-enabling conditions are defined by Answer Set Programming (ASP) rules, and which, thanks to the strong connections of ASP to symbolic learning, are directly learnable from data. We present such a learning approach in ASP and an incremental version thereof that trades optimality for efficiency and is capable to scale to large datasets. We evaluate our approach on two CER datasets and compare it to state-of-the-art automata learning techniques, demonstrating empirically a superior performance, both in terms of predictive accuracy and scalability.

Keywords: Automata Learning · Answer Set Programming · Complex Event Recognition

1 Introduction

Complex Event Recognition and forecasting (CER/F) systems [2,8,17] detect, or even forecast ahead of time, occurrences of *complex events* (CEs) in multivariate streaming input, defined as temporal combinations of *simple events*, e.g. sensor data. CE patterns are typically defined by domain experts in some *event specification language*. However, such patterns are not always known in advance, or they frequently need to be revised, as the characteristics of the input data change over time, making machine learning techniques capable of learning such patterns from data highly desirable in CER/F.

Despite the great diversity of existing event specification languages, a minimal set of basic constructs/operators that should be present in every such language have been identified [3,17,19,36], in the form of an *abstract event algebra*. The most important of these operators are the *sequence operator* and the closely related *iteration operator (Kleene Closure)*, implying respectively that some particular events should succeed one another temporally, or that an event should

© The Author(s), under exclusive license to Springer Nature Switzerland AG 2024
S. H. Muggleton and A. Tamaddoni-Nezhad (Eds.): ILP 2022, LNAI 13779, pp. 52–68, 2024.
https://doi.org/10.1007/978-3-031-55630-2_5

occur iteratively in a sequence, and the *selection* operator, which filters (selects) events that satisfy a set of predefined predicates. Taken together, these three operators already point to a computational model for CER/F based on symbolic automata [9], and indeed, in most existing CER/F systems CE patterns are either defined directly as symbolic automata, or are compiled into such at runtime [1,2,7,10–12,29,30,35,36]. In symbolic automata the transition-enabling conditions are predicates, rather than mere symbols, as in classical automata. In CER/F, the structure of such an automaton pattern corresponds to the conditions specified by the sequence/iteration operators in the CE pattern and their transition guards correspond to the pattern's selection predicates.

Learning such symbolic automata-based CE patterns is a challenging task that requires to combine automata structure identification techniques with reasoning about the satisfiability of the selection predicates. To address this issue we propose a family of symbolic automata, which we call *answer set automata (ASA)*, where the transition guards are defined by means of rules in Answer Set Programming (ASP), providing definitions for the selection predicates. Importantly, thanks to the strong connections of ASP with symbolic learning, ASA-based CE patterns are directly learnable from data. We present an approach that utilizes the power of ASP in declarative learning to automatically construct such patterns from data and we lift this approach to an incremental version that trades optimality for efficiency and allows our learning framework to scale to large datasets. We evaluate our approach on two CER datasets and compare it to state-of-the-art automata learning techniques, demonstrating empirically a superior performance, both in terms of predictive accuracy and scalability.

2   Related Work

Although the field of automata learning [20,34] has a long history in the literature [4,5,15,16,18,21,28,32,33], existing techniques that induce automata from positive & negative traces have several shortcomings, which limit their applicability in the CER/F domain. Most such algorithms either attempt to learn a model that perfectly discriminates between the positive/negative traces [4,5,15,16,18], or they use greedy techniques for *state merging* [21,28], a technique that generalizes from a large, tree-like automaton (the *Prefix Tree Acceptor – PTA*), generated from the entire training set. These approaches tend to learn large, overfitted models that generalize poorly. More recent techniques [31] replace the PTA generalization heuristics with exact, constraint-based automata identification methods, achieving higher generalization capacity. However, the issue remains that such techniques still need to encode the entire training set into a PTA, raising memory/scalability issues in large datasets.

All aforementioned algorithms learn classical automata. Although some of these algorithms could, in principle, be applied to the symbolic automata learning setting, e.g. via propositionalization, that would entail an explosion in alphabet size and the combinatorial complexity of the learning task. On the other hand, although some algorithms for symbolic automata induction do exist

[6,13,14,26], they are mostly based on "upgrading" existing classical automata identification techniques to richer alphabets, and they thus suffer from the limitations outlined above, i.e. poor generalization, intolerance to noise and limited scalability.

Learning automata and grammars has been an application domain for ILP since its early days, targeting mostly classical automata expressed as definite clause grammars. More recent ILP frameworks, such as meta-interpretative learning (MIL) and learning from answer sets (ILASP), have also been applied to the task [15,27]. However, both these approaches learn models that perfectly discriminate between positive and negative examples, therefore, they cannot deal with noise in the data. Moreover, the MIL approach of [27] learns classical automata, and although the ILASP-based approach of [15] does learn a form of symbolic automata, the transition guards therein are restricted to propositional clauses generated from combinations of the alphabet symbols, which falls short of the CER/F requirement for arbitrary selection predicates.

In contrast to the above-mentioned approaches, our symbolic automata learning framework utilizes the full expressive power of ASP in the definitions of transition guards and ASP's declarative learning capabilities to learn highly compressive models that generalize adequately. Moreover, its incremental learning version is able to scale to arbitrarily large datasets.

3   ASP Background

We assume some familiarity with ASP and refer to [23] for an in-depth account. In this section we review some basic ASP constructs that will be useful in what follows. Throughout, we use the Clingo[1] syntax for representing ASP expressions. A choice rule is an expression of the form $\{\alpha\} \leftarrow \delta_1, \ldots, \delta_n$, with the intuitive meaning that whenever the body $\delta_1, \ldots, \delta_n$ is satisfied by an answer set I of a program that includes the choice rule, instances of the head α are arbitrarily included in I (satisfied) as well. A weak constraint is an expression of the form $:\sim \delta_1, \ldots, \delta_n.[w@p, t_1, \ldots, t_k]$, where δ_i's are literals, called the body of the constraint, w and p are integers, called respectively the *weight* and the *priority level* of the constraint and $t_1, \ldots, t_k$ are ASP terms. A grounding/instance of a weak constraint c is an expression that results from c by replacing all variables in $\delta_1, \ldots, \delta_n, t_1, \ldots, t_k$ by constants. Such an instance is satisfied by an answer set I_Π of a program Π that includes c if I_Π satisfies c's ground body, which incurs a penalty of w on I_Π. I_Π's total cost is the sum of penalties resulting from each instance of c that is satisfied by I_Π. Inclusion of weak constraints in an ASP program triggers an optimization process that yields answer sets of minimum cost. Priority levels in weak constraints model the constraints' relative importance, since the aforementioned optimization process attempts to first minimize the total cost due to weak constraints of higher priority levels.

---

[1] https://potassco.org/.

4   The Problem Setting and a Running Example

We next set the scene for our proposed automata-based CE pattern learning framework. CER/F applications usually deal with multivariate input, i.e., input that arrives in multiple streams, each representing a "signal" obtained by the evolution of a relevant domain attribute in time. We illustrate the case using a running example from the domain of precision medicine, as formulated in the context of the INFORE EU-funded project[2].

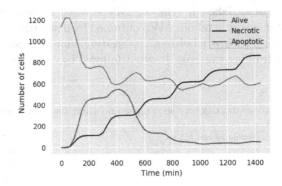

Fig. 1. A multi-cellular simulation of tumor evolution from the INFORE project.

Example 1 (*Running Example*). INFORE's precision medicine use-case utilizes CER/F techniques to assist the knowledge discovery process in personalized cancer treatment development. This process involves running a vast amount of complex, multi-cellular simulations to study the effects of various drug synergies on tumor growth. Such simulations are extremely demanding computationally and their majority ends-up in a negative result, signifying that a particular drug combination is not effective. Using CER/F to detect/forecast non-promising simulations at an early stage may thus speed up research by allowing to terminate non-interesting simulations early-on and allocate resources towards the exploration of more promising drug combinations. This calls for learning patterns of interesting/non-interesting outcomes from labeled, historical simulation data. Notably, the interpretability of such patterns is crucial in this domain. Therefore, mainstream black-box time-series classification methods, including deep learning techniques, are not an option. Figure 1 presents such a simulation generated by PhysiBoss [22], a bio-informatics simulation environment that allows to explore the results of several environmental and genetic alterations to populations of cells. Figure 1 presents tumor growth evolution over time, in terms of population sizes of three types of cell: the tumor's *alive* cells, its *apoptotic* cells, i.e. cells that are "programmed" to die, due to apoptosis, and the tumor's *necrotic* cells,

---

[2] https://www.infore-project.eu/.

i.e. cells that die due to the effects of an injected Tumor Necrosis Factor (TNF), i.e. a drug combination.

Multivariate time-series, such as the simulation data from Fig. 1, may be converted into symbolic multivariate sequences (MVSs), e.g. by using the Symbolic Aggregate Approximation (SAX) algorithm [24,25]. SAX converts time-series into symbolic sequences, by mapping numerical values to symbols, drawn from a fixed-length alphabet, such that each symbol in the converted sequence corresponds to a bin (value range) in the original time-series.

In the event pattern learning setting that we put forward we assume that the training data consist of labeled, symbolic MVSs, each representing a training example. For instance, the symbolic MVS obtained by discretizing the simulation data in Fig. 1, along with a label (e.g. *interesting/non-interesting* simulation) represents such a training example. In what follows, by MVS we always mean a symbolic MVS.

Table 1. Multivariate, discrete sequences and their logical representation.

(a) A toy training set consisting of two MVSs.	
Positive example (id_1):	**Negative example** (id_2):
Alive cells: eeeedcbbbb	*Alive cells:* eecdbbbbbb
Necrotic cells: aabbbcccde	*Necrotic cells:* aabbbbcccc
Apoptotic cells: bbbcdghhhh	*Apoptotic cells:* bbbcfghhhh

(b) The logical representation of MVS id_1:

$I_1^{id_1} = \{\text{obs}(id_1, \text{av}(alive, \text{e}), 1).\ \text{obs}(id_1, \text{av}(necrotic, \text{a}), 1).\text{obs}(id_1, \text{av}(apoptotic, \text{b}), 1).\}$

$I_2^{id_1} = \{\text{obs}(id_1, \text{av}(alive, \text{e}), 2).\ \text{obs}(id_1, \text{av}(necrotic, \text{a}), 2).\text{obs}(id_1, \text{av}(apoptotic, \text{b}), 2).\}$

$I_3^{id_1} = \{\text{obs}(id_1, \text{av}(alive, \text{e}), 3).\ \text{obs}(id_1, \text{av}(necrotic, \text{b}), 3).\text{obs}(id_1, \text{av}(apoptotic, \text{b}), 3).\}$

...

$I_{10}^{id_1} = \{\text{obs}(id_1, \text{av}(alive, \text{b}), 10).\ \text{obs}(id_1, \text{av}(necrotic, \text{e}), 10).\ \text{obs}(id_1, \text{av}(apoptotic, \text{h}), 10).\}$

Given an MVS S of maximum length n (i.e. the length of the largest sequence in S) we use a logical representation of S as a sequence of interpretations $I_1, \ldots, I_n$, where each I_t consists of ground facts that describe S's t-th coordinate. In particular, we assume that each sequence in S corresponds to a domain attribute and consists of symbols from a fixed alphabet Σ that represent the values of this attribute over time. Then, the interpretation I_t that corresponds to S's t-th coordinate consists of *observation facts* of the form $\text{obs}(SeqId, \text{av}(A, V), T)$, meaning that the attribute A of the MVS with unique id $SeqId$ has value V at time T.

*Example 2 (**Labeled MVS**).* Table 1(a) presents a minimal, toy training set with a single positive and a single negative example. Each example is an MVS consisting of three length-ten sequences regarding the evolution of cell populations for the different types of cell in our running example (Example 1). These sequences are short excerpts of longer simulation sequences, which have been discretized using SAX. Each symbol in a sequence corresponds to a bin of real values. Table 1(b) presents the logical representation of the positive example (MVS id_1) as a sequence of interpretations $I_1^{id}, \ldots, I_{10}^{id}$.

5   Answer Set Automata

We next define a family of symbolic automata that may be used to express CE patterns over MVSs. The transition guard predicates, which we shall call *transition features* and correspond to selection predicates in a CER/F context, will be defined by ASP rules, we therefore call the resulting automata *answer set automata* (ASA). Intuitively, a transition in an ASA is enabled when the body of the corresponding transition feature rule is satisfied by the input MVS. Note that ASA will be non-deterministic in principle. This is because to enforce determinism in the case of symbolic automata it must be ensured that the conditions that guard all outgoing transitions from some state q to a set of different states must be mutually exclusive. This is infeasible to guarantee in the ASA framework, since the transition features may encode arbitrary, domain-specific conditions that are deemed informative to synthesize automata with. The non-determinism of the ASA framework is in accordance with most event specification languages in the CER domain, where complex event patterns are defined as, or are eventually compiled into non-deterministic automata.

Definition 1 (Answer Set Automaton – ASA). An answer set automaton is a tuple $\mathcal{A} = \langle \Sigma, B, R, Q, q_0, F, \delta \rangle$, where: Σ is the alphabet, represented by a set of ASP facts; B is some background knowledge represented by an ASP program; R is a set of ASP rules, called the *transition features*; Q is a finite set of *states*; $q_0 \in Q$ is a designated *start state* and $F \subseteq Q$ is a designated set of *accepting states*; δ is a non-deterministic state transition function defined by means of a *feature mapping* $\delta_R : Q \times R \to Q$, where $\delta_R(q, r) = q'$ has the intuitive meaning that the transition from state q to q' is guarded by the transition feature r. Given a feature mapping δ_R, the transition function $\delta : Q \times 2^\Sigma \to 2^Q \cup \{\bot\}$ is defined as:

$$\delta(q, I) = \begin{cases} A_q = \{\delta_R(q,r) \in Q \mid I \cup B \vDash body(r)\}, \text{ if } A_q \neq \emptyset, \\ \Box \in \{\{q\}, \{\bot\}\}, \text{ else.} \end{cases} \quad (1)$$

The "alphabet" Σ in Definition 1 is defined as the set of ground facts that encode the simple events in the input, i.e., facts of the form $\mathsf{obs}(alive, \mathsf{a})$, as per our running example. The transition function δ operates on interpretations, i.e. subsets of Σ, as indicated by the powerset 2^Σ in δ's signature. Then, given a state q and an interpretation I, the "if" branch of δ in Eq. (1) maps q to its set of "next states" A_q. Each $q' \in A_q$ is obtained by the feature mapping δ_R, therefore, it is of the form $q' = \delta_R(q,r)$ and has the property that $I \cup B$ satisfies the body of the corresponding transition feature r.

If the set of next states is empty (i.e., if no transition feature associated with q is satisfied by I), the "else" branch encodes the different operational semantics that may be defined to govern the automaton's behavior in this case. Typical options for such semantics is either to self-loop on the current state, in which case $\delta(q, I) = \{q\}$, or to reject the input, by moving to an absorbing, "dead" state, which we denote by $\bot$. These semantics correspond to two different event consumption policies in CER/F, which are called *skip-till-any-match* and *strict contiguity* respectively [17].

The logical representation of an ASA consists of a set of facts of the form transition(s_1, f, s_2), meaning that the transition from state s_1 to s_2 is guarded by condition f. Figure 2 presents an example of this representation, which is explained in more detail in Example 3 below. Additionally, the accepting states in the ASA are specified via atoms of the form accepting(s).

Reasoning with ASA is performed via an interpreter that defines the desired ASA behavior. Such an interpreter is presented in Fig. 2 as part of the background knowledge B (also to be discussed in Example 3). The first rule in the interpreter states that for any example (input MVS) *SeqId* an ASA is initially (at time 1) in state q_0, i.e. q_0 is the start state. The second rule states that an ASA moves from state S_1 to state S_2 at time T, if there is a transition whose feature is satisfied by the current example (*SeqId*) at time T. This is the meaning of the satisfies/3 atom that appears in that rule. Finally, the third rule in the interpreter defines the accepting condition for the MVS *SeqId*, by demanding the ASA to be in an accepting state at the end of the MVS. Rejection of an input MVS is defined implicitly via closed-world assumption. Note that this interpreter implements the strict contiguity operational semantics, i.e. it rejects the input at time T if the set of next states A_q at T is empty. The skip-till-any match semantics may also be supported by adding to the interpreter an extra rule that allows to self-loop when $A_q = \emptyset$, e.g. by using count aggregates in ASP:

inState($Id, S, T + 1$) ← inState(Id, S, T), #count$\{F : $satisfies$(Id, F, T)\} = 0$.

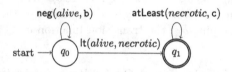

Logical representation:
transition(q_0, neg(*alive*, b), q_0). transition(q_0, lt(*alive, necrotic*), q_1).
transition(q_0, lt(*alive, necrotic*), q_1). accepting(q_1)

Background Knowledge B:
ASA Interpreter:
inState($SeqId, q_0, 1$) ← example(Id).
inState($SeqId, S_2, T + 1$) ← inState($ExmplId, S_1, T$), transition(S_1, F, S_2), satisfies($SeqId, F, T$).
accepted($SeqId$) ← inState($SeqId, S, T$), accepting(S), seqEnd($SeqId, T$).
Domain-specific background knowledge:
att(*alive; necrotic; apoptotic*).
val(a; b; c; d; e; f; g).

Transition Features R:
satisfies($SeqId$, neg(A, V), T) ← obs($SeqId$, av(A, V_1), T), $V \neq V_1$, att(A), val(V).
satisfies($SeqId$, lt(A_1, A_2), T) ← obs($SeqId$, av(A_1, V_1), T), obs(Id, av(A_2, V_2), T), $V_1 < V_2$.
satisfies($SeqId$, atLeast(A, V), T) ← obs($SeqId$, av(A, V_1), T), val(V_1), $V <= V_1$.

Fig. 2. An ASA that discriminates between the positive and negative MVSs of Fig. 1.

Transition Features. In this work the transition features are assumed to be defined beforehand (learning them, along with the corresponding ASA is a direction of future work) and are assumed to encode simple relations over attributes and values. Given that the goal is to check if the transition features are satisfied or not by the coordinates of an input MVS, we define them via the predicate satisfies/3 that is used by the interpreter. The bodies of such satisfies/3 rules consist of the conditions that should be satisfied in order for a transition to be triggered. These conditions are defined by means of attribute-value observation atoms (i.e., obs/3 atoms, as in Table 1) and comparison predicates that encode relations between such atoms.

*Example 3 (**Answer set automata & transition features**).* Figure 2 presents an ASA, its logical representation and its transition features R, along with some background knowledge B necessary to reason with the ASA. B consists of the ASA interpreter and the specification of attribute-value domain constants. We first discuss the transition features R before going into the details of the ASA and its functionality. The first rule in R specifies the conditions under which an MVS $SeqId$ satisfies, at time T, a predicate with signature $\mathsf{neg}(A, V)$, stating that at time T in $SeqId$ (i.e., in $SeqId$'s T-th coordinate), the attribute A does not have the value V. The next rule defines a predicate $\mathsf{lt}(A_1, A_2)$ stating that at time T the value of attribute A_1 is less than (hence, lt) the value of attribute A_2. Finally, the third rule in R defines $\mathsf{atLeast}(A, V)$ stating that at time T the value of attribute A is at least V.

Given these definitions, and based on the instances of the transition features that guard the edges of the ASA in Fig. 2, the behavior of the ASA is the following: It self-loops on q_0 for as long as the size of the alive cells population in the input – recall our running example – is not b; it transitions to the accepting state q_1 if an observation comes in, where the size of the alive cells population is smaller than that of the necrotic – an indication that a drug is promising; and it expects the necrotic cells population size to exceed a threshold (c) from that point on, by self-looping on the accepting state.

The ASA in Fig. 2 accepts the positive (id_1) and rejects the negative example (id_2) in Table 1. To see the former note the ASA self-loops on q_0 until time $T = 7$, when the value of $alive = \mathsf{b}$, causing $B \cup I_7^{id_1}$ to no longer satisfy the self-loop condition on q_0. However, at the same time point $necrotic = \mathsf{c}$, which exceeds the value of $alive$ (recall that the symbols in the running example represent bins of values and they are ordered by the lexicographic ordering, i.e. letters later in the alphabet represent bins of larger values). Therefore, $B \cup I_7^{id_1} \models \mathsf{lt}(alive, necrotic)$, causing the ASA to transition to the accepting state q_1. The values of $necrotic$ in the remaining time steps are at least c, thus the ASA self-loops on the accepting state for the rest of the input.

To see that the ASA rejects id_2 note that at time $T = 5$ in id_2 $alive = \mathsf{b}$, causing the condition that allows to self-loop on q_0 up to that point to fail. Moreover, the condition that allows to transition from q_0 to q_1 is also not satisfied, since $necrotic = \mathsf{b}$. Therefore, since the interpreter implements the strict contiguity semantics, the ASA is in no state at time $T = 6$ (i.e. it implicitly moves to the dead state) and the input is rejected.

6   Learning Answer Set Automata

We now turn to our approach to Answer Set Automata Learning (ASAL) in ASP. Our learning objective may be formulated as follows: Given a training set consisting of positive and negative MVSs S^+ and S^-, a set of transition features R, a "state budget" N and potentially, a set of structural and regularization constraints SC and RC respectively, learn an ASA $\mathcal{A}$ that uses the transition features in R, respects SC, optimizes RC, does not exceed N and minimizes the training error, defined as: $\sum_{s \in S^+} \text{rejects}(\mathcal{A}, s) + \sum_{s \in S^-} \text{accepts}(\mathcal{A}, s)$, i.e. the number of misclassified training examples.

Structural constraints may include e.g. requirements for accepting states being absorbing ones, starting states not being accepting states etc. Regularization constraints are typically related to learning simpler models, where simplicity in our case is measured by the total number of states and transitions in an automaton. Several other simplicity criteria may be considered. For instance, an *earliness bias* would favor automata that accept/reject their input as early as possible, the intuition being that initial segments of the input are often enough to learn a good model, while trying to fit the entire input could yield more complicated automata with inferior generalization capacity.

We cast the automata learning problem as an abductive reasoning task in ASP. In its simplest form, such a task may be defined as a tuple $\langle \Pi, IC, G, A \rangle$,

Table 2. Abductive ASA learning in ASP.

Generate ASA:

$\{\text{transition}(S_1, F, S_2)\} \leftarrow \text{state}(S_1), \text{state}(S_2), \text{feature}(F)$

$\text{feature}(\phi) \leftarrow \text{type}_1(var_\phi^1), \ldots, \text{type}_n(var_\phi^n)$

$\{\text{states}(S)\} \leftarrow \text{maxStates}(S)$

$\{\text{accepting}(S)\} \leftarrow \text{state}(S)$

$\text{maxStates}(1..q_N).\quad \text{start}(1)$

Minimize the training error:

$:\sim \text{ accepted}(SeqId), \text{negative}(SeqId). \ [w_{fp}@2, SeqId]$

$:\sim \textit{not } \text{accepted}(SeqId), \text{positive}(SeqId). \ [w_{fn}@2, SeqId]$

Example of regularization constraints:

$:\sim \text{ transition}(S_1, X, S_2). \ [1@1, S_1, S_2, X]$

$:\sim \text{ accepted}(SeqId, T). \ [T@1, SeqId, T]$

$\text{accepted}(SeqId, T) \leftarrow \text{inState}(SeqId, S, T), \text{accepting}(S)$

$\text{accepted}(SeqId) \leftarrow \text{accepted}(SeqId, \_)$

Example of structural constraints:

$\leftarrow \text{transition}(S, , S2), \text{accepting}, S2 \neq S.$

---

where Π is a logic program that represents some background knowledge, IC is a set of constraints that must be respected, G is a set of ground constraints, often called "goals" and A is a set of predicate signatures called abducibles. A solution to an abductive reasoning task is a set of ground logical facts Δ, such that $B \cup IC \cup \Delta \vDash G$.

In our case, the background knowledge program Π contains the ASA interpreter, the definitions of the transition features R and the training MVSs $S^+ \cup S^-$ in logical form; IC are the structural and regularization constraints, G is a set of ground constraints related to the acceptance/rejection of each MVS in S^+, S^- respectively and $A = \{\mathsf{transition}/3, \mathsf{accepting}/1\}$.

The abductive task is straightforward to specify and solve in ASP, via its generate-and-test methodology, according to which we generate automata via choice rules and test their performance via (weak) constraints. Table 2 presents an example formulation. The choice rules in the first block of rule generate ASA as collections of $\mathsf{transition}/3$ and $\mathsf{accepting}/3$ facts (as in Fig. 2). The $\mathsf{feature}/1$ rule is just a "type rule" added for each transition feature $r \in R$. For instance, for the transition feature $\mathsf{lt}(A, V)$ from Fig. 1, the corresponding type rule is $\mathsf{feature}(\mathsf{lt}(A, V)) \leftarrow \mathsf{att}(A), \mathsf{val}(V)$.

The next block of rules is a set of weak constraints that minimize the training error. Note that the $\mathsf{accepted}/1$ predicate is defined in the ASA interpreter in Fig. 2 and the $\mathsf{positive}/1$ and $\mathsf{negative}/1$ predicates are facts that carry the label of each training MVS. The constraints may be weighted differently, accounting e.g. for imbalances between positive/negative examples in the training set. The weights are w_{fp} for the first rule, which is the price paid for each false positive, and w_{fn} for the second rule, the price paid for each false negative. These constraints have a higher priority, relative to the ones that follow in Table 2, making training error minimization the primary objective.

The next block of rules presents an example of regularization biases in the form of weak constraints. The first constraint attempts to compress the generated automata as much as possible, by penalizing $\mathsf{transition}/3$ facts. The second rule attempts to maximize earliness by minimizing the length of the prefixes that an ASA needs to process before accepting[3]. The $\mathsf{accepted}/2$ predicate that is used in the earliness constraint simply monitors the number of steps needed to reach an accepting state, while the next rule defines acceptance in terms of such "partial" acceptance. To use the earliness bias constraint in ASAL these two rules should replace the third rule in the ASA interpreter in Fig. 2, while accepting states should be treated as absorbing. This essentially forces ASAL to learn an automaton that accepts from prefixes of the input, whose length is to be minimized by the earliness constraint. The last rule in Table 2 is a structural constraint ensuring that accepting states are absorbing.

---

[3] Maximizing earliness for input rejection, in addition to acceptance, would also be possible by modifying the ASA interpreter to not handle rejection via the closed-world assumption, but via explicit, absorbing dead states, and adding appropriate regularization constraints.

*Example 4 (**ASAL in Action**).* Let Π be the program consisting of the rules in Table 2, B and R from Fig. 2 and the logical representation of the two training examples in Table 1, as the union of the $I_t^{id_1}$'s and the $I_t^{id_2}$'s, along with the facts positive(id_1) and negative(id_2). Running Clingo on Π and filtering the transition/3 and the accepting/1 facts from the generated solutions yields the learnt ASA. One of these ASA is the one illustrated in Fig. 2, which is suboptimal, based on the constraints in Table 2. It can be seen that optimal ASA consist of two states and two transitions. e.g. the ASA

transition(q_0, at_least($alive$, e), q_0). transition(q_0, at_least($apoptotic$, d), q_1). accepting(q_1).

In addition to being smaller, it can be seen that this ASA accepts the positive example id_1 at step 6, in contrast to the ASA in Fig. 2, which accepts at step 8. If we drop the earliness constraint in Table 2 we may obtain a single-state ASA:

transition(q_0, neg($apoptotic$, f), q_0). accepting(q_0).

Although this ASA correctly classifies the examples, it is degenerate and has an unconventional behavior, always starting from an accepting state and failing later on to reject the negative examples (e.g. it moves to the implicit dead state at step 5 to reject id_2).

6.1   Incremental Learning & Automata Revision

ASAL is guaranteed to find an optimal, constraint-compliant solution to the abductive ASA learning task, given enough time and memory. The main drawback, however, is that the requirements for such resources grow exponentially with the complexity of the learning task (e.g. alphabet size, number of transition features etc.) and the size of the input (e.g. number and length of the training examples), making the approach infeasible for larger datasets. To alleviate this issue we give-up the requirement for optimal ASA and opt for an incremental learning strategy that simply learns ASA with a good fit in the training data. Additional strategies for improving ASAL's scalability, such as incorporating symmetry-breaking constraints, in order to ignore isomorphic ASA, are future work directions.

ASAL's incremental learning version operates on mini-batches of the training data, sufficiently small to allow for fast ASA induction from each batch and, ideally, sufficiently large and diverse to allow for learning relatively good ASA from samples of the training set. This is paired with an ASA revision technique, which tries to apply minimal structural modifications on existing automata, to improve their performance on new mini-batches. The algorithm – we omit the pseudocode due to space limitations – is a greedy, iterative hill-climbing search that works as follows: At each point in time, an initially empty, best-so-far ASA $\mathcal{A}$ is maintained. At each mini-batch D, if $\mathcal{A}$'s local classification performance on D is lower than a given error threshold, $\mathcal{A}$ is revised by running Clingo on a program Π similar to the one described in Example 4, augmented as follows: For each transition(q_i, ϕ_i, q_j) and each accepting(q_i) fact in the logical specification of $\mathcal{A}$ we add to Π the following:

existing(transition(q_i, ϕ_i, q_j)).
existing(accepting(q_i)).
:$\sim$ not transition(q_i, ϕ_i, q_j), existing(transition(q_i, ϕ_i, q_j)). [$-w_i$@1]
:$\sim$ not accepting(q_i), existing(accepting(q_i)). [1@1]

The first two facts simply state which facts already exist in the structural description of $\mathcal{A}$, while the weak constraints penalize their removal, thus fostering minimal revisions. The weight w_i in the first weak constraint is defined as $w_i = n - p$, where n, p are respectively the number of negative/positive examples throughout the entire training set, which are accepted by $\mathcal{A}$ and the acceptance paths use the corresponding transition feature ϕ_i. Note the "-" sign in front of w_i, which makes w_i positive (i.e., a penalty in the optimization process) if $n > p$ and negative (i.e. a reward) in the opposite case.

An ASP solver runs on the augmented program Π for a given time t, and the k best solutions found in that time are preserved, where the time-out t and k are run-time parameters. Subsequently, these k locally best solutions are evaluated on the entire training set (updating the aforementioned p, n counts for each transition/3 fact in these ASA). If an ASA $\mathcal{A}'$ is found after this process has a better global performance than $\mathcal{A}$, it replaces $\mathcal{A}$ as the new best ASA. The process is repeated for a given number of iterations, by shuffling and re-partitioning the training set into new mini-batches at the beginning of each iteration. The current best ASA that results from this process is returned in the output.

7   Experimental Evaluation

We empirically assess ASAL on two CER datasets from the domains of precision medicine and maritime monitoring. The former has already been outlined in Sect. 3. It consists of 644 time series, each containing three signals related to the *alive, necrotic* and *apoptotic* attributes, of length 49 each. The positive class (interesting simulations) amounts to the 20% of the data. In addition to this dataset, to which we refer as *Bio-small*, in order to test the scalability of the incremental version of ASAL, we also used a significantly larger dataset with the same characteristics, but with 50K training simulations.

The maritime dataset contains data from nine vessels that cruised around the port of Brest, France. There are five attribute signals for *longitude, latitude, speed, heading*, and *course over ground*. The positive class is related to whether a vessel eventually enters the port of Brest and there are 2,980 negative and 2,269 positive examples, a total of 5,249 multivariate examples, each of length 30. The maritime dataset has been previously used in CER research, we therefore refer to [2] for more details. Both datasets were discretized using SAX with ten bins.

Table 3. Experimental results.

	Method	F_1−score	#States	#Transitions	Time (min)
Bio Small-U	RPNI	0.702	13	292	**0.05**
	EDSM	0.722	12	278	**0.05**
	DISC	0.833	10	**13**	51
	$\text{ASAL}_{\text{classic}}^{\text{batch}}$	**0.887**	3	35	1 (time-out)
	$\text{ASAL}_{\text{classic}}^{\text{incr}}$	0.882	3	41	0.566
Bio Large-U	$\text{ASAL}_{\text{classic}}^{\text{incr}}$	0.858	3	57	13
Bio Small	$\text{ASAL}_{\text{classic}}^{\text{batch}}$	0.902	3	53	5 (time-out)
	$\text{ASAL}_{\text{classic}}^{\text{incr}}$	0.889	3	60	**2.7**
	$\text{ASAL}_{\text{symb}}^{\text{batch}}$	**0.968**	3	5	5 (time-out)
	$\text{ASAL}_{\text{symb}}^{\text{incr}}$	0.924	3	7	3.4
Bio Large	$\text{ASAL}_{\text{classic}}^{\text{incr}}$	0.852	3	12	**25**
	$\text{ASAL}_{\text{symb}}^{\text{incr}}$	**0.942**	3	8	39
Maritime	$\text{ASAL}_{\text{classic}}^{\text{incr}}$	0.892	3	15	**6**
	$\text{ASAL}_{\text{symb}}^{\text{incr}}$	**0.952**	3	8	18

We compared the following algorithms: (a) $\text{ASAL}_{\text{classic}}^{\text{batch}}$ and $\text{ASAL}_{\text{classic}}^{\text{incr}}$, the batch and incremental version of ASAL that learns ASA that resemble classical automata, by using no transition feature other that equality, i.e. an attribute having a particular value found in the data. This is similar to using a symbol for each attribute-value. This version of ASAL was evaluated to assess the merits of using relational transition features; (b) $\text{ASAL}_{\text{symb}}^{\text{batch}}$ and $\text{ASAL}_{\text{symb}}^{\text{incr}}$, the batch and incremental versions respectively of ASAL, as described in the previous sections. These were used with five predefined transition features, similar to those presented in Fig. 2; (c) RPNI [28] and an improved version thereof, EDSM [21], two widely used algorithms of the state-merging (SM) family, that compress a PTA (see Sect. 3) using greedy heuristics. Note that although these algorithms are quite old, the main ideas behind them are the SoA in SM-style learning and their LearrnLib[4] implementation used in the experiments is extremely efficient and frequently used by practitioners; (d) DISC [31], a recent algorithm that translates the PTA compression problem into a Mixed Integer Linear Programming problem, which it delegates to the off-the-shelf Gurobi solver. DISC is similar to ASAL in the sense that it is able to learn optimal automata, given enough time and memory.

The experimental setting was a five-fold cross validation with 80/20 training/testing set splits. The experiments were carried-out on a 3.6GHz processor (4 cores, 8 threads) and 16GB of RAM. Whenever $\text{ASAL}_{\text{classic}}^{\text{batch}}$ was used it was given a timeout (maximum allowed time), in order to obtain a solution in a feasible amount of time.

---

[4] https://learnlib.de/.

The results are presented in Table 3 in the form of average testing set F_1-scores, number of states and transitions, as well as training times for the algorithms compared. Note that RPNI, EDSM and DISC deal with single strings and cannot handle multivariate input. To compare to these algorithms we used a univariate version of the bio dataset, which contains the *alive* attribute only, as it is informative enough to learn a useful model. No such attribute has this property in the maritime dataset, we therefore did not experiment with RPNI, EDSM and DISC on it. Moreover, only the "classic" version of ASAL was used on the univarate bio dataset, since there are no cross-feature relations that could be captured by transition features in the symbolic version.

The first block in Table 3 concerns the small version of the univariate dataset. It can be seen that RPNI and EDSM are lightning-fast, learning a model in approx. three secs. On the other hand, they have significantly inferior predictive performance as compared to all other algorithms and they are significantly more complicated, as indicated by their size. DISC has a better F_1-score and learns slightly simpler models, as indicated by its states number (the reduced number of transitions for DISC is misleading, since DISC omits self loops). On the other hand, it takes a little less than an hour on average to train. $\text{ASAL}_{\text{classic}}^{\text{batch}}$ has the best predictive performance, achieved within 1 min. Its incremental version closely follows in predictive performance in almost half the time.

In the large version of the univiariate bio dataset (second block in Table 3) $\text{ASAL}_{\text{classic}}^{\text{incr}}$ was the only usable algorithm, since RPNI, EDSM and DISC terminated with memory errors, due to the size of the dataset. In contrast, thanks to its incremental learning strategy that never loads the entirety of the training data into memory, ASAL was able to learn a good model in approx. 13 min.

The results from the small version of the full bio dataset (containing all the features) in the next block in Table 3), highlight the advantages of learning symbolic automata. Indeed, both the batch and the incremental version of ASAL achieve significantly better results than the classical version of ASAL and learn automata with much fewer transitions. Note that the F_1-scores of the two versions of the batch ASAL version were achieved with the same time-out value and the incremental versions of ASAL have comparative training times. Therefore, the symbolic version learns better models without significantly compromising efficiency. The results from the large bio dataset (full, all features used) and the maritime dataset also seem to confirm this claim.

8   Conclusions and Future Work

We presented a methodology for learning symbolic automata where the transition guards are defined via ASP rules, and evaluated our approach on two CER datasets, demonstrating its efficacy. There are several directions for future work, including a more thorough experimental assessment on more datasets and settings, a formal characterization of the expressive power of ASA in relation to common event algebras used in CER, scalability improvements, e.g. via symmetry breaking, and jointly learning the transition features definitions, along with the automaton.

Acknowledgment. This work is supported by the project entitled "ARIADNE - AI Aided D-band Network for 5G Long Term Evolution", which has received funding from the European Union's Horizon 2020 research & innovation programme under grant agreement No 871464, and by the project entitled "INFORE: Interactive Extreme-Scale Analytics and Forecasting", which has received funding from the European Union's Horizon 2020 research & innovation programme under grant agreement No 825070.

References

1. Agrawal, J., Diao, Y., Gyllstrom, D., Immerman, N.: Efficient pattern matching over event streams. In: Proceedings of the 2008 ACM SIGMOD International Conference on Management of Data, pp. 147–160 (2008)
2. Alevizos, E., Artikis, A., Paliouras, G.: Complex event forecasting with prediction suffix trees. VLDB J. **31**(1), 157–180 (2022)
3. Alevizos, E., Skarlatidis, A., Artikis, A., Paliouras, G.: Probabilistic complex event recognition: a survey. ACM Comput. Surv. (CSUR) **50**(5), 1–31 (2017)
4. Angluin, D.: Learning regular sets from queries and counterexamples. Inf. Comput. **75**(2), 87–106 (1987)
5. Angluin, D., Eisenstat, S., Fisman, D.: Learning regular languages via alternating automata. In: Twenty-Fourth International Joint Conference on Artificial Intelligence (2015)
6. Argyros, G., D'Antoni, L.: The learnability of symbolic automata. In: Chockler, H., Weissenbacher, G. (eds.) CAV 2018. LNCS, vol. 10981, pp. 427–445. Springer, Cham (2018). https://doi.org/10.1007/978-3-319-96145-3_23
7. Cugola, G., Margara, A.: Tesla: a formally defined event specification language. In: Proceedings of the Fourth ACM International Conference on Distributed Event-Based Systems, pp. 50–61 (2010)
8. Cugola, G., Margara, A.: Processing flows of information: from data stream to complex event processing. ACM Comput. Surv. (CSUR) **44**(3), 15 (2012)
9. D'Antoni, L., Veanes, M.: The power of symbolic automata and transducers. In: Majumdar, R., Kunčak, V. (eds.) CAV 2017. LNCS, vol. 10426, pp. 47–67. Springer, Cham (2017). https://doi.org/10.1007/978-3-319-63387-9_3
10. Demers, A., Gehrke, J., Hong, M., Riedewald, M., White, W.: Towards expressive publish/subscribe systems. In: International Conference on Extending Database Technology, pp. 627–644. Springer (2006)
11. Demers, A.J., Gehrke, J., Panda, B., Riedewald, M., Sharma, V., White, W.M., et al.: Cayuga: a general purpose event monitoring system. In: Cidr, vol. 7, pp. 412–422 (2007)
12. Diao, Y., Immerman, N., Gyllstrom, D.: Sase+: an agile language for kleene closure over event streams. UMass Technical Report (2007)
13. Drews, S., D'Antoni, L.: Learning symbolic automata. In: International Conference on Tools and Algorithms for the Construction and Analysis of Systems, pp. 173–189. Springer (2017)
14. Fisman, D., Frenkel, H., Zilles, S.: Inferring symbolic automata (2021). arXiv preprint arXiv:2112.14252
15. Furelos-Blanco, D., Law, M., Jonsson, A., Broda, K., Russo, A.: Induction and exploitation of subgoal automata for reinforcement learning. J. Artif. Intell. Res. **70**, 1031–1116 (2021)
16. Giantamidis, G., Tripakis, S., Basagiannis, S.: Learning moore machines from input-output traces. Int. J. Softw. Tools Technol. Transfer **23**(1), 1–29 (2021)

17. Giatrakos, N., Alevizos, E., Artikis, A., Deligiannakis, A., Garofalakis, M.N.: Complex event recognition in the big data era: a survey. VLDB J. **29**(1), 313–352 (2020)
18. Gold, E.M.: Language identification in the limit. Inf. Control **10**(5), 447–474 (1967)
19. Grez, A., Riveros, C., Ugarte, M.: A formal framework for complex event processing. In: 22nd International Conference on Database Theory (ICDT 2019). Schloss Dagstuhl-Leibniz-Zentrum fuer Informatik (2019)
20. De la Higuera, C.: Grammatical inference: learning automata and grammars. Cambridge University Press (2010)
21. Lang, K.J., Pearlmutter, B.A., Price, R.A.: Results of the abbadingo one dfa learning competition and a new evidence-driven state merging algorithm. In: International Colloquium on Grammatical Inference. pp. 1–12. Springer (1998)
22. Letort, G., Montagud, A., Stoll, G., Heiland, R., Barillot, E., Macklin, P., Zinovyev, A., Calzone, L.: Physiboss: a multi-scale agent-based modelling framework integrating physical dimension and cell signalling. Bioinformatics **35**(7), 1188–1196 (2019)
23. Lifschitz, V.: Answer set programming. Springer (2019)
24. Lin, J., Keogh, E., Lonardi, S., Chiu, B.: A symbolic representation of time series, with implications for streaming algorithms. In: Proceedings of the 8th ACM SIGMOD Workshop on Research Issues in Data Mining and Knowledge Discovery, pp. 2–11 (2003)
25. Lin, J., Keogh, E., Wei, L., Lonardi, S.: Experiencing sax: a novel symbolic representation of time series. Data Min. Knowl. Disc. **15**(2), 107–144 (2007)
26. Maler, O., Mens, I.-E.: A generic algorithm for learning symbolic automata from membership queries. In: Aceto, L., Bacci, G., Bacci, G., Ingólfsdóttir, A., Legay, A., Mardare, R. (eds.) Models, Algorithms, Logics and Tools. LNCS, vol. 10460, pp. 146–169. Springer, Cham (2017). https://doi.org/10.1007/978-3-319-63121-9_8
27. Muggleton, S.H., Lin, D., Pahlavi, N., Tamaddoni-Nezhad, A.: Meta-interpretive learning: application to grammatical inference. Mach. Learn. **94**(1), 25–49 (2014)
28. Oncina, J., Garcia, P.: Identifying regular languages in polynomial time. In: Advances in Structural and Syntactic Pattern Recognition, pp. 99–108. World Scientific (1992)
29. Pietzuch, P.R., Shand, B., Bacon, J.: A framework for event composition in distributed systems. In: Endler, M., Schmidt, D. (eds.) Middleware 2003. LNCS, vol. 2672, pp. 62–82. Springer, Heidelberg (2003). https://doi.org/10.1007/3-540-44892-6_4
30. Schultz-Møller, N.P., Migliavacca, M., Pietzuch, P.: Distributed complex event processing with query rewriting. In: Proceedings of the Third ACM International Conference on Distributed Event-Based Systems, pp. 1–12 (2009)
31. Shvo, M., Li, A.C., Icarte, R.T., McIlraith, S.A.: Interpretable sequence classification via discrete optimization. In: Proceedings of the 35th AAAI Conference on Artificial Intelligence (AAAI), pp. 9647–9656 (2021)
32. Smetsers, R., Fiterău-Broştean, P., Vaandrager, F.: Model learning as a satisfiability modulo theories problem. In: Klein, S.T., Martín-Vide, C., Shapira, D. (eds.) LATA 2018. LNCS, vol. 10792, pp. 182–194. Springer, Cham (2018). https://doi.org/10.1007/978-3-319-77313-1_14
33. Ulyantsev, V., Zakirzyanov, I., Shalyto, A.: Bfs-based symmetry breaking predicates for dfa identification. In: International Conference on Language and Automata Theory and Applications. pp. 611–622. Springer (2015)
34. Wieczorek, W.: Grammatical Inference. Springer (2017)

35. Wu, E., Diao, Y., Rizvi, S.: High-performance complex event processing over streams. In: Proceedings of the 2006 ACM SIGMOD International Conference on Management of Data, pp. 407–418 (2006)
36. Zhang, H., Diao, Y., Immerman, N.: On complexity and optimization of expensive queries in complex event processing. In: Proceedings of the 2014 ACM SIGMOD International Conference on Management of Data, pp. 217–228 (2014)

Learning Hierarchical Problem Networks for Knowledge-Based Planning

Pat Langley[1,2(✉)]

[1] Institute for the Study of Learning and Expertise, Palo Alto, CA 94306, USA
patrick.w.langley@gmail.com
[2] Center for Design Research, Stanford University, Stanford, CA 94305, USA
http://www.isle.org/~langley/

Abstract. In this paper, we review hierarchical problem networks, which encode knowledge about how to decompose planning tasks, and report an approach to learning this expertise from sample solutions. In this framework, procedural knowledge comprises a set of conditional methods that decompose problems – sets of goals – into subproblems. Problem solving involves search through a space of hierarchical plans that achieve top-level goals. Acquisition involves creation of new methods, including state conditions for when they are relevant and goal conditions for when to avoid them. We describe HPNL, a system that learns new methods by analyzing sample hierarchical plans, using violated constraints to identify state conditions and ordering conflicts to determine goal conditions. Experiments with on-line learning in three planning domains demonstrate that HPNL acquires expertise that reduces search on novel problems and examine the importance of learning goal conditions. In closing, we contrast the approach with earlier methods for acquiring search-control knowledge, including explanation-based learning and inductive logic programming. We also discuss limitations and plans for future research.

Keywords: Learning for problem solving · Hierarchical planning · Search-control knowledge · Learning decomposition rules

1 Introduction

Three elements underlie classic accounts of intelligence in humans and machines: reasoning, search, and knowledge. Early work on AI saw rapid progress on the first two areas, but major applications were delayed until the advent of expert systems, which focused on the third topic. These saw widespread use but they were expensive to construct and maintain. Recognition of these drawbacks fostered increased research in machine learning, which aimed to automate the acquisition of such expertise. This movement saw rapid advances in the 1980s, which

ILP 2022, 31st International Conference on Inductive Logic Programming, Cumberland Lodge, Windsor, UK.

S. H. Muggleton and A. Tamaddoni-Nezhad (Eds.): ILP 2022, LNAI 13779, pp. 69–83, 2024.
https://doi.org/10.1007/978-3-031-55630-2_6

in turn led to early fielded applications (Langley & Simon, 1995). These grew more common with the automated collection of large data sets and delivery channels made possible by the World Wide Web.

However, the vast majority of learning applications have focused on classification and regression. For settings that require sequential decision making, such as plan generation, progress has been much slower. Recent successes of reinforcement learning have been limited to domains with accurate simulators that can carry out the thousands or millions of trials required. Instead, we desire mechanisms that acquire procedural expertise as efficiently as humans through reasoning about, and learning from, solutions to individual problems.

In this paper, we present a new approach to rapid learning of expertise for solving planning tasks. We start by reviewing hierarchical problem networks, a recently proposed formalism for encoding plan knowledge, and their use in solving complex problems through decomposition. After this, we describe an approach to acquiring such structures from sample hierarchical plans. Next we report the results of experiments that demonstrate its effectiveness in three planning domains. We conclude by reviewing earlier research on learning hierarchical knowledge for problem solving and outlining directions for future work in this important but understudied area.

2   A Review of Hierarchical Problem Networks

Breakthroughs in machine learning often follow the introduction of new representations for expertise and new mechanisms for using this content. For instance, inductive logic programming was not possible until formalisms like Prolog had been developed. In this section, we review a recent notation for knowledge about planning – *hierarchical problem networks* – and how this content supports efficient problem solving in sequential domains. The aim is akin to early work on search-control rules and more recent efforts on hierarchical task and goal networks, but we will see that the older frameworks differ in important ways.

2.1   Representing Hierarchical Problem Networks

A recurring theme in both human and machine cognition is decomposition of complex problems into simpler ones. This idea is central to logic programming (Lloyd, 1984), which organizes knowledge into hierarchical structures, with nonterminal symbols serving as connective tissue. This notion is also key to hierarchical task networks (Nau et al., 2003), which encode knowledge about how to decompose sequential activities into subactivities, using task names to link across levels. In both cases, nonterminal symbols support modularity and reuse, much like subroutine names in traditional programming languages. But reliance on nonterminals is also a drawback in that learning requires creation of intermediate predicates, which is more challenging than identifying rule conditions.

Hierarchical problem networks (HPNs) offer a way to encode planning knowledge that sidesteps this complication. Like other formalisms, they divide content

Table 1. Four methods for logistics planning that include a head, state conditions, an operator, a subproblem, and optional goal conditions. These partially encode an HPN procedure that solves problems in the logistics domain efficiently. The notation assumes that distinct variables will match against different constant expressions. Bold and italic fonts for some conditions denote sources of learning discussed later.

((at ?o1 ?l3))	
conditions:	((object ?o1) (truck ?t1) (location ?l3) (location ?l2)
	(location ?l1) (in-city ?l3 ?c1) (in-city ?l2 ?c1) (in-city ?l1 ?c1)
	(at ?t1 ?l2) (at ?o1 ?l1))
operator:	(unload-truck ?o1 ?t1 ?l3)
subproblem:	((at ?t1 ?l3) (in ?o1 ?t1))
((at ?t1 ?l1))	
conditions:	((truck ?t1) (location ?l2) (location ?l1) (city ?c1)
	(in-city ?l2 ?c1) (in-city ?l1 ?c1) **(at ?t1 ?l2))**
operator:	(drive-truck ?t1 ?l2 ?l1 ?c1)
subproblem:	((at ?t1 ?l2))
unless-goals	((in ?o ?t1))
((in ?o1 ?t1))	
conditions:	((object ?o1) (truck ?t1) (location ?l1) *(location ?l2)*
	(in-city ?l1 ?c1) (in-city ?l2 ?c1) **(at ?t1 ?l2) (at ?o1 ?l1))**
operator:	(load-truck ?o1 ?t1 ?l1)
subproblem:	((at ?t1 ?l1) (at ?o1 ?l1))
((in ?o1 ?t1)	
:conditions	((object ?o1) (truck ?t1) (location ?l1) *(airport ?l1)*
	(location ?l2) (location ?l3) (in-city ?l1 ?c1) (in-city ?l2 ?c1)
	(in-city ?l3 ?c2) **(at ?t1 ?l2) (at ?o1 ?l3))**
:operator	(load-truck ?o1 ?t1 ?l1)
:subproblem	((at ?t1 ?l1) (at ?o1 ?l1))

into rules or *methods*, each indicating how to decompose a class of problems into simpler ones. More specifically, each HPN method includes a head that describes a goal to be achieved and an operator that accomplishes it. A method also contains a subproblem based on the operator's conditions that should be solved before one applies it. In addition, each method includes *state* conditions specifying relations that must hold for the decomposition to be appropriate. Teleoreactive logic programs (Langley & Choi, 2006) and hierarchical goal networks (Shivashankar et al., 2012; Fine-Morris et al., 2020) also index methods by goals they achieve, but neither defines subproblems in terms of operator conditions.

Table 1 shows four methods from a hierarchical problem network for logistics planning, a domain that has been widely used in the literature. The first method indicates that, to achieve *(at ?o1 ?l3)*, we apply *(unload-truck ?o1 ?t1 ?l3)*, but only if we first satisfy this operator's two conditions *(at ?t1 ?l3)* and *(in ?o1 ?t1)*. Moreover, this decomposition is only relevant when the truck *?t1* is located in the same city as the object *?o1* that we want to transport. The second method specifies how to achieve *(at ?t1 ?l1)* by applying *(drive-truck ?t1 ?l2 ?l1 ?c1)*, but

Table 2. Three operators for the logistics planning domain, each specifying an action (head), conditions, and effects. The domain also includes operators (not shown) for unloading an airplane, flying an airplane between cities, and loading an airplane.

```
((unload-truck ?o ?t ?l)
 :conditions ((object ?o)(truck ?t)(location ?l)(at ?t ?l)(in ?o ?t))
 :effects    ((at ?o ?l)(not (in ?o ?t))))
((drive-truck ?t ?l1 ?l2 ?c)
 :conditions ((truck ?t)(location ?l1)(location ?l2)(city ?c)
              (in-city ?l1 ?c)(in-city ?l2 ?c)(at ?t ?l1))
 :effects    ((at ?t ?l2)(not (at ?t ?l1))))
((load-truck ?o ?t ?l)
 :conditions ((object ?o)(truck ?t)(location ?l)(at ?t ?l)(at ?o ?l))
 :effects    ((in ?o ?t)(not (at ?o ?l))))
```

again only when its current and desired location are in the same city. The last two methods detail where to load an object into a truck, with one for situations when they are in the same city and another when they differ.

However, HPN methods can also include an optional field that specifies when we should **not** invoke them. This refers not to the current state but rather to other goals in the current problem that are unsatisfied in the state. The second method in Table 1 includes such an *unless-goals* condition, which indicates that we should not attempt to achieve *(at ?t1 ?l1)* by driving truck *?t1* if *(in ?o ?t1)* is an open goal. The reasoning is straightforward: any package that we want in the truck should already be in the vehicle before we move it. Such constraints are similar in spirit to rejection rules in problem solvers like PRODIGY (Minton, 1988), but they are embedded in methods rather than stored separately.

Naturally, an HPN knowledge base also requires definitions for the domain operators that appear in methods. As in other AI planning frameworks, these give the name and arguments for an action, its effects in terms of added and deleted relations, and the conditions under which these effects occur. Table 2 presents operator descriptions for three actions from the logistics domain: unloading a truck, driving a truck, and loading a truck. The domain knowledge also includes three analogous actions for unloading an airplane at an airport, flying it from one airport to another, and loading it at an airport. Instances of these operators serve as terminal nodes in hierarchical plans, whereas instances of HPN methods correspond to nonterminal nodes.

2.2 Hierarchical Problem Decomposition

The HPN framework assumes the presence of a problem solver that can use available methods to generate plans. We can specify this performance task more explicitly in terms of inputs and outputs:

- *Given*: A set of HPN *methods* and associated domain *operators*;
- *Given*: An *initial state* specified as a conjunctive set of *relations*;

- *Given*: A *problem* specified as a conjunctive set of *goals*;
- *Find*: A *hierarchical plan* that transforms the initial state into one that satisfies all problem goals.

Two supporting structures, the *problem stack* and the *state sequence*, are altered during the problem-solving process. The first is simply a stack of problems and their ancestors, whereas the latter is a list of states in reverse order of generation.

Plan generation recursively decomposes the top-level problem into subproblems. The decomposition mechanism relies on three main subprocesses: method matching, method selection, and method expansion. Problem solving iteratively examines the topmost element on the problem stack and, if necessary, uses HPN methods to place new subproblems above it. These are popped when satisfied, which in turn allows application of the associated operator. This produces a new state that may lead to new subproblems. Before adding a subproblem or applying an operator, the procedure checks the stack for problem loops (with identical goals) and state loops (with identical states), rejecting a candidate if either occurs. The overall process is similar to that used with hierarchical task networks and goal networks. The key difference is that it relies on a stack of *problems* rather than tasks or individual goals, which supports checking of *unless* conditions that avoid goal interactions. Langley and Shrobe (2021) describe HPD, a hierarchical planner that implements these processing postulates.

In summary, planning in this framework involves search through a space of decompositions defined by methods, operators, problem goals, and an initial state. The need for backtracking can arise when the HPN's methods have overly general state conditions or when they lack necessary *unless-goals* conditions. However, given appropriate knowledge about a domain, the HPD problem solver mimics a deterministic procedure in that it selects a useful decomposition at each step. Langley and Shrobe reported this behavior experimentally in three planning domains, as well as the search that results when state and goal conditions are omitted from the knowledge base.

3   Learning HPNs from Sample Solutions

Now that we have described hierarchical problem networks as a representational framework and their use in efficient generation of hierarchical plans, we can turn to the acquisition of this knowledge. As with the performance task, we specify the learning problem in terms of inputs and outputs:

- *Given*: A set of domain operators that specify conditional effects of actions;
- *Given*: A set of training tasks comprising initial states and conjunctive goals;
- *Given*: A hierarchical plan for each task that achieves its associated goals;
- *Find*: A hierarchical problem network that solves the training tasks efficiently and that generalizes well to new cases.

This statement does not specify precisely the two measures of success, 'efficiently' or 'generalizes well'. Naturally, we desire learned knowledge that solves planning tasks with little or no search, and we want improvement on this front to occur rapidly, but these are empirical issues, not definitional ones.

In this section, we present an approach to addressing the problem of acquiring hierarchical problem networks from sample solutions. First we describe the inputs to the learning process more clearly and introduce an example that we draw upon later. After this, we explain how the structure of training problems maps onto new HPN methods and how the approach extracts state and goal conditions for each method. We also report an implementation of these ideas in the HPNL system, which builds on the existing HPD problem solver.

3.1 Inputs to HPN Learning

As we have seen, one input to the learning process is a set of domain operators, each of which describes the conditional effects of some action. Table 2 presented three such operators from the logistics domain for unloading an object from a truck, driving a truck from one location to another, and loading a package into a truck. In addition, each operator-effect pair maps onto a naive HPN method that indicates how one can achieve the effect by first achieving the operator's conditions and then applying it. Thus, we can generate a naive hierarchical problem network from the operators alone, but it can still require substantial search to solve problems. To move beyond this incomplete knowledge, we need experience with specific training problems (i.e., initial states with goal descriptions). In addition, we need hierarchical plans that decompose the top-level problems into subproblems to make contact with their starting situations. Each component of these plans links some goal to a conjunction of subgoals through an operator instance, with terminal literals corresponding to elements of the initial state.

Figure 1 depicts a hierarchical plan for a simple logistics problem with the single goal *(at o1 l3)* and an initial state containing *(at o1 l1)*, *(at t1 l2)*, and static relations like *(location l1)* and *(in-city l1 c1)*. The plan indicates that, to achieve *(at o1 l2)*, we can apply the operator instance *(unload-truck o1 t1 l2)*, which in turn requires solving subgoals *(in o1 t1)* and *(at t1 l3)*. Furthermore, to achieve *(in o1 t1)*, we can apply *(load-truck o1 t1 l1)*, which means addressing the subgoals *(at t1 l1)* and *(at o1 l1)*. The latter holds in the initial state and *(at t1 l1)* can be satisfied by invoking *(drive-truck t1 l2 l1 c1)*, provided that *(at t1 l2)*, which is true at the outset. In addition, we can achieve *(at t1 l3)* by applying *(drive-truck t1 l1 l3 c1)*. The plan does not mention other locations, trucks, packages, or relations that are not relevant to the solution. We might instead require the learner to find its own hierarchical plan for each training problem, as in early work on learning for search control (Sleeman et al., 1982). However, the learner would still need to transform the resulting hierarchical plans into a set of HPN methods, so we have chosen to focus on this central issue rather than on such preprocessing steps.

3.2 Identifying HPN Structure

Classic research on learning for hierarchical decomposition has addressed three questions. The first concerns how to break a sample solution into segments in order to identify the structure of new methods. The second issue deals with when to associate the same head or task name with distinct methods. The final

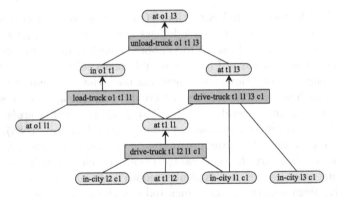

Fig. 1. A hierarchical plan for a simple logistics task that involves four problem decompositions and associated operator instances.

matter involves what conditions to place on each method. Different approaches to learning hierarchical procedures address these design choices in different ways, but the HPN framework offers straightforward answers to the first two questions.

Recall that sample problem solutions, whether provided by a human or generated through search, specify a hierarchical plan. Each literal in this structure (except for terminal nodes) is associated with an operator instance that achieves it and the instantiated set of conditions for that operator. Each triple of this sort maps onto a candidate HPN method. For instance, the topmost goal *(at o1 l3)* in Fig. 1, the operator *(unload-truck o1 t1 l3)* that achieves it, and the latter's conditions together map onto the first method in Table 1. The operator's static conditions, such as *(object o1)*, contribute to the method's state conditions, although we will see soon that others may augment them. Dynamic conditions, such as *(at t1 l3)* and *(in o1 t1)*, become elements of the *:subproblem* field. Constant arguments of predicates are replaced with variables in a consistent way throughout the method. The four operator instances in Fig. 1 correspond to four distinct methods that such a process might add to the knowledge base.

The second issue, when to assign a common head to different methods, also has a simple response in the HPN framework. Because each method refers to a goal that it achieves, every structure that addresses the same goal will have the same head. For instance, three methods constructed from the hierarchical plan in Fig. 1 would both have heads with the predicate *at*, even though one involves the *unload* operator and the others invoke the *drive* operator. This approach is very different from techniques for learning classical hierarchical task networks, whose heads include task names that are distinct from state predicates. However, it is similar to early mechanisms for learning teleoreactive logic programs (Langley & Choi, 2006; Nejati et al., 2006).

3.3 Inferring State Conditions

The organization of each sample solution determines the structure of the learned HPN, but we must still identify the conditions under which to apply each rule.

Let us start with state-related conditions. One option would use *explanation-based learning* to analyze logical dependencies and identify conditions from each sample solution, which would seem to support rapid learning. For example, for the top-level decomposition in Fig. 1, it would collect all terminal nodes in the hierarchical plan as conditions for a new method. However, empirical studies revealed that such analytic techniques can create complex, specific rules that are expensive to match and generalize poorly. This leads to a *utility problem*, where learning reduces search but increases planning time (Minton, 1988). Another response would use *inductive logic programming* or similar schemes for relational learning. These often carry out general-to-specific search for conditions that find simpler, more general rules, but typically require multiple examples to discriminate positive from negative cases, which reduces the learning rate. We desire a way to identify state conditions on HPN methods that combines learning from individual training solutions with an inductive bias toward generality.

Remember that a key purpose of state conditions in the HPN framework is to ensure that all arguments of a method's operator are bound. Some of these variables are already specified in the head, but others may remain unconstrained. For instance, the third method in Table 1 says that we can achieve *(in ?o1 ?t1)* by applying *(load-truck ?o1 ?t1 ?l1)*, so the object and truck appear in the head, but not the location. Information about argument types (e.g., that *?l1* is a location) do not suffice to eliminate ambiguity. Fortunately, we can combine knowledge implicit in operators with details about the state in which a decomposition occurs to infer additional conditions. Figure 1 reveals that *(in o1 t1)* is achieved by *(load-truck o1 t1 l1)*, which has *(at t1 l1)* as one of its conditions. The latter relation is achieved in turn by *(drive-truck t1 l2 l1 c1)*, which deletes *(at t1 l2)* and adds *(at t1 l1)*, so the two literals are mutually exclusive, at least in this context. This suggests *(at t1 l2)*, appropriately generalized, as a state condition for the third method, as denoted by bold font in the table.

We can use operator specifications to identify constraints for this purpose: any relation that an operator deletes and replaces with another implies a mutual exclusion. Examples include *(load-truck ?o ?t ?l)*, which removes the literal *(at ?o ?l)* with *(in ?o ?t)*, and *(unload-truck ?o ?t ?l)*, which does the opposite. Three such constraints arise in the logistics domain: an entity cannot be *at* two places, it cannot be *in* two vehicles, and it cannot be *at* a place and *in* a vehicle. To find state conditions for a method M with operator O, for each argument of O not bound in M's head, we can note which relations held when the sample decomposition occurred but are inconsistent with O's conditions.

Unfortunately, the resulting conditions may not suffice and static literals may be necessary to ensure proper argument bindings. For instance, in Logistics the conditions *(in-city ?l2 ?c1)* and *(in-city ?l1 ?c1)* in Table 1's third method indicate that *?l2*, the truck's location, and *?l1*, the package's location, must be in the same city. The fourth method specifies a different configuration in which we should load the truck at an airport when the package is in a different city. We can identify such static conditions by chaining outward from unbound arguments in a sample solution. For the state in which a decomposition occurs, we find literals that contain such an argument, note any new arguments that are introduced, and find relations that contain them. This process continues until no new arguments arise, at which point we replace constants with variables in a consistent manner. Table 1 uses italics to highlight conditions found through this mechanism. The second method, for achieving *(at ?t ?l1)* with *drive-truck*, does not include any because it inherits all necessary static conditions from its operator.

3.4 Identifying Goal Conditions

Now let us turn to the construction of *unless-goals* conditions. These serve to constrain the order in which methods are selected during hierarchical decomposition. The only example of an unless condition in Table 1 occurs in the second method, which indicates that one should not attempt to achieve *(at ?t1 ?l1)* with *(drive-truck ?t1 ?l2 ?l1 ?c1)* if there is an unsatisfied goal of the form *(in ?o ?t1)*. To identify such priorities, we examine the sample solution to find which state literals held when each goal decomposition took place. We then note which operator instance achieved each goal and calculate its composed conditions and effects, much as in techniques for forming macro-operators (e.g., Iba, 1989). When two goals appear as siblings in the sample hierarchical plan, we see whether the composed effects of the subplan carried out later would 'clobber' the composed conditions of the one carried out earlier. If so, then we add an *unless-goals* condition that requires the method learned from the later subplan **not** be selected when the goal achieved by the earlier subplan still remains unsatisfied.

For example, the goals *(in o1 t1)* and *(at t1 l3)* in Fig. 1 each have associated subplans that achieve them. The composed conditions of the first subplan include the state literal *(at t1 l1)*, which is needed for loading *o1* into *t1*. However, the composed effects of the second subplan includes deletion of *(at t1 l1)* because this is a necessary result of driving *t1* from *l1* to *l3*. Thus, carrying out the two subplans in reverse order will not succeed and, to avoid this negative interaction, we add the *unless-goals* condition *(in ?o ?t1)* to the second method in Table 1. A different sample solution that involves flying an airplane from one city to another would lead to a similar goal condition, although a method for this goal-operator combination does not appear in the table.

3.5 Implementation Details

We have implemented this approach to learning hierarchical problem networks in Steel Bank Common Lisp. The resulting system – HPNL – inputs domain operators, training problems with associated hierarchical plans, and constraints about which relations are mutually exclusive. The program processes sample solutions one at a time, adding new methods as suggested by these traces. Before the system creates a method, it compares the candidate with existing structures to see if they are structurally isomorphic by checking whether their heads, state conditions, and operators map onto each other. In such cases, it increments a counter rather than adding a duplicate and the HPD problem solver uses these scores to select among multiple matches, favoring methods with higher counts.

HPNL acquires hierarchical methods in an incremental, monotonic manner that is unaffected by the order of training problems. In practice, it constructs only a few methods from each solution trace, as subplans often have similar structures, and in some cases none are created at all. For classic planning domains, handcrafted programs can require only one or two methods per operator-effect pair. Nevertheless, HPNL treats each hierarchical plan as a potential learning experience, as new configurations of initial states and goals are always possible. When the implementation detects a goal interaction, it adds an analogous *unless-goals* condition to each method with the same goal-operator pair.

4   Empirical Evaluation

Our approach to learning hierarchical problem networks holds promise for rapid acquisition of planning expertise, but we must still demonstrate its effectiveness. To this end, we designed and ran experiments that studied the learning behavior of the HPNL implementation. For a given domain, we manually created a set of methods that solved problems with little or no search. We also generated a set of state-goal configurations and used the expert knowledge to generate a hierarchical plan for each such problem. We primed HPNL with content about domain operators and constraints,[1] then presented sample problems and plans sequentially, using each one first as a test case and then as a training case. We were concerned with two measures of performance – number of decompositions and CPU time – which we recorded on each run. We were also interested in rate of improvement, so we collected learning curves that plotted performance against number of training samples, averaged across different training orders.

We evaluated HPNL's learning behavior on three different problem-solving domains to provide evidence of generality. These settings will be very familiar to readers of the AI planning literature:

- **Blocks World** involves changing an initial configuration of blocks into a target configuration. States were encoded with six dynamic predicates affected by four operators – *stack*, *unstack*, *putdown*, and *pickup*. The expert HPN program for this domain included six methods, two for *holding* and one each for other dynamic predicates. Problems involved four to six blocks and ranged from four to six goals, while solution lengths were six to 16 steps.
- **Logistics** requires transporting packages from initial to target locations. States involved seven static relations but only two dynamic predicates – *at* and *in* – that were altered by six operators. The expert knowledge base included seven methods, four for achieving the *at* relation and three for the *in* predicate. Tasks included two packages and two goals in one or two cities, each with three locations, with solutions varying from four to 19 steps.
- **Depots** involves moving crates from some pallets to others and stacking them in specified towers. There were six static predicates and six dynamic relations – *available*, *lifting*, *at*, *on*, *in*, and *clear* – influenced by five operators. Expert knowledge comprised eight methods, two for *on*, two for *lifting*, and one each for other dynamic predicates. Problems contained two or three depots, three to four crates, and three to four goals, while solutions were seven to 21 steps.

---

[1] We constructed these constraints manually, although in principle they could have been extracted automatically from the operators' definitions.

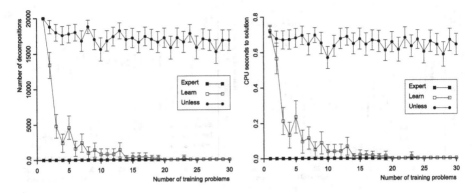

Fig. 2. Number of decompositions (left) and CPU time (right) needed to solve problems in the Blocks World by an expert HPN knowledge base, HPN methods learned from sample plans, and learned methods that lack *unless-goals* conditions. Each curve reports mean values with 95% confidence intervals over 100 random problem orders.

For each domain, we trained and tested the system on 30 distinct problems, limiting effort on each task to 20,000 method decompositions (i.e., nodes visited in the search tree). We also limited plan length to 30 steps in the Blocks World and 50 steps in the other domains. For each run, we recorded both CPU seconds and the decompositions carried out, assigning the maximum number if the system failed to find a solution. To factor out order effects, we called the system 100 times with random problem sequences and averaged performance across runs.

For this initial study, we wanted to understand HPNL's rate of learning, how acquired expertise compares to handcrafted methods, and how important goal conditions are to success. For these reasons, we examined three experimental conditions – handcrafted structures, learned methods, and the same methods without *unless-goals* conditions. We did not compare the HPNL's behavior to other systems for acquiring plan knowledge because, in most cases, their inputs would not be comparable. Moreover, our aim was not to show which approach is superior but to demonstrate the viability of our new framework.

Figure 2 presents results for the Blocks World. The left graph plots the number of decompositions required to solve each task, whereas the right displays the CPU times. As expected, the manually created HPN for this domain solved each problem with little or no search and took negligible processing time. More important, the HPNL system, which started with overly general methods, initially needed substantial search to find solutions, but it acquired expertise rapidly and its performance on both measures reached near expert level by the 20th task.

The figure also shows HPNL's behavior when we removed the ability to test *unless-goals* conditions on learned methods, and thus the ability to master goal orderings. The lesioned system's performance improved slightly with training but continued to require massive search, which indicates that goal conditions are crucial for expert behavior in this domain. In addition, note that the learning curves for the number of decompositions and time have very similar shapes. This

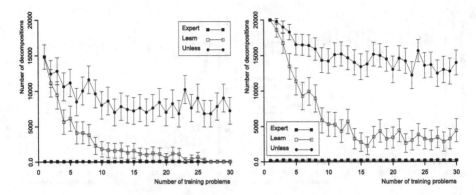

Fig. 3. Number of decompositions needed to solve problems in Logistics (left) and Depots (right) by an expert HPN knowledge base, HPN methods learned from sample plans, and learned methods that lack *unless-goals* conditions. Each curve reports means and 95% confidence intervals over 100 random problem orders.

suggests that HPNL does not suffer from the classic utility problem, in which learning reduces search but actually slows processing. This phenomenon arose in recursive domains like the Blocks World, so its absence here is encouraging.

The leftmost graph in Fig. 3 shows results for the Logistics domain. As before, the handcrafted knowledge base solves all problems very rapidly with almost no search. In this case, learning reduces the number of decompositions more slowly, only reaching expert level by the 26th training problem. Again, the asymptote is substantially higher when the system does not use *unless-goals* conditions, although it fares better than in the Blocks World. Although not shown, the learning curve for CPU time again parallels the one for number of decompositions. Results for the Depots domain, in the rightmost graph of Fig. 3, are less impressive in that HPNL never quite reaches the expert level and some search through the space of hierarchical plans remains. This suggests that the constraint-based learning mechanism is finding overly specific conditions that do not generalize to new problems as much as desired.

Examination of structures acquired in the three domains is consistent with this interpretation. For the Blocks World, HPNL created only six methods and these were nearly identical to the six handcrafted ones. In contrast, the system learned 29 methods for Logistics and 30 for Depots, substantially more than the 11 and 10 rules in their expert knowledge bases. Further inspection revealed that many methods were idiosyncratic variants of the handcrafted ones. For instance, the system learned 11 different Logistics methods for achieving the *at* relation with *unload-truck*: when the target and truck locations are the same, when the truck is at the airport, and others. We posit two reasons for this behavior: direct replacement of constants with variables introduces identities that are not logically required and the technique for adding static relations finds conditions not needed to constrain variables. Neither issue arose in the Blocks World, which is why the system found fewer, more general methods in that domain.

In summary, our experimental findings were mixed. In two domains, HPNL achieved expert-level performance from under 30 sample plans, but learning did not eliminate search in the third domain and specialized conditions reduced its generalization. Another issue was that the learned methods sometimes found much longer solutions than did handcrafted ones. Thus, our approach to learning expertise for hierarchical planning achieved some but not all of our original aims.

5 Related Research

Our approach to learning expertise for problem solving incorporates ideas from the previous literature, but it also makes novel contributions. Langley and Shrobe (2021) have reviewed the HPN framework's relation to other hierarchical formalisms, so we will focus here on the acquisition of expertise. Some early work on learning search-control knowledge (Sleeman et al., 1982) emphasized induction of state-related conditions on when to apply operators, whereas later efforts on learning search-control rules (e.g., Minton, 1988) and macro-operators (Iba, 1989) invoked explanation-based techniques. Most relied on forward search from states, but some systems chained backward from goals, as in our framework.

A few early researchers addressed the acquisition of hierarchical structures for planning and problem solving. Ruby and Kibler's (1991) SteppingStone and Marsella and Schmidt's (1993) PRL acquired decomposition rules, but they did not associate operators with them. Shavlik (1990) reported an approach that learned hierarchical rules, some recursive, using analytic techniques, but it worked within the situation calculus. The closest relative to our work from this era was Reddy and Tadepalli's (1997) X-Learn, which also learned rules for decomposing goals but used inductive logic programming to identify conditions.

There has also been research on learning hierarchical task networks and related structures. For instance, Ilghami et al. (2002) used successful HTN plans as training cases, invoking a version-space technique to induce conditions on methods. Hogg et al. (2008) instead used a form of explanation-based learning to derive conditions on methods from definitions of operators used in sample traces. In this arena, the nearest kin is Nejati et al.'s (2006) work on learning goal-driven teleoreactive logic programs from sample plans, which also acquired methods from individual problems but used simpler analysis than other efforts.

Schmid and Kitzelmann (2011) present a very different approach that learns recursive programs by detecting and generalizing patterns in a small set of sample traces. Their formulation differs from ours but shares the aim of rapidly acquiring search-free procedures. Finally, Cropper and Muggleton (2015) report a system that uses meta-interpretive learning, which combines abductive reasoning with abstract knowledge, to create hierarchical rules for sequential behavior with invented nonterminal symbols. In contrast, our approach to learning hierarchical problem networks avoids the need for such predicates because it indexes acquired methods by goals they achieve. In summary, our framework shares features with earlier research on procedural learning but also has some important differences.

6   Concluding Remarks

In this paper, we reviewed hierarchical problem networks and presented a novel approach to learning them from sample plans. A primary innovation was the use of domain constraints to identify simple conditions on hierarchical methods from single subplans, which avoids both the overly complex rules generated by explanation-based techniques and the reliance of relational induction on multiple training cases. Another important contribution was a means for learning *unless-goals* conditions on methods that ensure goals are tackled in the proper order. Experiments in three domains provided evidence that this approach leads to effective planning knowledge which substantially reduces both search and problem-solving time on novel problems from the same domain.

Despite the progress that we have reported here, our mechanisms for acquiring plan knowledge require further development to improve their rate of learning. One promising approach involves abandoning simple substitution of constants with variables, which encodes accidental identities, and instead propagates dependencies through sample plans. This should reduce the number of idiosyncratic methods and improve generalization to new problems. Another response is to replace the chaining technique that finds static relations with a specialized form of inductive logic programming. Recall that state conditions serve to distinguish desirable bindings for operator arguments that will achieve the method's goal from ones that will not. Each sample decomposition offers one positive instance of such bindings and typically provides multiple negative cases that to support induction of conditions about dynamic and static relations.

We intend to implement both techniques in future research and run experiments that identify the conditions under which they are effective. We should also compare our approach to classic methods for analytic learning, including macro-operator formation, and to inductive logic programming. Finally, we should examine learning mechanisms' behaviors on additional planning domains to further demonstrate their generality and to uncover any unexpected drawbacks. Nevertheless, our initial results have been encouraging and suggest that our computational framework for acquiring expertise in hierarchical planning merits additional study.

Acknowledgements. This research was supported by Grant N00014-20-1-2643 from the US Office of Naval Research, which is not responsible for its contents. We thank Howie Shrobe, Boris Katz, Gary Borchardt, Sue Felshin, Mohan Sridharan, and Ed Katz for discussions that influenced the ideas reported here.

References

Cropper, A., Muggleton, S.H.: Learning efficient logical robot strategies involving composable objects. In: Proceedings of the Twenty-Fourth International Joint Conference on Artificial Intelligence, Buenos Aires, Argentina, pp. 3423–3429. AAAI Press (2015)

Fine-Morris, M., et al.: Learning hierarchical task networks with landmarks and numeric fluents by combining symbolic and numeric regression. In: Proceedings of the Eighth Annual Conference on Advances in Cognitive Systems. Cognitive Systems Foundation (2020)

Hogg, C., Muñoz-Avila, H., Aha, D.W.: HTN-Maker: learning HTNs with minimal additional knowledge engineering required. In: Proceedings of the Twenty-Third National Conference on Artificial Intelligence. AAAI Press (2008)

Iba, G.A.: A heuristic approach to the discovery of macro-operators. Mach. Learn. **3**, 285–317 (1989)

Ilghami, O., Nau, D.S., Muñoz-Avila, H., Aha, D.W.: CaMeL: learning method preconditions for HTN planning. In: Proceedings of the Sixth International Conference on AI Planning and Scheduling, Toulouse, France, pp. 131–141. AAAI Press (2002)

Langley, P., Choi, D.: Learning recursive control programs from problem solving. J. Mach. Learn. Res. **7**, 493–518 (2006)

Langley, P., Shrobe, H.E.: Hierarchical problem networks for knowledge-based planning. In: Proceedings of the Ninth Annual Conference on Advances in Cognitive Systems. Cognitive Systems Foundation (2021)

Langley, P., Simon, H.A.: Applications of machine learning and rule induction. Commun. ACM **38**(November), 55–64 (1995)

Lloyd, J.W.: Foundations of logic programming. Springer, Heidelberg (1984). https://doi.org/10.1007/978-3-642-96826-6

Marsella, S.C., Schmidt, C.F.: A method for biasing the learning of nonterminal reduction rules. In: Minton, S. (ed.), Machine learning methods for planning. Morgan Kaufmann: San Francisco, CA (1993)

Minton, S.: Quantitative results concerning the utility of explanation-based learning. In: Proceedings of the Seventh National Conference on Artificial Intelligence, St. Paul, MN, pp. 564–569. Morgan Kaufmann (1988)

Nau, D., et al.: SHOP2: An HTN planning system. J. Artif. Intell. Res. **20**, 379–404 (2003)

Nejati, N., Langley, P., Könik, T.: Learning hierarchical task networks by observation. In: Proceedings of the Twenty-Third International Conference on Machine Learning, Pittsburgh, PA, pp. 665–672 (2006)

Reddy, C., Tadepalli, P.: Learning goal-decomposition rules using exercises. In: Proceedings of the Fourteenth International Conference on Machine Learning, Nashville, TN, pp. 278–286. Morgan Kaufmann (1997)

Ruby, D., Kibler, D.: SteppingStone: An empirical and analytical evaluation. In: Proceedings of the Tenth National Conference on Artificial Intelligence, Menlo Park, CA, pp. 527–532. AAAI Press (1991)

Schmid, U., Kitzelmann, E.: Inductive rule learning on the knowledge level. Cogn. Syst. Res. **12**, 237–248 (2011)

Shavlik, J.: Acquiring recursive and iterative concepts with explanation-based learning. Mach. Learn. **5**, 39–70 (1990)

Shivashankar, V., Kuter, U., Nau, D., Alford, R.: A hierarchical goal-based formalism and algorithm for single-agent planning. In: Proceedings of the Eleventh International Conference on Autonomous Agents and Multiagent Systems, Valencia, Spain, pp. 981–988 (2012)

Sleeman, D., Langley, P., Mitchell, T.: Learning from solution paths: An approach to the credit assignment problem. AI Mag. **3**, 48–52 (1982)

Combining Word Embeddings-Based Similarity Measures for Transfer Learning Across Relational Domains

Thais Luca[1](✉)[iD], Aline Paes[2][iD], and Gerson Zaverucha[1][iD]

[1] Department of Systems Engineering and Computer Science, Universidade Federal do Rio de Janeiro, Rio de Janeiro, RJ, Brazil
{tluca,gerson}@cos.ufrj.br
[2] Institute of Computing, Universidade Federal Fluminense, Niteroi, RJ, Brazil
alinepaes@ic.uff.br

Abstract. Statistical relational learning (SRL) algorithms have succeeded in many real-world applications as real-world data is relational and consists of different entities characterized by different sets of attributes. Real-world data can also be noisy and have incomplete information. Like traditional machine learning models, SRL models also assume training and testing data are sampled from the same distribution. If distributions differ, a new model must be trained using newly collected data. Employing Transfer Learning to machine learning models has become a great asset in handling such issues. It aims to leverage the knowledge learned in a source domain to train a model in a target domain. Moreover, SRL models may suffer from insufficient high-quality data instances and a long training time. Recent work has shown that applying transfer learning is suitable for SRL models as it admits training and testing data sampled from different distributions. However, an essential challenge is how to transfer the learned structure, mapping the vocabulary across different domains. This work relies on a previous approach that uses the similarity between pre-trained word embeddings to guide the mapping and applies theory revision to improve its inferential capacities. However, choosing the most suitable similarity metrics for a specific pair of source and target datasets is not trivial. Thus, we propose to combine different similarity metrics to map predicates. Experimental results showed that combining distinct similarity metrics has improved or equated performance compared to previous methods. It also requires less training time for some experiments.

Keywords: Transfer learning · Statistical relational learning · Word embeddings

Supported by CAPES, FAPERJ, and CNPq.

S. H. Muggleton and A. Tamaddoni-Nezhad (Eds.): ILP 2022, LNAI 13779, pp. 84–99, 2024.
https://doi.org/10.1007/978-3-031-55630-2_7

1 Introduction

Traditional machine learning models assume data to be independent and identically distributed (i.i.d.). However, most real-world data is relational and consists of different types of entities characterized by different sets of attributes [13]. Entities may be related to each other by relations, and exploring this relational structure of the data allows for finding solutions to more complex problems [6].

Statistical Relational Learning (SRL) [10] is a machine learning branch that combines statistical and relational modeling elements. It attempts to represent, reason, and learn in domains with complex relational and rich probabilistic structures. SRL models have succeeded in many real-world applications because they can handle uncertainty inherent to real-world data that may have missing, partially observed, or noisy information. SRL models do not assume data to be i.i.d., as traditional methods. However, traditional and SRL models assume training and testing data are sampled from the same distribution [25]. If distribution changes, a new model must be trained from scratch using newly collected data.

As data can be expensive or even impossible to collect, Transfer Learning [30] may be the key to handling such scenarios. It aims to leverage knowledge learned by a model in a source domain to train a new model in a different target domain. Besides, most SRL models may only succeed when trained using large amounts of data and may suffer from low quantities of high-quality data instances. Transfer learning can also help accelerate the learning process since SRL models may have a long training time. Previous works [1,8,15,18,20,21] have shown that transfer learning also succeeds in SRL models as it makes learning a new task less time- and data-consuming.

The last years have witnessed an explosion of new methods and successful results when employing transfer learning with Deep Learning applications [17], as it reduces the effort to adapt a model to a distinct domain or target task and reduces the need for extensive datasets. Unlike the usual Deep Learning applications, SRL models have a rich vocabulary composed of different classes, objects, properties, and relationships [9]. Thus, the remaining challenge for transferring SRL models is how to transfer the learned structure, mapping the vocabulary across different domains. TransBoostler [18] is a Relational Dependency Boosting (RDN-B) [23] framework that proposes to map predicates to a Vector Space Model (VSM) [26], as predicates' names usually have a semantic connotation. It takes advantage of the context in which predicates appear to find suitable mappings by similarity. After transference, it relies on Theory Revision [29] to improve its inferential capacities. Nevertheless, as presented by [18], no similarity measure leads the algorithm to its best performance for all experiments.

In this work, we propose combining different similarity metrics to map predicates to improve TransBoostler's performance. Also, mapping predicates by similarity may increase the revision time for some experiments. We propose to use majority voting and Borda Count [7] to combine measures to try to make fewer modifications to the transferred theory. We call it TransBoostler+[1] and it combines the similarity measures used by [18] to transfer Relational Dependency Networks (RDNs) [24]. After transferring, it performs theory revision to increase its accuracy. We performed a set of experiments to evaluate TransBoostler+ benefits in real-world relational datasets compared to three baseline models. Two of them perform transfer learning, and one learns from data from scratch. The first experiment simulates a scenario of few data available and training is performed on one single fold and testing on the remaining folds. Then, we compare TransBoostler+ performance for different amounts of target data using cross-validation. Our results demonstrate that the proposed algorithm can successfully transfer learned theories across different domains by combining similarity measures, performing equally or better than TransBoostler and other methods.

The rest of the paper is organized as follows. Section 2 contains the necessary background. Section 3 compares our proposal to previous works. Section 4 presents our proposed method. Section 5 describes experimental results of TransBoostler+ for different datasets. Finally, Sect. 6 presents our conclusions.

2 Background

This section revises functional gradient boosting to learn RDNs, transfer learning, word embeddings, and Borda Count.

2.1 Functional Gradient Boosting of Relational Dependency Networks

Much machine learning research has focused on "flattened" propositional data. It ignores the relational structure of the data, which contains crucial information such as characteristics of heterogeneous objects and the relations among these objects. Relational models extend the flat propositional representation of the variables and conditional dependencies among them to relational representation [10]. Exploring this relational structure of the data allows for finding solutions to more complex problems [6].

To represent relations between objects, we follow first-order logic (FOL). Relations are represented as logical facts, while domains are represented using constants, variables, and predicates. *movie(titanic,leonardo)* is a logical fact that represents a relation between a movie identified by *titanic* and an actor named *leonardo* who starred in that movie. *movie* is the name of the predicate that consists of two arguments. *titanic* and *leonardo* are constants that represent entities of the domain. Several relational learning algorithms associate arguments with a type of language bias. For example, *titanic* is associated with the type *title* and *leonardo* is associated with the type *person*. The predicate *movie* has two arguments, so we say its arity is two or it is a binary predicate. Predicates can also

---

[1] The source code and experiments are publicly available at https://github.com/MeLL-UFF/TransBoostler.

represent properties of an object in the domain. For instance, *actor(leonardo)* states that *leonardo* is an actor and *director(cameron)* states that *cameron* is a director. Both predicates have one single argument of type *person*, so we say their arity is one. A predicate applied to terms is called an atom. A term can be a variable, constant, or function symbol applied to terms. The atom *movie(title, person)* is called the ground atom because it asserts a relationship among constants. Lastly, a literal can be an atom or a negated atom. A disjunction of literals with only one positive literal is a definite clause.

SRL is a combination of statistical learning and relational modeling that attempts to represent, reason, and learn in domains with complex relational and rich probabilistic structures [10]. SRL models aim to represent probabilistic dependencies among attributes of different related objects. RDNs can express and reason over dependencies by approximating the joint distribution of a set of random variables as a product of conditional distributions over a ground atom. Besides, RDNs allow representing cyclic dependencies which are required to express and exploit autocorrelation. RDNs consist of a set of predicates and function symbols. They associate each predicate Y_i in the domain to a conditional probability distribution $P(Y_i|\mathbf{Pa}(Y_i))$, the distribution over the values of Y_i given its parents' values $\mathbf{Pa}(Y_i)$ [24] in the RDN.

RDN-B [23] proposes to use functional gradient boosting to learn RDNs. It builds a set of *relational regression trees* using gradient-based boosting instead of representing the conditional distribution for each relation as a single relational probability tree. Boosting is a nonparametric approach, so the number of parameters grows with the number of training episodes. Interactions between random variables are introduced as needed, and the large search space is not explicitly considered. Besides, both structure and parameters are learned simultaneously.

2.2 Transfer Learning

Transfer learning aims to reutilize the knowledge learned in one domain to another domain by exploiting a pre-trained model. Following the notations introduced by [25]: a domain $\mathcal{D}$ consists of a feature space $\mathcal{X}$ and a marginal probability distribution $P(X)$, where $X = \{x_1, \cdots, x_n\} \in \mathcal{X}$. Given a specific domain $D = \{\mathcal{X}, P(X)\}$, a task consists of a label space $\mathcal{Y}$ and a objective predictive function $f(\cdot)$, and it is denoted by $\mathcal{T} = \{\mathcal{Y}, f(\cdot)\}$. Given a source domain D_S and a learning task T_S, a target domain D_T, and a learning task T_T, transfer learning aims to help to improve the learning of a target predictive function $f_T(\cdot)$ in D_T using the knowledge in D_S and T_S (where $D_S \neq D_T$ or $T_S \neq T_T$). Exploiting the knowledge learned from one or more previous tasks avoids learning from scratch one specific domain. Besides, SRL models may suffer from low quantities of high-quality data instances and a long training time. Transfer learning reduces the re-calibration effort to train a new model and makes learning a new task less time- and data-consuming [25]. However, the main challenge in SRL is transferring the learned structure by mapping the vocabulary across different domains.

2.3 Word Embeddings

Word embeddings are the most popular way to represent words as dense vectors of fixed length [28]. Words are encoded such that words close in the vector space have similar meanings. Word embeddings follow the distributional semantics that state that words used and occurring in the same contexts tend to have similar meanings [12]. For instance, words like *actor* and *movie* must appear close to each other as they usually appear in the same context. *Embedding* is the term commonly used when referring to word representations induced with neural networks. One of such methods is fast-Text [3]. It focuses on predicting words in the surrounding context given a target word. It also creates embeddings from sub-words to handle out-of-vocabulary words.

2.4 Borda Count

In a decision-making process with more than one option, choosing the candidate with more than half of the votes is natural. However, majority voting may not be the most adequate solution when choosing between multiple options. Borda Count [7] is a voting scheme designed for scenarios where there are more than two candidates. In Borda Count, each voter lists candidates according to his preference, i.e., the first candidate is a voter's preferred, and the last is the least preferred. In this way, each position in the voter's list of preferences corresponds to a score. If there are n candidates, the candidate in the i-th position on the list has a score of $n - i$. The best one would have $n - 1$ points, and the worst would have zero points. Suppose three voting ballots and four candidates A, B, C, and D. In this case, the preferred candidate receives three points. If two voters elected candidate A as the preferred, it receives $2*3 = 6$ points; if the third voter elected candidate A as the second preferred, it receives $1*2 = 2$ points. Candidate A final score is $6+2 = 8$ points. The winner is the one with the highest score.

3 Related Work

Regarding SRL models, one remaining challenge is how to transfer vocabulary considering different domains. LTL [15] tries to transfer theories by type-matching while TAMAR [20] proposes to transfer Markov Logic Networks across domains by using weighted pseudo-log-likelihood. Both GROOT [8] and Tree-Boostler [1] focus on transferring RDNs. The former relies on a genetic algorithm, while the latter performs an exhaustive search to find suitable mappings. Both TAMAR, GROOT, and TreeBoostler use theory revision to improve their accuracy. In this work, we rely on TransBoostler [18] a transfer learning-based framework that uses the similarity between pre-trained word embeddings to guide the mapping as predicates names usually have a semantic connotation that can be mapped to a VSM. This approach leads to a richer mapping as it takes advantage of the context of embeddings to choose mappings, and no searching is applied. It also revises those trees by pruning and expanding nodes to improve their inferential capacities. Since choosing the most suitable similarity metrics for a specific pair of source and target datasets is not trivial, we propose to modify its mapping component by combining different similarity metrics.

4 TransBoostler+

This section presents our proposed method. TransBoostler+ relies on a transfer learning-based framework that uses word embeddings to guide mapping to transfer RDNs. It combines different similarity measures to improve performance. It also revises its trees by pruning and expanding nodes after transference.

4.1 Transferring and Revising the Structure

TransBoostler adopts the local mapping approach introduced by [20], also adopted by TreeBoostler. It consists of mapping predicates as they appear in each clause. Mapping is performed separately and independently of how other clauses were mapped. It is a more scalable approach since the number of predicates in a single clause is smaller than the total number of predicates in the entire source domain.

We can see each path from the root to the leaf in a relational regression tree as a clause in a logic program. These paths may share the same inner nodes with different trees. Also, RDN-B works on a set of relational trees that may share the same predicates in nodes. They cannot be interpreted individually and are not independent of each other. Thus, once the algorithm maps a predicate, this mapping is used for the entire structure as it just translates predicates the first time they appear in the structure.

When performing transfer learning, one may expect that knowledge from source and target domains come from distinct distributions; hence, just mapping predicates is usually not enough [20]. After mapping the vocabulary, the algorithm relies on Theory Revision [29] to improve its inferential capacities. It searches for paths in trees that are responsible for misclassifying examples, which are called revision points. Revision points may be specialization or generalization points. If a positive example is not covered by the theory, we have a generalization point. It means the theory is too specific and needs to be generalized. If the theory covers negative examples, we have a specialization point. It means the theory is too general and needs to be specialized. These points must be modified to increase accuracy. Modifications are proposed by revision operators. The pruning operator may generalize the theory by deleting nodes from a tree to increase the coverage of examples (generalization operator). The expansion operator may decrease the coverage of examples by expanding nodes in each tree (specialization operator). First, the revision algorithm applies the Pruning operator to work recursively by pruning the tree from the bottom to the top. It removes nodes whose children are leaves marked as revision points. Next, it applies the Expansion operator, which also works recursively by adding nodes that give the best split in a leaf marked as a revision point. If the pruning operator prunes an entire tree, the revision algorithm would have to expand nodes from an empty tree. In the case of pruning resulting in a null model, i.e., deletion of all trees, the operator is ignored as if it was never applied. The revision algorithm uses conditional log-likelihood (CLL) to score both transferred and revised theory and implements the one with the best score.

4.2   Combining Similarity Measures

We rely on the mapping component proposed by [18], briefly described in the following. We propose modifying TransBoostler's mapping component by combining different similarity measures to perform the mapping. As presented in [18], finding the best similarity measure to map predicates is not trivial since no similarity metric was unanimously better than the others.

TransBoostler assumes predicates have meaningful names and takes advantage of the semantics of pre-trained word vectors to map predicates by similarity. It starts from the root node of the first source tree and works recursively to map predicates. First, it splits each predicate into its component words since predicates can be made of one, two, or more words in relational domains. Next, it uses a pre-built dictionary to replace all shortened words with their full forms and it turns verbs into their base form. After the preprocessing step, every predicate is represented in the VSM using word vectors pre-trained on Wikipedia with fast-Text Skip-gram [22]. Relational datasets have a limited vocabulary, so pre-trained word vectors contribute to finding similar predicates by the context they appear in [18]. Words not belonging to the pre-trained model vocabulary are represented as null vectors.

TransBoostler maps a source predicate to a target predicate if they have the highest similarity value compared to other targets. However, taking one of the transfer experiments as an example, we have two different mappings for the source predicate *teamplaysinleague*: *cityhascompanyoffice* and *bankbankincountry*. From a semantic point of view, both mappings make sense. Both describe something that belongs somewhere. Also, two measures agree that *teamplaysinleague* is most similar to *bankbankincountry*. Inspired by the success of ensemble learning, we propose to combine different similarity measures to find suitable mappings for predicates. The most intuitive and naive way to combine different similarity measures is majority voting. In majority voting, a target predicate is chosen as the corresponding mapping to a given source predicate if it has the majority of the similarity measures' votes, as presented in Algorithm 1. As majority voting may not be efficient for multiple options, we also propose using Borda Count. When using Borda Count, each similarity measure casts a ballot: a list of the most to least similar target predicates to a given source predicate. The target predicate with the highest score is the corresponding mapping to the given source. Following [18], we only map predicates of same arity to maintain variables' consistency, and it is not permitted to have two source predicates mapped to a same target predicate. If there is a tie, we follow alphabetical order.

Also, if the algorithm cannot find a compatible mapping for a given source, it is mapped to "empty".

After transfer, three possible scenarios are modeled by [1]. In the first scenario, all literals in an inner node have a non-empty predicate mapping. This is the best scenario because we have the same number of literals in the transferred tree. Another possible scenario is when an inner node has some predicate mapped to "empty," and at least one mapped to non-empty. In this case, the ones mapped to empty are discarded. The third and last possible scenario is the worst case. If an inner node has all its literals mapped to an empty predicate, discarding all literals results in an empty node and affects the tree structure. In this case, the algorithm discards the empty node, promotes its left child, and appends its right child to the right-most path of the subtree. If the left child is a leaf, the right child is promoted. If both are leaves, it is discarded.

Algorithm 1: Majority voting mapping approach. Inputs are an ordered list of source predicates and a list of all target predicates.

Function MAJORITY_VOTING(srcPreds, tarPreds):

    $mappings \leftarrow \{\}$

    for $srcPred \in srcPreds$ **do**

        $candidates \leftarrow \{\}$

        for $sim \in similarity\_metrics$ **do**

            $similarities \leftarrow$ sim(srcPred,tarPreds)

            Sort $similarities$

            $mostSimilar \leftarrow$ get most similar target predicate using $similarities$

            Insert $mostSimilar$ to $candidates$

        end

        $mostVoted \leftarrow$ get the most frequent predicate in $candidates$

        Insert $(srcPred, mostVoted)$ in $mappings$

    end

return mappings

---

5 Experimental Results

This section presents the experiments performed to evaluate TransBoostler+. We compare our results with TransBoostler [18], a word embeddings-based similarity framework to transfer RDNs, TreeBoostler [1], which is another SRL transfer learning-based framework, and RDN-B [23], which learns from data from scratch.

We follow the same experimental setup as TransBoostler [18]. We set the depth limit of trees to be 3, the number of leaves to be 8, the number of regression trees to be 10, the maximum number of literals per node to be 2, and the initial potential to be -1.8, which is the same experimental setup for TreeBoostler. We subsample negative examples in a ratio of 2 negatives for one positive, and testing is done with all the negative examples. TransBoostler+ combines the three similarity metrics used by [18], which are the most common when it comes to the similarity between word embeddings: Soft Cosine [27], which is a modification of the traditional Cosine Similarity that also considers the similarities between words, Euclidean distance, and Word Mover's Distance (WMD) [16], which computes the "travel cost" to move a given document d to a document d'. We use majority voting and Borda Count to combine similarities. We compare two versions of our algorithm to evaluate results with no theory revision. One version considers only mapping and parameter learning (TransBoostler*+), and the completed version applies theory revision (TransBoostler+).

To evaluate TransBoostler, we used six real-world relational datasets paired as in previous literature [1,8,15,18,20,21]: IMDB dataset [21] is divided into five mega-examples that present information about four movies. The objective is to predict which actor has worked for a director by learning the *workedunder* relation; Cora dataset [2] contains information about Computer Science research papers. It is divided into five mega-examples, and its goal is to predict if two venues represent the same conference by learning the *samevenue* relation; UW-CSE [14] contains information about the Department of Computer Science and Engineering at the University of Washington (UW-CSE) to predict if a student is advised by a professor. It is also divided into five mega-examples; Yeast protein [19] is a dataset obtained from MIPS Comprehensive Yeast Genome Database. It contains protein information and is divided into four folds independent of each other to predict if a protein is associated with a class; Twitter [11] is a dataset of tweets about Belgian soccer matches. It is divided into two independent folds to predict the account type; NELL [4] is a system that uses machine learning to extract information from web texts and converts it into a probabilistic knowledge base. We consider the domains NELL Sports and NELL Finances. The objective of NELL Sports is to predict which sport a team plays, and the objective of NELL Finances is to predict if a company belongs to an economic sector. We split the target data randomly into three different folds.

To compare performance between our proposed method and previous works, we used conditional log-likelihood (CLL), area under the ROC curve (AUC ROC), area under the PR curve (AUC PR) [5], and training time. All results are averaged over n runs. For every run, a new learned source model is used for transference. Following [18], we did not consider the time required to load the fast-Text model but did consider the time to calculate similarities between predicates. Because we combine three similarity measures, the time to compute similarities is the sum of the time required for each similarity measure. We used the same environment as [18] for all experiments.

First, we simulate a transfer learning scenario with a reduced set of data available. We follow previous literature, train TransBoostler+ on one fold, and test it on the remaining n-1 folds. Tables 1 and 2 present the transfer experiments for pairs IMDB and Cora, and Yeast and Twitter, respectively. Each dataset was treated as source and target domains on each turn. Table 3 presents the results for IMDB → UW-CSE and NELL Sports → NELL Finances. Results for transferring from UW-CSE to IMDB are omitted because it is too easy. NELL

Finances to NELL Sports transfer experiment is also omitted because Tree-Boostler cannot find useful mappings. We measured the statistical significance between TransBoostler and the baselines using a paired t-test with $p \leq 0.05$. In tables, T, R, S, E, W indicate when TransBoostler+ is significantly better than TreeBoostler, RDN-B, TransBoostler Soft Cosine, TransBoostler Euclidean, and TransBoostler WMD, respectively.

Results show that TransBoostler+ performs equally or better than Trans-Boostler. Combining similarity measures improved performance for some experiments. It also has competitive results with TreeBoostler and outperforms RDN-B. However, it still depends on theory revision to succeed. For IMDB $\rightarrow$ Cora, both voting schemes find the same mappings as found by the Euclidean distance. As pointed out by [18], IMDB has only one predicate of arity two, while Cora only has predicates of arity two. Thus, the only source predicate to be mapped is *movie*. Even combining different similarity measures, we still have a different mapping from *venue*, which is the one found by TreeBoostler. For Yeast $\rightarrow$ Twitter experiments, both voting schemes also find the same mappings as found by TransBoostler when using the Euclidean distance. For IMDB $\rightarrow$ UW-CSE, we have a different mapping from TransBoostler's similarity measures, which might explain the improvement in TransBoostler+ results. In this way, Trans-Boostler+ mappings are also different from TreeBoostler. For Cora $\rightarrow$ IMDB and Twitter $\rightarrow$ Yeast, TransBoostler+ finds the same mappings as TransBoostler as all similarity measures find the same mappings. The former has the same mappings found by TreeBoostler, while the latter has different mappings. For NELL Sports $\rightarrow$ NELL Finances, all mappings are different from both baselines, and results for both methods show it is difficult to transfer across NELL domains. TreeBoostler can only map four predicates out of seven, and all mappings do not make sense from a semantic point of view. It still improves performance for AUC ROC when using majority voting compared to TransBoostler using Soft Cosine, Euclidean distance, and WMD. Even though TransBoostler+ calculates more similarities than TransBoostler, the mapping time is neglectable compared to learning and revision times. For most experiments, it takes more time due to revising the theory to have a better performance.

Figures 1, 2, 3, 4, 5, and 6 present the results for TransBoostler+ for different amounts of target data. We follow traditional cross-validation methodology, so training is performed on n-1 folds and testing on one fold. We incrementally increase the amount of target data to evaluate our algorithm's performance. Training data is shuffled and divided into five sequence parts. All curves were obtained by averaging the results over n runs. To better visualize the results, we took the average over the three similarity measures for TransBoostler. As can be seen, TransBoostler+ has competitive results compared to TransBoostler for most experiments. It also has competitive or better results compared to TreeBoostler and RDN-B for some experiments. It underperforms TreeBoostler for IMDB $\rightarrow$ Cora and Twitter $\rightarrow$ Yeast experiments, and NELL Sports $\rightarrow$ NELL Finances for AUC ROC.

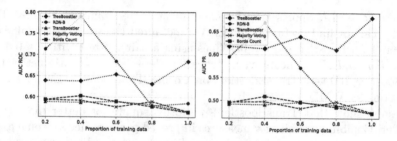

Fig. 1. Learning curves for AUC ROC (left) and AUC PR (right) for IMDB → Cora transfer experiment.

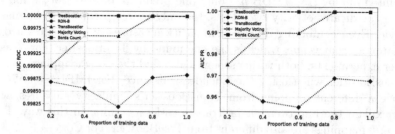

Fig. 2. Learning curves for AUC ROC (left) and AUC PR (right) for Cora → IMDB transfer experiment.

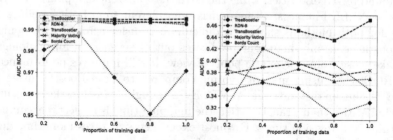

Fig. 3. Learning curves for AUC ROC (left) and AUC PR (right) for Yeast → Twitter transfer experiment.

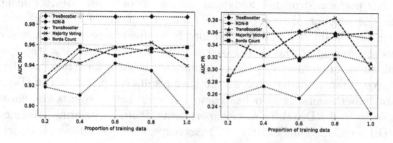

Fig. 4. Learning curves for AUC ROC (left) and AUC PR (right) for Twitter → Yeast transfer experiment.

Table 1. Comparison between TransBoostler+ and baselines for IMDB and Cora datasets.

	IMDB → Cora				Cora → IMDB			
	CLL	AUC ROC	AUC PR	Run-time(s)	CLL	AUC ROC	AUC PR	Run-time(s)
RDN-B	−0.693	0.558	0.426	76.97	−0.075	1.000	1.000	2.89
TreeBoostler	−0.659	0.606	0.530	45.74	−0.075	0.999	0.954	4.29
TransBoostler Soft Cosine	−0.675	0.599	0.464	51.18	−0.074	1.000	1.000	4.36
TransBoostler Euclidean	−0.677	0.589	0.453	52.61	−0.076	0.999	0.927	4.42
TransBoostler WMD	−0.668	0.600	0.463	54.44	−0.076	0.999	0.948	4.43
TransBoostler+ Majority Voting	−0.678	0.589	0.453	51.37	−0.074	1.000^T	1.000	4.15
TransBoostler+ Borda Count	$−0.681^T$	0.578	0.442	51.66	−0.075	1.000^T	1.000	4.27
TreeBoostler*	−0.659	0.574	0.518	1.63	−0.115	0.982	0.888	0.95
TransBoostler* Soft Cosine	−0.699	0.500	0.379	2.20	−0.306	0.868	0.092	1.94
TransBoostler* Euclidean	−0.699	0.500	0.379	2.15	−0.304	0.868	0.092	1.90
TransBoostler* WMD	−0.699	0.500	0.379	2.23	−0.308	0.868	0.092	1.92
TransBoostler*+ Majority Voting	−0.699	0.500	0.379	1.23	$−0.388^{TRS}$	0.500	0.026	0.76
TransBoostler*+ Borda Count	−0.699	0.500	0.379	1.28	$−0.394^{TRS}$	0.500	0.026	0.77

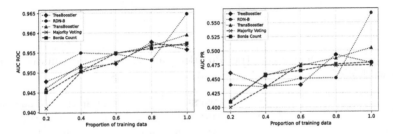

Fig. 5. Learning curves for AUC ROC (left) and AUC PR (right) for IMDB → UW-CSE transfer experiment.

Table 2. Comparison between TransBoostler+ and baselines for Yeast and Twitter datasets.

	Yeast → Twitter				Twitter → Yeast			
	CLL	AUC ROC	AUC PR	Run-time(s)	CLL	AUC ROC	AUC PR	Run-time(s)
RDN-B	−0.122	0.990	0.347	23.45	−0.253	0.926	0.230	15.55
TreeBoostler	−0.096	0.994	0.395	86.63	−0.166	0.986	0.267	34.96
TransBoostlter Soft Cosine	−0.127	0.994	0.382	23.38	−0.280	0.920	0.169	20.39
TransBoostlter Euclidean	−0.107	0.994	0.389	26.09	−0.282	0.894	0.325	13.05
TransBoostlter WMD	−0.107	0.994	0.374	24.55	−0.240	0.953	0.282	19.64
TransBoostlter+ Majority Voting	−0.102	0.994	0.367	43.10	−0.245	0.952^E	0.290^S	22.59
TransBoostlter+ Borda Count	−0.102	0.994	0.389^S	59.96	$−0.239^T$	0.951^{SE}	0.320^S	21.77
TreeBoostlter*	−0.103	0.993	0.334	7.17	−0.166	0.986	0.267	2.17
TransBoostlter* Soft Cosine	−0.154	0.993	0.339	4.51	−0.336	0.820	0.299	3.35
TransBoostlter* Euclidean	−0.110	0.994	0.405	5.65	−0.336	0.820	0.307	2.44
TransBoostlter* WMD	−0.110	0.994	0.391	4.45	−0.336	0.820	0.304	2.51
TransBoostlter*+ Majority Voting	−0.111	0.994	0.386	2.65	$−0.334^{TR}$	0.820	0.303	1.20
TransBoostlter*+ Borda Count	−0.109	0.994	0.400	2.72	$−0.335^{TR}$	0.820	0.309	1.23

Table 3. Comparison between TransBoostler+ and baselines for pairs of datasets IMDB and UW-CSE and NELL Sports and NELL Finances.

	IMDB → UW-CSE				NELL Sports → NELL Finances			
	CLL	AUC ROC	AUC PR	Run-time(s)	CLL	AUC ROC	AUC PR	Run-time(s)
RDN-B	−0.257	0.940	0.282	8.74	−0.323	0.692	0.062	24.86
TreeBoostler	−0.247	0.939	0.302	4.78	−0.165	0.980	0.071	124.59
TransBoostlter Soft Cosine	−0.255	0.936	0.284	5.94	−0.321	0.721	0.087	62.70
TransBoostlter Euclidean	−0.254	0.936	0.275	6.44	−0.320	0.750	0.069	54.04
TransBoostlter WMD	−0.247	0.936	0.274	5.89	−0.324	0.741	0.079	53.81
TransBoostlter+ Majority Voting	$−0.254^W$	0.938	0.270	6.13	$−0.318^T$	0.753	0.077	51.71
TransBoostlter+ Borda Count	−0.253	0.939	0.298	6.79	$−0.331^{TW}$	0.712	0.066	55.02
TreeBoostlter*	−0.267	0.930	0.293	0.63	−0.315	0.979	0.068	8.85
TransBoostlter* Soft Cosine	−0.385	0.608	0.035	1.17	−0.366	0.531	0.001	6.92
TransBoostlter* Euclidean	−0.296	0.906	0.131	1.53	−0.365	0.558	0.002	5.88
TransBoostlter* WMD	−0.288	0.906	0.131	1.19	−0.365	0.540	0.002	5.66
TransBoostlter+* Majority Voting	$−0.291^T$	0.906^S	0.131	0.64	$−0.367^{TR}$	0.558	0.002	2.46
TransBoostlter+* Borda Count	$−0.289^R$	0.906	0.131	0.68	$−0.367^{TR}$	0.559	0.002	2.57

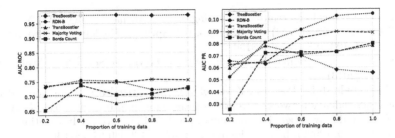

Fig. 6. Learning curves for AUC ROC (left) and AUC PR (right) for NELL Sports → NELL Finances transfer experiment.

6   Conclusions

This paper proposes TransBoostler+, an algorithm that transfers Boosted RDNs across different domains. It relies on a previous SRL transfer learning method named TransBoostler, which uses pre-trained word embeddings to guide the mapping between predicates. Choosing the best similarity measure is not trivial, so we propose combining different similarity measures using majority voting and Borda Count. Experimental results show that combining measures has a good performance, performing better than one of the baselines. It is also less time-consuming than at least one of the baselines. However, it remains a future investigation on how to know the best pair of source and target datasets to transfer in advance. One possible future direction is combining pre-trained word vectors from different contexts to find better mappings.

References

1. Azevedo Santos, R., Paes, A., Zaverucha, G.: Transfer learning by mapping and revising boosted relational dependency networks. Mach. Learn. **109**(7), 1435–1463 (2020). https://doi.org/10.1007/s10994-020-05871-x
2. Bilenko, M., Mooney, R.J.: Adaptive duplicate detection using learnable string similarity measures. In: Proceedings of the Ninth ACM SIGKDD International Conference on Knowledge Discovery and Data Mining, pp. 39–48. KDD 2003, Association for Computing Machinery, New York, NY, USA (2003). https://doi.org/10.1145/956750.956759
3. Bojanowski, P., Grave, E., Joulin, A., Mikolov, T.: Enriching Word Vectors with Subword Information. Trans. Assoc. Comput. Linguist. **5**, 135–146 (2017). https://doi.org/10.1162/tacl_a_00051
4. Carlson, A., Betteridge, J., Kisiel, B., Settles, B., Hruschka, E.R., Mitchell, T.M.: Toward an architecture for never-ending language learning. In: Proceedings of the Twenty-Fourth AAAI Conference on Artificial Intelligence, pp. 1306–1313. AAAI 2010, AAAI Press (2010)
5. Davis, J., Goadrich, M.: The relationship between precision-recall and roc curves. In: Proceedings of the 23rd International Conference on Machine Learning, pp. 233–240. ICML 2006, Association for Computing Machinery, New York, NY, USA (2006). https://doi.org/10.1145/1143844.1143874

6. Raedt, L.: Logical and relational learning. In: Zaverucha, G., da Costa, A.L. (eds.) SBIA 2008. LNCS (LNAI), vol. 5249, pp. 1–1. Springer, Heidelberg (2008). https://doi.org/10.1007/978-3-540-88190-2_1

7. Emerson, P.: The original borda count and partial voting. Soc. Choice Welf. **40**(2), 353–358 (2013)

8. de Figueiredo, L.F., Paes, A., Zaverucha, G.: Transfer learning for boosted relational dependency networks through genetic algorithm. In: Katzouris, N., Artikis, A. (eds.) Inductive Logic Programming, pp. 125–139. Springer International Publishing, Cham (2022). https://doi.org/10.1007/978-3-030-97454-1_9

9. Friedman, N., Getoor, L., Koller, D., Pfeffer, A.: Learning probabilistic relational models. In: Proceedings of the 16th International Joint Conference on Artificial Intelligence, vol. 2, pp. 1300–1307. IJCAI 1999, Morgan Kaufmann Publishers Inc., San Francisco, CA, USA (1999)

10. Getoor, L., Taskar, B.: Introduction to Statistical Relational Learning (Adaptive Computation and Machine Learning). The MIT Press, Cambridge (2007)

11. Haaren, J.V., Kolobov, A., Davis, J.: Todtler: two-order-deep transfer learning. In: Proceedings of the Twenty-Ninth AAAI Conference on Artificial Intelligence, pp. 3007–3015. AAAI 2015, AAAI Press (2015)

12. Harris, Z.S.: Distributional structure. Word **10**(2–3), 146–162 (1954)

13. Khosravi, H., Bina, B.: A survey on statistical relational learning. In: Farzindar, A., Kešelj, V. (eds.) AI 2010. Lecture Notes in Computer Science (Lecture Notes in Artificial Intelligence), vol. 6085, pp. 256–268. Springer, Heidelberg (2010). https://doi.org/10.1007/978-3-642-13059-5_25

14. Khosravi, H., Schulte, O., Hu, J., Gao, T.: Learning compact Markov logic networks with decision trees. In: Muggleton, S.H., Tamaddoni-Nezhad, A., Lisi, F.A. (eds.) Inductive Logic Programming, pp. 20–25. Springer, Heidelberg (2012). https://doi.org/10.1007/s10994-012-5307-6

15. Kumaraswamy, R., Odom, P., Kersting, K., Leake, D., Natarajan, S.: Transfer learning via relational type matching. In: 2015 IEEE International Conference on Data Mining, pp. 811–816 (2015). https://doi.org/10.1109/ICDM.2015.138

16. Kusner, M., Sun, Y., Kolkin, N., Weinberger, K.: From word embeddings to document distances. In: Bach, F., Blei, D. (eds.) Proceedings of the 32nd International Conference on Machine Learning Research, vol. 37, pp. 957–966. PMLR, Lille, France, 07–09 July 2015

17. LeCun, Y., Bengio, Y., Hinton, G.: Deep learning. Nature **521**(7553), 436–444 (2015)

18. Luca, T., Paes, A., Zaverucha, G.: Mapping across relational domains for transfer learning with word embeddings-based similarity. In: Katzouris, N., Artikis, A. (eds.) Inductive Logic Programming, pp. 167–182. Springer International Publishing, Cham (2022). https://doi.org/10.1007/978-3-030-97454-1_12

19. Mewes, H.W., et al.: MIPS: a database for genomes and protein sequences. Nucleic Acids Res. **28**, 37–40 (2000). https://doi.org/10.1093/nar/28.1.37

20. Mihalkova, L., Huynh, T., Mooney, R.J.: Mapping and revising Markov logic networks for transfer learning. In: Proceedings of the 22nd National Conference on Artificial Intelligence - Volume 1, pp. 608–614. AAAI 2007, AAAI Press (2007)

21. Mihalkova, L., Mooney, R.J.: Bottom-up learning of Markov logic network structure. In: Proceedings of the 24th International Conference on Machine Learning, pp. 625–632. ICML 2007, Association for Computing Machinery, New York, NY, USA (2007). https://doi.org/10.1145/1273496.1273575

22. Mikolov, T., Grave, E., Bojanowski, P., Puhrsch, C., Joulin, A.: Advances in pre-training distributed word representations. In: Proceedings of the Eleventh International Conference on Language Resources and Evaluation (LREC 2018). European Language Resources Association (ELRA), Miyazaki, Japan (May 2018). https://aclanthology.org/L18-1008

23. Natarajan, S., Khot, T., Kersting, K., Gutmann, B., Shavlik, J.: Gradient-based boosting for statistical relational learning: the relational dependency network case. Mach. Learn. **86**(1), 25–56 (2012). https://doi.org/10.1007/s10994-011-5244-9

24. Neville, J., Jensen, D.: Relational dependency networks. J. Mach. Learn. Res. **8**, 653–692 (2007)

25. Pan, S.J., Yang, Q.: A survey on transfer learning. IEEE Trans. Knowl. Data Eng. **22**(10), 1345–1359 (2010). https://doi.org/10.1109/TKDE.2009.191

26. Salton, G., Wong, A., Yang, C.S.: A vector space model for automatic indexing. Commun. ACM **18**(11), 613–620 (1975)

27. Sidorov, G., Gelbukh, A., Gomez Adorno, H., Pinto, D.: Soft similarity and soft cosine measure: similarity of features in vector space model. Computación y Sistemas **18**, 491–504 (2014). https://doi.org/10.13053/cys-18-3-2043

28. Torregrossa, F., Allesiardo, R., Claveau, V., Kooli, N., Gravier, G.: A survey on training and evaluation of word embeddings. Int. J. Data Sci. Anal. **11**, 1–19 (2021)

29. Wrobel, S.: First order theory refinement. Adv. Induct. Logic Program. **32**, 14–33 (1996)

30. Yang, Q., Zhang, Y., Dai, W., Pan, S.J.: Transfer Learning. Cambridge University Press, Cambridge (2020). https://doi.org/10.1017/9781139061773

Learning Assumption-Based Argumentation Frameworks

Maurizio Proietti[1]([✉]) [iD] and Francesca Toni[2] [iD]

[1] IASI-CNR, Rome, Italy
maurizio.proietti@iasi.cnr.it
[2] Imperial College London, London, UK
ft@ic.ac.uk

Abstract. We propose a novel approach to logic-based learning which generates *assumption-based argumentation (ABA) frameworks* from positive and negative examples, using a given background knowledge. These ABA frameworks can be mapped onto logic programs with negation as failure that may be non-stratified. Whereas existing argumentation-based methods learn exceptions to general rules by interpreting the exceptions as *rebuttal attacks*, our approach interprets them as *undercutting attacks*. Our learning technique is based on the use of transformation rules, including some adapted from logic program transformation rules (notably *folding*) as well as others, such as *rote learning* and *assumption introduction*. We present a general strategy that applies the transformation rules in a suitable order to learn stratified frameworks, and we also propose a variant that handles the non-stratified case. We illustrate the benefits of our approach with a number of examples, which show that, on one hand, we are able to easily reconstruct other logic-based learning approaches and, on the other hand, we can work out in a very simple and natural way problems that seem to be hard for existing techniques.

Keywords: Logic-based learning · Assumption-based argumentation · Logic program transformation

1 Introduction

Various forms of *computational argumentation*, notably abstract argumentation [Dun95] and assumption-based argumentation (ABA) [BDKT97, DKT09, Ton14] and [CFST17], have been advocated as unifying frameworks for various forms of non-monotonic reasoning, including logic programming. However, with very few early exceptions (notably [DK95]), computational argumentation has received little attention as a basis to support logic-based learning. Here, we fill this gap by proposing a novel approach to logic-based learning which generates ABA frameworks from examples, using background knowledge also in ABA format.

In general, ABA frameworks amount to a *deductive system* (consisting of a logical *language* to specify sentences and of a set of inference *rules* built from

ILP 2022, 31st International Conference on Inductive Logic Programming, Cumberland Lodge, Windsor, UK.

S. H. Muggleton and A. Tamaddoni-Nezhad (Eds.): ILP 2022, LNAI 13779, pp. 100–116, 2024.
https://doi.org/10.1007/978-3-031-55630-2_8

these sentences), a set of *assumptions* (which are sentences with a special status) and their *contraries* (which are sentences). Rules are then used to construct *arguments*, which support claims by means of assumptions, and *attacks* between assumptions/arguments are achieved by means of arguments supporting contraries of assumptions. The semantics of ABA frameworks is then defined in terms of various notions of *(dialectically) acceptable extensions*, amounting to sets of assumptions/arguments that can be deemed to defend themselves against attacks, in some sense (see Sect. 2). Thus, the goal of *ABA learning* amounts to identifying rules, assumptions and their contraries (adding to those in the given background knowledge) that cover argumentatively the positive examples and none of the negative examples according to some chosen semantics (see Sect. 3).

Logic programs can be seen as restricted instances of ABA frameworks (where assumptions are negation as failure literals, and the contrary of $not\, p$ is p) [BDKT97]. Moreover, ABA frameworks of a special kind (namely when all sentences are atomic and no assumption occurs in the head of rules) can be mapped to logic programs. These mappings hold under a range of semantics for ABA and for logic programming [BDKT97]. Thus, learning ABA frameworks can be seen as learning logic programs. However, given that ABA frameworks admit several other non-monotonic reasoning instances [BDKT97], learning ABA frameworks can also in principle provide a way to learn other forms of non-monotonic logics.

Our approach to learning ABA frameworks relies upon transformation rules applied to ABA frameworks (to obtain new ones, see Sect. 4): some of these transformation rules are adapted from logic programming, such as *folding* [PP94], whereas others are new, such as *rote learning* and *assumption introduction*. We define the transformation rules and outline a general strategy for applying them (see Sect. 6) in order to learn ABA frameworks that achieve the goal of ABA learning. We also illustrate, with the use of examples (see Sect. 5 and 7), the benefits of ABA learning in comparison with existing methods. We focus on similarly inspired methods, notably [DK95] and [SSG17]: the former learns argumentation frameworks of a different kind (where arguments are built from clauses and preferences over them), whereas the latter learns logic programs with negation as failure, but can be seen as being guided by argumentative principles (while not being explicitly so). Both these methods learn exceptions to general rules by interpreting the exceptions as *rebuttal attacks* (namely attacks between arguments with conflicting claims), and result in stratified logic programs [ABW88]. Instead, our approach interprets exceptions as *undercutting attacks* (from an argument to the support of another) while also accommodating rebuttal attacks, and may give rise to logic programs with non-stratified negation as failure.

Related Work. Several approaches to learning logic programs with negation as failure exist, in addition to the aforementioned [DK95,SSG17]. These include methods for learning exceptions to default rules [IK97], Sakama's inverse entailment [Sak00] and brave induction [SI09] in non-monotonic logic programs, and induction from answer sets [Sak05]. Answer sets are also the target of other logic-learning methods, notably as in ILASP [LRB14]. These approaches learn non-stratified logic programs, rather than ABA frameworks. ABA can be seen as performing abductive reasoning (in that assumptions are hypotheses open for debate). Whereas other approaches combine abductive and inductive learning [Ray09], again, they do not learn ABA frameworks. Some approaches learn abductive logic programs [IH00], which rely upon assumptions, like ABA frameworks. Overall, providing a formal comparison between our method and existing methods learning instances of ABA frameworks is left for future work. Finally, several existing works use argumentation to perform learning (e.g., see overview in [CT16]) while others learn argumentation frameworks (e.g., recently, [CSCT20]): we differ from the former in that our method learns ABA frameworks rather than using argumentation to aid learning, and from the latter in that we learn a different type of argumentation frameworks.

2   Background: Assumption-Based Argumentation (ABA)

An *Assumption-based argumentation (ABA) framework* (as originally proposed in [BDKT97], but presented here following recent accounts in [DKT09, Ton14] and [CFST17]) is a tuple $\langle \mathcal{L}, \mathcal{R}, \mathcal{A}, \overline{} \rangle$ where

- $\langle \mathcal{L}, \mathcal{R} \rangle$ is a deductive system, where $\mathcal{L}$ is a *language* and $\mathcal{R}$ is a set of *(inference) rules* of the form $s_0 \leftarrow s_1, \ldots, s_m$ ($m \geq 0, s_i \in \mathcal{L}$, for $1 \leq i \leq m$);
- $\mathcal{A} \subseteq \mathcal{L}$ is a (non-empty) set of *assumptions*;[1]
- $\overline{}$ is a total mapping from $\mathcal{A}$ into $\mathcal{L}$, where $\overline{a}$ is the *contrary* of a, for $a \in \mathcal{A}$.

Given a rule $s_0 \leftarrow s_1, \ldots, s_m$, s_0 is the *head* and $s_1, \ldots, s_m$ is the *body*; if $m = 0$ then the body is said to be *empty* (represented as $s_0 \leftarrow$ or $s_0 \leftarrow true$). If assumptions are not heads of rules then the ABA framework is called *flat*.

Elements of $\mathcal{L}$ can be any sentences, but in this paper we will focus on (flat) ABA frameworks where $\mathcal{L}$ is a set of ground atoms. However, in the spirit of logic programming, we will use *schemata* for rules, assumptions and contraries, using variables to represent compactly all instances over some underlying universe.

Example 1. Let $\mathcal{L} = \{p(X), q(X), r(X), a(X), b(X) | X \in \{1, 2\}\}$. Then, an ABA framework may be $\langle \mathcal{L}, \mathcal{R}, \mathcal{A}, \overline{} \rangle$ with the other components defined as follows:

$$\mathcal{R} = \{p(X) \leftarrow a(X), \quad q(X) \leftarrow b(X), \quad r(1) \leftarrow true\};$$
$$\mathcal{A} = \{a(X), b(X)\};$$
$$\overline{a(X)} = q(X), \quad \overline{b(X)} = r(X).$$

In ABA, *arguments* are deductions of claims using rules and supported by assumptions, and *attacks* are directed at the assumptions in the support of arguments. More formally, following [DKT09, Ton14, CFST17]:

---

[1] The non-emptiness requirement can always be satisfied by including in $\mathcal{A}$ a *bogus assumption*, with its own contrary, neither occurring elsewhere in the ABA framework. For conciseness, we will not write this assumption and its contrary explicitly.

- *An argument for (the claim) $s \in \mathcal{L}$ supported by $A \subseteq \mathcal{A}$ and $R \subseteq \mathcal{R}$* (denoted $A \vdash_R s$) is a finite tree with nodes labelled by sentences in $\mathcal{L}$ or by *true*, the root labelled by s, leaves either *true* or assumptions in A, and non-leaves s' with, as children, the elements of the body of some rule in R with head s'.
- Argument $A_1 \vdash_{R_1} s_1$ *attacks* argument $A_2 \vdash_{R_2} s_2$ iff $s_1 = \overline{a}$ for some $a \in A_2$.

Example 2 (Example 1 cntd). Let rules in $\mathcal{R}$ be named $\rho_1(X)$, $\rho_2(X)$, ρ_3, respectively. Then, arguments include $\{b(1)\} \vdash_{\{\rho_2(1)\}} q(1)$, $\emptyset \vdash_{\{\rho_3\}} r(1)$, and $\{a(1)\} \vdash_\emptyset a(1)$,[2] where, for example, $\emptyset \vdash_{\{\rho_3\}} r(1)$ attacks $\{b(1)\} \vdash_{\{\rho_2(1)\}} q(1)$.

Given argument $\alpha = A \vdash_R s$, we will refer to the single rule $\rho \in R$ such that the sentences in ρ's body label s' children in α as the *top rule* of the argument.

Note that, in ABA, attacks are carried out by *undercutting* some of their supporting premises (the assumptions). Other forms of attacks can be also represented in ABA, including attacks by *rebuttal*, where arguments disagree on their claim (see [Ton14] for details).

Given a flat ABA framework $\langle \mathcal{L}, \mathcal{R}, \mathcal{A}, \overline{} \rangle$, let *Args* be the set of all arguments and $Att = \{(\alpha, \beta) \in Args \times Args \mid \alpha \text{ attacks } \beta\}$, for 'arguments' and 'attacks' defined as above. Then $(Args, Att)$ is an Abstract Argumentation (AA) framework [Dun95] and standard semantics for the latter can be used to determine the semantics of the ABA framework [Ton14].[3] For example, $S \subseteq Args$ is a *stable extension* iff (i) $\nexists \alpha, \beta \in S$ such that $(\alpha, \beta) \in Att$ (i.e. S is *conflict-free*) and (ii) $\forall \beta \in Args \setminus S, \exists \alpha \in S$ such that $(\alpha, \beta) \in Att$ (i.e. S "attacks" all arguments it does not contain).

In the following example and in the remainder we will omit to specify the supporting rules in arguments (because these rules play no role when determining extensions, as attacks only depend on supporting assumptions and claims). Thus, e.g., argument $\{b(1)\} \vdash_{\{\rho_2(1)\}} q(1)$ in Example 2 is written simply as $\{b(1)\} \vdash q(1)$.

Example 3 (Example 2 cntd). The AA framework is $(Args, Att)$ with *Args* as given earlier and $Att = \{(\emptyset \vdash r(1), \{b(1)\} \vdash q(1)), (\emptyset \vdash r(1), \{b(1)\} \vdash b(1))\} \cup \{((\{b(X)\} \vdash q(X), \{a(X)\} \vdash p(X)), (\{b(X)\} \vdash q(X), \{a(X)\} \vdash a(X))) \mid X \in \{1, 2\}\}$. Then, $\{\emptyset \vdash r(1), \{a(1)\} \vdash p(1), \{a(1)\} \vdash a(1), \{b(2)\} \vdash q(2), \{b(2)\} \vdash b(2)\}$ is the only stable extension. This captures the "model" $\{r(1), p(1), a(1), q(2), b(2)\}$, amounting to all the claims of accepted arguments in the stable extension [Ton14].

Note that, in general, ABA frameworks may admit several stable extensions, in which case one can reason *credulously* or *sceptically*, by focusing respectively on (claims of arguments accepted in) a single or all stable extensions.

---

[2] The other (ground) arguments are $\{a(1)\} \vdash_{\{\rho_1(1)\}} p(1)$, $\{a(2)\} \vdash_{\{\rho_1(2)\}} p(2)$, $\{b(2)\} \vdash_{\{\rho_2(2)\}} q(2)$, $\{a(2)\} \vdash_\emptyset a(2)$, $\{b(1)\} \vdash_\emptyset b(1)$, and $\{b(2)\} \vdash_\emptyset b(2)$.

[3] ABA semantics were originally defined in terms of sets of assumptions and attacks between them [BDKT97], but can be reformulated, for flat ABA frameworks, in terms of sets of arguments and attacks between them (see [Ton14]), as given here.

Example 4. Given $\langle \mathcal{L}, \mathcal{R}, \mathcal{A}, ^{\frown} \rangle$ as in Example 1, consider $\langle \mathcal{L}, \mathcal{R}', \mathcal{A}, ^{\frown} \rangle$, where $\mathcal{R}' = \mathcal{R} \cup \{r(2) \leftarrow a(2)\}$. Now, there are two stable extensions: the same as in Example 3 as well as $\{\emptyset \vdash r(1), \{a(1)\} \vdash p(1), \{a(1)\} \vdash a(1), \{a(2)\} \vdash p(2), \{a(2)\} \vdash a(2), \{a(2)\} \vdash r(2)\}$, with accepted claims $\{r(1), a(1), p(1), a(2), p(2), r(2)\}$. Then, e.g., $r(1)$ is sceptically accepted whereas $r(2)$ is only credulously accepted.

Finally, note that ABA frameworks of the form considered here can be naturally mapped onto logic programs where assumptions are replaced by the negation as failure of their contraries, such that, in particular, stable extensions of the former correspond to stable models [GL88] of the latter.[4]

Example 5 (Example 4 cntd). For instance, $\langle \mathcal{L}, \mathcal{R}', \mathcal{A}, ^{\frown} \rangle$ from Example 4 can be mapped onto the logic program[5]

$$p(X) \leftarrow not\, q(X), \quad q(X) \leftarrow not\, r(X), \quad r(1) \leftarrow, \quad r(2) \leftarrow not\, q(2).$$

This admits two stable models, identical to the claims accepted in the two stable extensions for the ABA framework.

Thus, learning ABA frameworks of the form we consider amounts to a form of inductive logic programming (ILP).

In the remainder, without loss of generality we leave the language component of all ABA frameworks implicit, and use, e.g., $\langle \mathcal{R}, \mathcal{A}, ^{\frown} \rangle$ to stand for $\langle \mathcal{L}, \mathcal{R}, \mathcal{A}, ^{\frown} \rangle$ where $\mathcal{L}$ is the set of all sentences in $\mathcal{R}$, $\mathcal{A}$ and in the range of $^{\frown}$. We will also use $\langle \mathcal{R}, \mathcal{A}, ^{\frown} \rangle \models s$ to indicate that $s \in \mathcal{L}$ is the claim of an argument accepted in all or some stable extensions (depending on the choice of reasoning) of $\langle \mathcal{R}, \mathcal{A}, ^{\frown} \rangle$.

3 The ABA Learning Problem

We define the core ingredients of ABA learning, in a similar vein as in ILP.

Definition 1. *A* positive/negative example *(for a predicate p with arity $n \geq 0$) is a ground atom of the form $p(c)$, for c a tuple of n constants.*

The predicate amounts to the *concept* that inductive ABA aims to learn (in the form of an ABA framework whose language component includes the examples amongst its sentences). Positive and negative examples, albeit having the same syntax, play a very different role in ABA learning, as expected. Like standard ILP, ABA learning is driven by a (*non-empty*) set of positive examples and a (*possibly empty*) set of negative examples, with the help of some *background knowledge* compactly providing information about the examples, as follows:

Definition 2. *The* background knowledge *is an ABA framework.*

An illustration of possible background knowledge $\langle \mathcal{R}, \mathcal{A}, ^{\frown} \rangle$ and examples for a simple inductive ABA task is shown in Fig. 1 (adapted from [DK95]). Then, in

$$\mathcal{R} = \{bird(X) \leftarrow penguin(X), \quad penguin(X) \leftarrow superpenguin(X),$$
$$bird(a) \leftarrow, \ bird(b) \leftarrow, \quad penguin(c) \leftarrow, \ penguin(d) \leftarrow,$$
$$superpenguin(e) \leftarrow, \ superpenguin(f) \leftarrow\}$$

Positive Examples: $\{flies(a), flies(b), flies(e), flies(f)\}$
Negative Examples: $\{flies(c), flies(d)\}$

Fig. 1. A simple illustration of background knowledge as an ABA framework $\langle \mathcal{R}, \mathcal{A}, \overline{} \rangle$ (showing only $\mathcal{R}$, with $\mathcal{A}$ consisting of a single bogus assumption), and of positive/negative examples for ABA learning of concept $flies/1$.

ABA learning, we establish whether examples are *(not) covered* argumentatively:

Definition 3. *Given an ABA framework* $\langle \mathcal{R}, \mathcal{A}, \overline{} \rangle$, *an example* e *is* covered *by* $\langle \mathcal{R}, \mathcal{A}, \overline{} \rangle$ *iff* $\langle \mathcal{R}, \mathcal{A}, \overline{} \rangle \models e$ *and is* not covered *by* $\langle \mathcal{R}, \mathcal{A}, \overline{} \rangle$ *iff* $\langle \mathcal{R}, \mathcal{A}, \overline{} \rangle \not\models e$.

In the case of Fig. 1, none of the examples is covered by the background knowledge (no matter what $\models$ is, as no arguments for any of the examples exist).

Definition 4. *Given background knowledge* $\langle \mathcal{R}, \mathcal{A}, \overline{} \rangle$, *positive examples* $\mathcal{E}^+$ *and negative examples* $\mathcal{E}^-$, *with* $\mathcal{E}^+ \cap \mathcal{E}^- = \emptyset$, *the goal of ABA learning is to construct* $\langle \mathcal{R}', \mathcal{A}', \overline{}' \rangle$ *such that* $\mathcal{R} \subseteq \mathcal{R}'$, $\mathcal{A} \subseteq \mathcal{A}'$, *and, for all* $\alpha \in \mathcal{A}$, $\overline{\alpha}' = \overline{\alpha}$, *such that:*
(Existence) $\langle \mathcal{R}', \mathcal{A}', \overline{}' \rangle$ *admits at least one extension under the chosen ABA semantics,*
(Completeness) for all $e \in \mathcal{E}^+$, $\langle \mathcal{R}', \mathcal{A}', \overline{}' \rangle \models e$, *and*
(Consistency) for all $e \in \mathcal{E}^-$, $\langle \mathcal{R}', \mathcal{A}', \overline{}' \rangle \not\models e$.

This definition is parametric wrt the choice of semantics, and also whether this is used credulously or sceptically. For choices of semantics other than stable extensions (e.g., grounded or preferred extensions [CFST17]) the Existence requirement may be trivially satisfied (as these extensions always exist).

$$\mathcal{R}' = \{flies(X) \leftarrow bird(X), \alpha_1(X),$$
$$c\text{-}\alpha_1(X) \leftarrow penguin(X), \alpha_2(X),$$
$$c\text{-}\alpha_2(X) \leftarrow superpenguin(X)\} \cup \mathcal{R}$$
$$\mathcal{A}' = \{\alpha_1(X), \alpha_2(X)\} \quad \text{with } \overline{\alpha_1(X)}' = c\text{-}\alpha_1(X), \quad \overline{\alpha_2(X)}' = c\text{-}\alpha_2(X)$$

Fig. 2. An ABA framework $\langle \mathcal{R}', \mathcal{A}', \overline{}' \rangle$ achieving the goal of ABA learning, given the background knowledge and examples in Fig. 1.

---

[4] The correspondence also holds under other semantics, omitted here for simplicity.
[5] We use the same notation for ABA rules and logic programs as, indeed, logic programming is an instance of ABA [BDKT97].

The ABA framework $\langle \mathcal{R}', \mathcal{A}', \overline{}' \rangle$ in Fig. 2 admits a single stable extension and covers all positive examples and none of the negative examples in Fig. 1 (for either the sceptical or credulous version of $\models$). Thus, this $\langle \mathcal{R}', \mathcal{A}', \overline{}' \rangle$ achieves the goal of ABA learning. But how can this ABA framework be obtained? In the remainder we will outline our method for achieving the goal of ABA learning.

4   Transformation Rules for ABA Frameworks

Our method for solving the ABA learning problem makes use of transformation rules, some of which are borrowed from the field of logic program transformation [AD95, PP94, Sek91, TK96], while others are specific for ABA frameworks.

We assume that, for any ABA framework, the language $\mathcal{L}$ contains all equalities between elements of the underlying universe and $\mathcal{R}$ includes all rules $a = a \leftarrow$, where a is an element of the universe. We also assume that all rules in $\mathcal{R}$ (except for the implicit equality rules) are *normalised*, i.e. they are written as:

$$p_0(X_0) \leftarrow eq_1, \ldots, eq_k, p_1(X_1), \ldots, p_n(X_n)$$

where $p_i(X_i)$, for $0 \leq i \leq n$, is an atom (whose ground instances are) in $\mathcal{L}$ and eq_i, for $1 \leq i \leq k$, is an equality whose variables occur in the tuples $X_0, X_1, \ldots, X_n$. The body of a normalised rule can be freely rewritten by using the standard axioms of equality, e.g., $Y_1 = a, Y_2 = a$ can be rewritten as $Y_1 = Y_2, Y_2 = a$.

Given an ABA framework $\langle \mathcal{R}, \mathcal{A}, \overline{} \rangle$, a *transformation rule* constructs a new ABA framework $\langle \mathcal{R}', \mathcal{A}', \overline{}' \rangle$. We use transformation rules R1–R5 below, where we mention explicitly only the components of the framework that are modified.

R1. Rote Learning. Given atom $p(t)$, add $\rho : p(X) \leftarrow X = t$ to $\mathcal{R}$. Thus, $\mathcal{R}' = \mathcal{R} \cup \{\rho\}$.

In our learning strategy, Rote Learning is typically applied with $p(t)$ a positive example. The added rule allows us to obtain an argument for $p(t)$.

Example 6. Let us consider the learning problem of Fig. 1. By four applications of R1, from the positive examples $flies(a), flies(b), flies(e), flies(f)$, we get

$$\mathcal{R}_1 = \mathcal{R} \cup \{flies(X) \leftarrow X = a, flies(X) \leftarrow X = b,$$
$$flies(X) \leftarrow X = e, flies(X) \leftarrow X = f\}.$$

R2. Equality Removal. Replace a rule $\rho_1 : H \leftarrow eq_1, Eqs, B$ in $\mathcal{R}$, where eq_1 is an equality, Eqs is a (possibly empty) set of equalities, and B is a (possibly empty) set of atoms, by rule $\rho_2 : H \leftarrow Eqs, B$. Thus, $\mathcal{R}' = (\mathcal{R} \setminus \{C_1\}) \cup \{C_2\}$.

Equality Removal allows us to generalise a rule by deleting an equality in its body. We will see an example of application of this rule in Sect. 5.

R3. Folding. Given rules

$$\rho_1 : H \leftarrow Eqs_1, B_1, B_2 \quad \text{and} \quad \rho_2 : K \leftarrow Eqs_1, Eqs_2, B_1$$

in $\mathcal{R}$, replace ρ_1 by ρ_3: $H \leftarrow Eqs_2, K, B_2$. Thus, $\mathcal{R}' = (\mathcal{R} \setminus \{\rho_1\}) \cup \{\rho_3\}$.

Folding is a form of *inverse resolution* [Mug95], used for generalising a rule by replacing some atoms in its body with their 'consequence' using a rule in $\mathcal{R}$.

Example 7. By R3 using rule $bird(X) \leftarrow X = a$ in $\mathcal{R}$, rule $flies(X) \leftarrow X = a$ in $\mathcal{R}_1$ (see Example 6) is replaced by $flies(X) \leftarrow bird(X)$, giving $\mathcal{R}_2 = \mathcal{R} \cup \{flies(X) \leftarrow bird(X), flies(X) \leftarrow X = b, flies(X) \leftarrow X = e, flies(X) \leftarrow X = f\}$.

R4. Subsumption. Suppose that $\mathcal{R}$ contains rules
$$\rho_1 : H \leftarrow Eqs_1, B_1 \quad \text{and} \quad \rho_2 : H \leftarrow Eqs_2, B_2$$
such that, for every ground instance $H' \leftarrow Eqs'_2, B'_2$ of ρ_2, there exists a ground instance $H' \leftarrow Eqs'_1, B'_1$ of ρ_1 (with the same head) such that, if for each atom B in Eqs'_2, B'_2 there is an argument $S \vdash_{\mathcal{R}} B$, then for each atom A in Eqs'_1, B'_1 there is an argument $S' \vdash_{\mathcal{R}'} A$ with $S' \subseteq S$. Thus, ρ_2 is *subsumed* by ρ_1 and can be deleted from $\mathcal{R}$, and hence $\mathcal{R}' = \mathcal{R} \setminus \{\rho_2\}$.

In particular, R4 generalises the usual logic program transformation that allows the removal of a rule which is θ-subsumed by another one [PP94].

Example 8. Rule $flies(X) \leftarrow X = b$ in $\mathcal{R}_2$ (from Example 7) is subsumed by $flies(X) \leftarrow bird(X)$. Indeed, b is the only ground x such that $\emptyset \vdash_{\{x=b\leftarrow\}} x = b$, and when x is b, we have $\emptyset \vdash_{\{bird(x)\leftarrow x=b, x=b\leftarrow\}} bird(x)$. Similarly, rules $flies(X) \leftarrow X = e$ and $flies(X) \leftarrow X = f$ are subsumed by $flies(X) \leftarrow bird(X)$. Thus, we derive $\mathcal{R}_3 = \mathcal{R} \cup \{flies(X) \leftarrow bird(X)\}$.

R5. Assumption Introduction. Replace $\rho_1 : H \leftarrow Eqs, B$ in $\mathcal{R}$ by $\rho_2 : H \leftarrow Eqs, B, \alpha(X)$ where X is a tuple of variables taken from $vars(H) \cup vars(B)$ and $\alpha(X)$ is a (possibly new) assumption with contrary $\chi(X)$. Thus, $\mathcal{R}' = (\mathcal{R} \setminus \{\rho_1\}) \cup \{\rho_2\}$, $\mathcal{A}' = \mathcal{A} \cup \{\alpha(X)\}$, $\overline{\alpha(X)}' = \chi(X)$, and $\overline{\beta}' = \overline{\beta}$ for all $\beta \in \mathcal{A}$.

Example 9. By applying R5, we get $\mathcal{R}_4 = \mathcal{R} \cup \{flies(X) \leftarrow bird(X), \alpha_1(X)\}$, with $\overline{\alpha_1(X)}' = c\text{-}\alpha_1(X)$. Now, we complete this example to show, informally, that other approaches based on learning exceptions [DK95,SSG17] can be recast in our setting. For the newly introduced $c\text{-}\alpha_1(X)$, we have positive examples $\mathcal{E}_1^+ = \{c\text{-}\alpha_1(c), c\text{-}\alpha_1(d)\}$, corresponding to the exceptions to $flies(X) \leftarrow bird(X)$, and negative examples $\mathcal{E}_1^- = \{c\text{-}\alpha_1(a), c\text{-}\alpha_1(b), c\text{-}\alpha_1(e), c\text{-}\alpha_1(f)\}$, corresponding to the positive examples for $flies(X)$ to which $flies(X) \leftarrow bird(X)$ correctly applies. Then, starting from these examples, we can learn rules for $c\text{-}\alpha_1(X)$ similarly to what we have done for *flies*. By Rote Learning, we get $\mathcal{R}_5 = \mathcal{R} \cup \{flies(X) \leftarrow bird(X), \alpha_1(X), c\text{-}\alpha_1(X) \leftarrow X = c, c\text{-}\alpha_1(X) \leftarrow X = d\}$. The rules for $c\text{-}\alpha_1(X)$ can be viewed as rebuttal attacks against $flies(X) \leftarrow bird(X)$, as c and d are birds that do not fly. By Folding and Subsumption, we generalise the rules for $c\text{-}\alpha_1(X)$ and obtain $\mathcal{R}_6 = \mathcal{R} \cup \{flies(X) \leftarrow bird(X), \alpha_1(X), c\text{-}\alpha_1(X) \leftarrow penguin(X)\}$. The new rule also covers the negative examples $c\text{-}\alpha_1(e)$ and $c\text{-}\alpha_1(f)$, and hence we introduce a new assumption $\alpha_2(X)$ with contrary $c\text{-}\alpha_2(X)$

having c-$\alpha_2(e)$ and c-$\alpha_2(f)$ as positive examples. By one more sequence of applications of Rote Learning, Folding and Subsumption, we get exactly the ABA framework in Fig. 2.

In the field of logic program transformation, the goal is to derive new programs that are *equivalent*, wrt a semantics of choice, to the initial program. Various results guarantee that, under suitable conditions, transformation rules such as Unfolding and Folding indeed enforce equivalence (e.g., wrt the least Herbrand model of definite programs [PP94] and the stable model semantics of normal logic programs [AD95]). These results have also been generalised by using argumentative notions [TK96].

In the context of ABA learning, however, program equivalence is not a desirable objective, as we look for sets of rules that generalise positive examples and avoid to cover negative examples. In particular, as shown by the examples of this and next section, the generalisation of positive examples is done by applying the Folding, Equality Removal, and Subsumption transformations, while the exceptions due to negative examples are learned by Assumption Introduction and Rote Learning. A general strategy for applying the transformation rules will be presented in Sect. 6. The requirements that R2–R4 should preserve positive examples, while R1 and R5 should be able to avoid negative examples, are formalised by the following two properties that we require to hold. These properties are sufficient to show that, when the learning process terminates, it indeed gets a solution of the ABA learning problem given in input.

Property 1. *Let $\langle \mathcal{R}', \mathcal{A}', \overline{}' \rangle$ be obtained by applying any of Folding, Equality Removal and Subsumption to $\langle \mathcal{R}, \mathcal{A}, \overline{} \rangle$ to modify rules with p in the head. If $\langle \mathcal{R}, \mathcal{A}, \overline{} \rangle \models p(t)$ then $\langle \mathcal{R}', \mathcal{A}', \overline{}' \rangle \models p(t)$.*

Property 2. *Let $p(t_1), p(t_2)$ be atoms such that $p(t_1) \neq p(t_2)$ and $\langle \mathcal{R}, \mathcal{A}, \overline{} \rangle$ be such that $\langle \mathcal{R}, \mathcal{A}, \overline{} \rangle \models p(t_1)$ and $\langle \mathcal{R}, \mathcal{A}, \overline{} \rangle \models p(t_2)$. Then there exists $\langle \mathcal{R}', \mathcal{A}', \overline{}' \rangle$ obtained from $\langle \mathcal{R}, \mathcal{A}, \overline{} \rangle$ by applying Assumption Introduction to modify rules with p in the head and then applying Rote Learning to add rules for the contraries of the assumption atoms, such that $\langle \mathcal{R}, \mathcal{A}, \overline{} \rangle \models p(t_1)$ and $\langle \mathcal{R}', \mathcal{A}', \overline{}' \rangle \not\models p(t_2)$.*

We leave to future work the identification of conditions that enforce Properties 1 and 2 wrt ABA semantics. However, note that, even though we cannot directly apply the results about logic program transformations to prove these properties, we can leverage the proof methodology and adapt some partial results, and specifically the ones developed by using argumentative notions [TK96].

5   Learning by Rebuttal and Undercutting Attacks

Some approaches [DK95, SSG17] propose learning techniques for non-monotonic logic programs based on the idea of learning default rules with exceptions.

Default rules are learned by generalising positive examples, and exceptions to those rules are learned by generalising negative examples. This process can be iterated by learning exceptions to the exceptions. From an argumentative perspective, these approaches can be viewed as learning rules that attack each other by rebuttal, because their heads are 'opposite'. We have illustrated through the *flies* example in Sect. 4 that our transformation rules can easily reconstruct learning by rebuttal. Through another example, in this section we show that our transformation rules can also learn undercutting attacks, which in contrast seem hard for other approaches that learn by rebuttal.

Suppose that a robot moves through locations $1, \ldots, 6$. Let atom $step(X, Y)$ mean that the robot can take a step from location X to location Y. Some locations are busy, and the robot cannot occupy them. Consider the background knowledge with $\mathcal{R}$ as follows (and a single bogus assumption):

$$\mathcal{R} = \{step(1, 2) \leftarrow, step(1, 3) \leftarrow, step(2, 4) \leftarrow, step(2, 5) \leftarrow,$$
$$step(4, 6) \leftarrow, step(5, 2) \leftarrow, busy(3) \leftarrow, busy(6) \leftarrow\}.$$

We would like to learn the concept $free(X)$, meaning that the robot is free to proceed from X to a non-busy, successor location. Let

$$\mathcal{E}^+ = \{free(1), free(2), free(5)\}, \quad \mathcal{E}^- = \{free(3), free(4), free(6)\}.$$

be the positive and negative examples, respectively. Let us see how we can solve this ABA learning problem by our transformation rules. We start off by applying Rote Learning and introducing the rule

$\qquad free(X) \leftarrow X = 1$ $\hfill (1)$

and hence $\mathcal{R}_1 = \mathcal{R} \cup \{(1)\}$. Then, by Folding using the (normalised) rule $step(X, Y) \leftarrow X = 1, Y = 2$ in $\mathcal{R}$, we learn

$\qquad free(X) \leftarrow Y = 2, step(X, Y)$ $\hfill (2)$

and $\mathcal{R}_2 = \mathcal{R} \cup \{(2)\}$. By Equality Removal, we get

$\qquad free(X) \leftarrow step(X, Y)$ $\hfill (3)$

and $\mathcal{R}_2 = \mathcal{R} \cup \{(3)\}$. Rule (3) covers all positive examples, but it also covers the negative example $free(4)$. To exclude this, we construct an undercutting attack to rule (3). We apply Assumption Introduction to obtain $\alpha(X, Y)$ with contrary $c\text{-}\alpha(X, Y)$, and we replace rule (3) by

$\qquad free(X) \leftarrow step(X, Y), \alpha(X, Y)$ $\hfill (4)$

and $\mathcal{R}_3 = \mathcal{R} \cup \{(4)\}$. The assumption $\alpha(X, Y)$ represents *normal* values of (X, Y), for which it is legitimate to use default rule (4), while $c\text{-}\alpha(X, Y)$ represents exceptions to rule (4). Then, we add positive and negative examples for $c\text{-}\alpha(X, Y)$:

$$\mathcal{E}_1^+ = \{c\text{-}\alpha(4, 6)\}, \quad \mathcal{E}_1^- = \{c\text{-}\alpha(1, 2), c\text{-}\alpha(2, 4), c\text{-}\alpha(2, 5), c\text{-}\alpha(5, 2)\}.$$

By Rote Learning, we get $\mathcal{R}_4 = \mathcal{R} \cup \{(4), (5)\}$ with

$\qquad c\text{-}\alpha(X, Y) \leftarrow X = 4, Y = 6$ $\hfill (5)$

Finally, by Folding, using $busy(Y) \leftarrow Y = 6$, and Equality Removal, we get

$\qquad c\text{-}\alpha(X, Y) \leftarrow busy(Y)$ $\hfill (6)$

which can be viewed as an undercutting attack to a premise of rule (4). The final learnt set of rules is $\mathcal{R} \cup \{(4), (6)\}$, which indeed are a very compact and general definition of the sought concept $free(X)$.

Now we will show that the approaches based on rebuttal encounter difficulties in our robot example. More specifically, we consider the approach proposed by Dimopoulos and Kakas in [DK95]. Their formalism consists of rules of the form $L_0 \leftarrow L_1, \ldots, L_n$ where $L_0, L_1, \ldots, L_n$ are positive or explicitly negative literals. These rules are understood as default rules that admit exceptions. An exception is viewed as a rule whose head is the negation of some default rule it attacks, i.e., a rule of the form $\overline{L_0} \leftarrow M_1, \ldots, M_k$. Attacks are formalised by a priority relation between rules, whereby the default rule has higher priority with respect to the exception. As already mentioned, this type of attack is a rebuttal, in the sense that the default rule and the exception have opposite conclusions. This type of rules with priorities can easily be translated into an ABA framework, which in turn can be mapped to a normal logic program (see Sect. 2) with *stratified* negation, as the priority relation is assumed to be irreflexive and antisymmetric.

Now, from rule (3) the Dimopoulos-Kakas algorithm generates a new learning problem for the concept $\neg free(X)$ with positive and negative examples as follows:
$$\mathcal{E}_1^+ = \{\neg free(4)\}, \quad \mathcal{E}_1^- = \{\neg free(1), \neg free(2), \neg free(5)\}.$$
The new positive example is the exception to rule (3), and the new negative examples are the positive examples covered by rule (3), which we would like not be covered by the rules for $\neg free(X)$. The learning algorithm computes the rule[6]
$$\neg free(X) \leftarrow step(X, Y), busy(Y) \tag{7}$$
which indeed covers the positive example in $\mathcal{E}_1$, but unfortunately also covers all examples in $\mathcal{E}_1^-$. Now, the algorithm should learn the exceptions to the exceptions, which, however, are equal to the initial positive examples. To avoid entering an infinite loop, the algorithm will just enumerate these exceptions to rule (7) by adding the set of rules $E = \{free(1) \leftarrow, free(2) \leftarrow, free(5) \leftarrow\}$. The rules in E attack rule (7), which in turn attacks rule (3).

We argue that this result of the Dimopoulos-Kakas algorithm is due to the fact that, by rebuttal, it looks for Xs, i.e., the variable of the head of rule (3) that are exceptions to the rule. In contrast, our approach also looks for exceptions that are instances of Y, which does not occur in the head of the rule.

6   A Learning Strategy

The transformation rules from Sect. 4 need to be guided to solve an ABA learning problem in a satisfactory way. For instance, by using our transformation rules as shown in Sect. 5 we can learn a very good solution to our robot problem. However, by using the transformation rules in a different way, we could also

---

[6] In fact the Dimopoulos-Kakas algorithm is just sketched and we have conjectured what we believe to be a reasonable result of this learning step.

learn an ABA framework isomorphic to the unsatisfactory Dimopoulos-Kakas solution. In this section we present a template of a general strategy for learning through our transformation rules (see Fig. 3). This strategy is non-deterministic at several points and different choices may lead to different final results.

Input: ABA framework $\langle \mathcal{R}, \mathcal{A}, \overline{} \rangle$ (background knowledge); Training data $\mathcal{E}^+$ and $\mathcal{E}^-$, with $\mathcal{E}^+ \cap \mathcal{E}^- = \emptyset$, for concept p_0 to be learnt.

Repeat the following steps **until** all examples in $\mathcal{E}^+$ are covered and all examples in $\mathcal{E}^-$ are not covered.

Step 1 [Rote Learn] Select a predicate p such that $\exists p(c) \in \mathcal{E}^+$ and, for each positive example $p(c)$ in $\mathcal{E}^+$, add the rule $p(X) \leftarrow X = c$ to $\mathcal{R}$ by Rote Learning;

Step 2 [Generalise] For each rule in $\mathcal{R}$, perform one of the following transformations:
1. apply Subsumption and, possibly, remove the rule from $\mathcal{R}$;
2. repeatedly apply Folding and Equality Removal until all constants are removed;

Step 3 [Introduce Assumptions] Repeatedly apply Assumption Introduction as follows. Select a rule $\rho: p(X) \leftarrow Eqs, B$ (w.l.o.g. $X \subseteq vars(B)$) in $\mathcal{R}$ such that there is an argument for $p(d) \in \mathcal{E}^-$ with ρ as top rule; then:
1. select a (minimal) set $A = \{a_1(Y_1), \ldots, a_k(Y_k)\} \subseteq B$ (w.l.o.g. $a_1, \ldots, a_k$ are distinct) such that $\exists$ disjoint sets A^+, A^- of ground instances of A such that:
   (a) for every example $p(e) \in \mathcal{E}^+$ covered by $\langle \mathcal{R}, \mathcal{A}, \overline{} \rangle$, there exist an argument for $p(e)$ having (a ground instance of) ρ as top rule and $\{a_1(e_1), \ldots, a_k(e_k)\} \in A^+$ such that $a_1(e_1), \ldots, a_k(e_k)$ are children of $p(e)$;
   (b) for every example $p(e) \in \mathcal{E}^-$ covered by $\langle \mathcal{R}, \mathcal{A}, \overline{} \rangle$ and for every argument for $p(e)$ having (a ground instance of) ρ as top rule, there exists $\{a_1(e_1), \ldots, a_k(e_k)\} \in A^-$ such that $a_1(e_1), \ldots, a_k(e_k)$ are children of $p(e)$;
2. Replace ρ by $p(X) \leftarrow Eqs, B, \alpha(Y_1, \ldots, Y_k)$ where $\alpha(Y_1, \ldots, Y_k)$ is a new assumption with contrary $\chi(Y_1, \ldots, Y_k)$;
   Add $\alpha(Y_1, \ldots, Y_k)$ to $\mathcal{A}$ and extend $\overline{}$ by setting $\overline{\alpha(Y_1, \ldots, Y_k)} = \chi(Y_1, \ldots, Y_k)$;
3. For every $\{a_1(e_1), \ldots, a_k(e_k)\} \in A^+$, add $\chi(e_1, \ldots, e_k)$ to $\mathcal{E}^-$;
   For every $\{a_1(e_1), \ldots, a_k(e_k)\} \in A^-$, add $\chi(e_1, \ldots, e_k)$ to $\mathcal{E}^+$;

Step 4: Remove from $\langle \mathcal{E}^+, \mathcal{E}^- \rangle$ all examples for p.

Fig. 3. ABA Learning Strategy

Let us briefly comment on the strategy.

After Step 1, all positive examples for p are covered and no negative example for p is covered by maximally specific rules that enumerate all positive examples.

At the end of Step 2.2, equalities between variables may be left. After Step 2, by Property 1, all positive examples for p are still covered, but some negative example might also be covered.

At Step 3, the condition $X \subseteq vars(B)$ on $p(X) \leftarrow Eqs, B$ can always be met by adding to its body atoms $true(X')$ for any missing variables X'. After Step 3, by Property 2, we get a set of rules still covering all positive examples for p and, after Rote Learning at the next iteration, covers no negative example.

As it stands the ABA learning strategy might not terminate, as it could keep introducing new assumptions at each iteration. However, if we assume a finite universe, divergence can be detected by comparing the sets of positive/negative examples (modulo the predicate names) generated for new assumptions wrt those of "ancestor" assumptions. In that case we can just stop after Step 1 and generate the trivial solution for the predicate at hand by Rote Learning. An alternative way of enforcing termination is to allow the application of Assumption Introduction using assumptions already introduced at previous steps. This variant of the strategy enables learning *circular debates* as shown in the next section.

7   Learning Circular Debates

Existing argumentation-based approaches (notably [DK95]) are designed to learn "stratified" knowledge bases. Instead, in some settings, it is useful and natural to learn to conduct circular debates, where opinions may not be conclusively held. As an illustration, we work out a version of the Nixon-diamond example [RC81]. *Background Knowledge.* $\langle \mathcal{R}, \mathcal{A}, \overline{} \rangle$ with bogus assumption and

$$\mathcal{R} = \{quacker(X) \leftarrow X = a, republican(X) \leftarrow X = a,$$
$$quacker(X) \leftarrow X = b, republican(X) \leftarrow X = b\}.$$

Positive Examples: $\mathcal{E}^+ = \{pacifist(a)\}$, *Negative Examples:* $\mathcal{E}^- = \{pacifist(b)\}$. Note that this example can be seen as capturing a form of *noise*, whereby two rows of the same table (one for a and one for b) are characterised by exactly the same attributes (amounting to being quackers and republicans) but have different labels (one is pacifist, the other is not). In non-monotonic reasoning terms, this requires reasoning with contradictory rules [RC81]. In argumentative terms, this boils down to building circular debates. In the remainder, we show how the ABA learning strategy is able to learn these contradictory rules, in a way that circular debates can be supported.

First Iteration of the ABA Learning Strategy. At Step 1, we consider the positive example $pacifist(a)$ and by Rote Learning we add to $\mathcal{R}$:

$$pacifist(X) \leftarrow X = a \tag{1}$$

At Step 2, we generalise by Folding using $quacker(X) \leftarrow X = a$ in the background knowledge, and replace (1) with:

$$pacifist(X) \leftarrow quacker(X) \tag{2}$$

Note that other folds are possible, leading to different ABA frameworks.

At Step 3, there is an argument for the negative example $pacifist(b)$, because $quacker(X)$ holds for $X = b$. Thus, we apply the Assumption Introduction rule to replace (2) with:

$$pacifist(X) \leftarrow quacker(X), normal\_quacker(X) \tag{3}$$

with $\overline{normal\_quacker(X)} = abnormal\_quacker(X)$. The new examples for *abnormal_quacker* are:

$\mathcal{E}_1^+ = \{abnormal\_quacker(b)\}$,　　　　　　$\mathcal{E}_1^- = \{abnormal\_quacker(a)\}$.

Second Iteration of the ABA Learning Strategy. We learn the *abnormal_quacker* predicate. At Step 1, by Rote Learning we add to $\mathcal{R}$:

$\quad abnormal\_quacker(X) \leftarrow X = b$ ⟶(4)

At Step 2, we fold using $republican(X) \leftarrow X = b$:

$\quad abnormal\_quacker(X) \leftarrow republican(X)$ ⟶(5)

There is an argument for the negative example $abnormal\_quacker(a)$, and then, at Step 3, we use the Assumption Introduction rule to replace (5) with:

$\quad abnormal\_quacker(X) \leftarrow republican(X), normal\_republican(X)$ ⟶(6)

with $\overline{normal\_republican(X)} = abnormal\_republican(X)$.

Third Iteration of the ABA Learning Strategy. We learn the abnormal_republican predicate from the examples:

$\mathcal{E}_2^+ = \{abnormal\_republican(a)\}$,　　　　$\mathcal{E}_2^- = \{abnormal\_republican(b)\}$.

By Rote Learning we add:

$\quad abnormal\_republican(X) \leftarrow X = a$ ⟶(7)

We then fold using $quacker(X) \leftarrow X = a$ and we get:

$\quad abnormal\_republican(X) \leftarrow quacker(X)$ ⟶(8)

Since there is an argument for the negative example $abnormal\_republican(b)$, we use the Assumption Introduction rule to obtain:

$\quad abnormal\_republican(X) \leftarrow quacker(X), normal\_quacker(X)$ ⟶(9)

Note that here we use the same assumption as in (3): this is allowed by the definition of R5 and is useful given that rule (8) has the same body as (2), which was replaced by rule (3) earlier on. Then, by Folding using rule (3), we get:

$\quad abnormal\_republican(X) \leftarrow pacifist(X)$ ⟶(10)

This leads to an ABA framework with final set of learnt rules $\{(3), (6), (10)\}$, encompassing a circular debate whereby an argument for being pacifist is attacked by one for being non-pacifist (and vice versa). This ABA framework has (among others) the following stable extension (corresponding to the choice, as the accepted set of assumptions, of $\{normal\_quacker(a), normal\_republican(b)\}$):

$\quad \{\{normal\_quacker(a)\} \vdash pacifist(a),$

$\quad \{normal\_quacker(a)\} \vdash normal\_quacker(a),$

$\quad \{normal\_quacker(a)\} \vdash abnormal\_republican(a),$

$\quad \{normal\_republican(b)\} \vdash abnormal\_quacker(b),$

$\quad \{normal\_republican(b)\} \vdash normal\_republican(b),$

$\quad \emptyset \vdash quacker(a), \emptyset \vdash republican(a), \emptyset \vdash quacker(b), \emptyset \vdash republican(b)\}$.

Here, a is pacifist and b is not, thus achieving the goal of ABA learning under credulous reasoning. Note that there are three other stable extensions of the resulting ABA framework (one where b is pacifist and a is not, one where both are pacifist and one where neither is), and thus sceptical reasoning would not work.

8   Conclusions

We have presented a novel approach to learning ABA frameworks from positive and negative examples, using background knowledge. A notable feature of our method is that it is able to learn exceptions to general rules that can be interpreted as undercutting attacks, besides the more traditional rebuttal attacks. Our learning technique is based on transformation rules, borrowing a well established approach from logic program transformation. We have presented a general strategy that applies these transformation rules in a suitable order and we have shown through some examples that we are able, on one hand, to reconstruct other logic-based learning approaches that learn stratified rules and, on the other hand, to also learn rules enacting non-stratified, circular debates.

Our approach can be expanded in several directions. First of all, we need to study conditions guaranteeing that our transformation rules always derive a correct solution (see Properties 1 and 2). To do that we may build upon results available in the field of logic program transformation. At present, our learning strategy is a template relying on several non-deterministic choices that need to be realised to obtain a concrete algorithm. Then, we plan to conduct experiments on existing benchmarks in comparison with other systems. In particular, for comparison, we plan to use FOLD [SSG17], which learns stratified normal logic programs, and ILASP [LRB14], which learns Answer Set Programs. We also plan to explore whether solutions to our ABA learning problems are better suited, than existing approaches to ILP, to provide explanations, leveraging on several existing approaches to argumentative XAI [CRA+21].

Acknowledgements. We thank the anonymous reviewers for useful comments. We also thank Mark Law for advice on the ILASP system. F. Toni was partially funded by the European Research Council (ERC) under the European Union's Horizon 2020 research and innovation programme (grant agreement No. 101020934) and by J.P. Morgan and the Royal Academy of Engineering under the Research Chairs and Senior Research Fellowships scheme. M. Proietti is a member of the INdAM-GNCS research group.

References

ABW88. Apt, K.R., Blair, H.A., Walker, A.: Towards a theory of declarative knowledge. In: Foundations of Deductive Databases and Logic Programming, pp. 89–148. Morgan Kaufmann (1988)

AD95.   Aravindan, C., Dung, P.M.: On the correctness of unfold/fold transformation of normal and extended logic programs. J. Log. Program. **24**(3), 201–217 (1995)

BDKT97. Bondarenko, A., Dung, P.M., Kowalski, R.A., Toni, F.: An abstract, argumentation-theoretic approach to default reasoning. Artif. Intell. **93**, 63–101 (1997)

CFST17. Cyras, K., Fan, X., Schulz, C., Toni, F.: Assumption-based argumentation: disputes, explanations, preferences. FLAP **4**(8), 2407–2455 (2017)

CRA+21. Cyras, K., Rago, A., Albini, E., Baroni, P., Toni, F.: Argumentative XAI: a survey. In: IJCAI, pp. 4392–4399 (2021)

CSCT20. Cocarascu, O., Stylianou, A., Cyras, K., Toni, F.: Data-empowered argumentation for dialectically explainable predictions. In: ECAI, pp. 2449–2456 (2020)

CT16. Cocarascu, O., Toni, F.: Argumentation for machine learning: a survey. In: COMMA, pp. 219–230 (2016)

DK95. Dimopoulos, Y., Kakas, A.: Learning non-monotonic logic programs: learning exceptions. In: Lavrac, N., Wrobel, S. (eds.) ECML 1995. LNCS, vol. 912, pp. 122–137. Springer, Heidelberg (1995). https://doi.org/10.1007/3-540-59286-5_53

DKT09. Dung, P.M., Kowalski, R.A., Toni, F.: Assumption-based argumentation. In: Simari, G., Rahwan, I. (eds.) Argumentation in Artificial Intelligence, pp. 199–218. Springer, Boston (2009). https://doi.org/10.1007/978-0-387-98197-0_10

Dun95. Dung, P.M.: On the acceptability of arguments and its fundamental role in nonmonotonic reasoning, logic programming and n-person games. Artif. Intell. **77**(2), 321–358 (1995)

GL88. Gelfond, M., Lifschitz, V.: The stable model semantics for logic programming. In: ICLP, pp. 1070–1080. MIT Press (1988)

IH00. Inoue, K., Haneda, H.: Learning abductive and nonmonotonic logic programs. In: Abduction and Induction: Essays on their Relation and Integration, pp. 213–231. Kluwer Academic (2000)

IK97. Inoue, K., Kudoh, Y.: Learning extended logic programs. In: IJCAI, pp. 176–181. Morgan Kaufmann (1997)

LRB14. Law, M., Russo, A., Broda, K.: Inductive learning of answer set programs. In: Fermé, E., Leite, J. (eds.) JELIA 2014. LNCS (LNAI), vol. 8761, pp. 311–325. Springer, Cham (2014). https://doi.org/10.1007/978-3-319-11558-0_22

Mug95. Muggleton, S.: Inverse entailment and Progol. N. Gener. Comput. **13**(3–4), 245–286 (1995)

PP94. Pettorossi, A., Proietti, M.: Transformation of logic programs: foundations and techniques. J. Log. Program. **19**(20), 261–320 (1994)

Ray09. Ray, O.: Nonmonotonic abductive inductive learning. J. Appl. Log. **7**(3), 329–340 (2009)

RC81. Reiter, R., Criscuolo, G.: On interacting defaults. In: IJCAI, pp. 270–276. William Kaufmann (1981)

Sak00. Sakama, C.: Inverse entailment in nonmonotonic logic programs. In: Cussens, J., Frisch, A. (eds.) ILP 2000. LNCS (LNAI), vol. 1866, pp. 209–224. Springer, Heidelberg (2000). https://doi.org/10.1007/3-540-44960-4_13

Sak05. Sakama, C.: Induction from answer sets in nonmonotonic logic programs. ACM Trans. Comput. Log. **6**(2), 203–231 (2005)

Sek91. Seki, H.: Unfold/fold transformation of stratified programs. Theoret. Comput. Sci. **86**, 107–139 (1991)

SI09. Sakama, C., Inoue, K.: Brave induction: a logical framework for learning from incomplete information. Mach. Learn. **76**(1), 3–35 (2009)

SSG17. Shakerin, F., Salazar, E., Gupta, G.: A new algorithm to automate inductive learning of default theories. TPLP **17**(5–6), 1010–1026 (2017)

TK96. Toni, F., Kowalski, R.A.: An argumentation-theoretic approach to logic program transformation. In: Proietti, M. (ed.) LOPSTR 1995. LNCS, vol. 1048, pp. 61–75. Springer, Heidelberg (1996). https://doi.org/10.1007/3-540-60939-3_5

Ton14. Toni, F.: A tutorial on assumption-based argumentation. Arg. Comput. 5(1), 89–117 (2014)

Diagnosis of Event Sequences with LFIT

Tony Ribeiro[1(✉)], Maxime Folschette[2], Morgan Magnin[3,4], Kotaro Okazaki[5], Lo Kuo-Yen[5], and Katsumi Inoue[4]

[1] Vivy, France
`tony.ribeiro@ls2d.fr`
[2] Univ. Lille, CNRS, Centrale Lille, UMR 9189 CRIStAL, 59000 Lille, France
[3] Univ. Nantes, CNRS, Centrale Nantes, UMR 6004 LS2N, 44000 Nantes, France
[4] National Institute of Informatics, 2-1-2 Hitotsubashi, Chiyoda-ku, Tokyo 101-8430, Japan
[5] SONAR Inc., 8-16-6, Ginza, Chuo-Ku, Tokyo 104-0061, Japan

Abstract. Diagnosis of the traces of executions of discrete event systems is of interest to understand dynamical behaviors of a wide range of real world problems like real-time systems or biological networks. In this paper, we propose to address this challenge by extending Learning From Interpretation Transition (LFIT), an Inductive Logic Programming framework that automatically constructs a model of the dynamics of a system from the observation of its state transitions. As a way to tackle diagnosis, we extend the theory of LFIT to model event sequences and their temporal properties. It allows to learn logic rules that exploit those properties to explain sequences of interest. We show how it can be done in practice through a case study.

Keywords: dynamic systems · logical modeling · explainable artificial intelligence

1 Introduction

Discrete event systems have been formalized as a wide range of paradigms, e.g., Petri nets [6], to model dynamical behaviors. In this paper, we propose to focus on learning dynamical properties from the trace of executions of such system, i.e., sequences of events. Such a setting can be related to fault diagnosis, which has been the subject of much interest [5]. It consists of identifying underlying phenomena that result in the failure of a system. It takes as input a model and a set of observations of the system under the form of event sequences. In our case, we only consider the event sequences as input and propose a method independent of the model paradigm.

Since its first establishment in the 80s and 90s, Inductive Logic Programming (ILP) has been identified as a promising approach to tackle such a diagnosis problem [4] and several works followed [3,10]. Learning From Interpretation Transition (LFIT) [2] is an ILP framework that automatically builds a model of the dynamics of a system from the observation of its state transitions. Our goal

---

T. Ribeiro—Independent Researcher.

S. H. Muggleton and A. Tamaddoni-Nezhad (Eds.): ILP 2022, LNAI 13779, pp. 117–126, 2024.
https://doi.org/10.1007/978-3-031-55630-2_9

here is to extend LFIT to exploit temporal properties to explain event sequences of interest. Figure 1 illustrates the general LFIT learning process. Given some raw data, like time-series of gene expression, a discretization of those data in the form of state transitions is assumed. From those state transitions, according to the semantics of the system dynamics, several inference algorithms modeling the system as a logic program have been proposed.

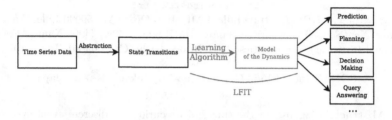

Fig. 1. Assuming a discretization of time series data of a system as state transitions, we propose a method to automatically model the system dynamics.

In [8], we extended this framework to learn system dynamics independently of its update semantics. For this purpose, we proposed a modeling of discrete memory-less multi-valued systems as logic programs in which each rule represents the possibility for a variable to take some value in the next state. This modeling permits to characterize optimal programs independently of the update semantics, allowing to model the dynamics of a wide range of discrete systems. To learn such semantic-free optimal programs, we proposed **GULA**: the General Usage LFIT Algorithm that now serves as the core block to several methods of the framework. In this paper, we show how to use **GULA** in order to learn logic rules that combine temporal patterns to explain event sequences of interest. We use a case study to show some of the difficulties and interests of the method.

2   Dynamical Multi-valued Logic Program

In this section, the concepts necessary to understand the modeling we propose in this paper are formalized. Let $\mathcal{V} = \{v_1, \cdots, v_n\}$ be a finite set of $n \in \mathbb{N}$ variables, $\mathcal{V}al$ the set in which variables take their values and dom : $\mathcal{V} \to \wp(\mathcal{V}al)$ a function associating a domain to each variable, with $\wp$ the power set. The atoms of *multi-valued logic* ($\mathcal{M}$VL) are of the form v^{val} where $v \in \mathcal{V}$ and $val \in$ dom(v). The set of such atoms is denoted by $\mathcal{A} = \{v^{val} \in \mathcal{V} \times \mathcal{V}al \mid val \in$ dom$(v)\}$. Let $\mathcal{F}$ and $\mathcal{T}$ be a partition of $\mathcal{V}$, that is: $\mathcal{V} = \mathcal{F} \cup \mathcal{T}$ and $\mathcal{F} \cap \mathcal{T} = \emptyset$. $\mathcal{F}$ is called the set of *feature* variables, which values represent the state of the system at the previous time step $(t-1)$, and $\mathcal{T}$ is called the set of *target* variables, which values represent the state of the system at the current time step (t). A $\mathcal{M}$VL *rule* R is defined by:

$$R = v_0^{val_0} \leftarrow v_1^{val_1} \wedge \cdots \wedge v_m^{val_m}$$

where $m \in \mathbb{N}$, and $\forall i \in [\![0; m]\!], \mathrm{v}_i^{val_i} \in \mathcal{A}$; furthermore, every variable is mentioned at most once in the right-hand part: $\forall j, k \in [\![1; m]\!], j \neq k \Rightarrow \mathrm{v}_j \neq \mathrm{v}_k$. The rule R has the following meaning: the variable v_0 can take the value val_0 in the next dynamical step if for each $i \in [\![1; m]\!]$, variable v_i has value val_i in the current dynamical step. The atom on the left side of the arrow is called the *head* of R, denoted $\mathrm{head}(R) := \mathrm{v}_0^{val_0}$, and is made of a target variable: $\mathrm{v}_0 \in \mathcal{T}$. The notation $\mathrm{var}(\mathrm{head}(R)) := \mathrm{v}_0$ denotes the variable that occurs in $\mathrm{head}(R)$. The conjunction on the right-hand side of the arrow is called the *body* of R, written $\mathrm{body}(R)$, and all variables in the body are feature variables: $\forall i \in [\![1; m]\!], \mathrm{v}_i \in \mathcal{F}$. In the following, the body of a rule is assimilated to the set $\{\mathrm{v}_1^{val_1}, \cdots, \mathrm{v}_m^{val_m}\}$; we thus use set operations such as $\in$ and $\cap$ on it, and we denote $\emptyset$ an empty body. A *dynamical multi-valued logic program* ($\mathcal{DMVLP}$) is a set of $\mathcal{MVL}$ rules.

Definition 1 (Rule Domination). *Let R_1, R_2 be $\mathcal{MVL}$ rules. R_1 dominates R_2, written $R_1 \geq R_2$ if $\mathrm{head}(R_1) = \mathrm{head}(R_2)$ and $\mathrm{body}(R_1) \subseteq \mathrm{body}(R_2)$.*

The dynamical system we want to learn the rules of, is represented by a succession of *states* as formally given by Definition 2. We also define the "compatibility" of a rule with a state in Definition 3, and with a transition in Definition 4.

Definition 2 (Discrete state). *A discrete state s on a set of variables $\mathcal{X}$ of a $\mathcal{DMVLP}$ is a function from $\mathcal{X}$ to $(\mathrm{dom}(\mathrm{v}))_{\mathrm{v} \in \mathcal{X}}$. It can be equivalently represented by the set of atoms $\{\mathrm{v}^{s(\mathrm{v})} \mid \mathrm{v} \in \mathcal{X}\}$ and thus we can use classical set operations on it. We write $\mathcal{S}^{\mathcal{X}}$ to denote the set of all discrete states of $\mathcal{X}$.*

Often, $\mathcal{X} \in \{\mathcal{F}, \mathcal{T}\}$. In particular, a couple of states $(s, s') \in \mathcal{S}^{\mathcal{F}} \times \mathcal{S}^{\mathcal{T}}$ is called a *transition*.

Definition 3 (Rule-state matching). *Let $s \in \mathcal{S}^{\mathcal{F}}$. The $\mathcal{MVL}$ rule R matches s, written $R \sqcap s$, if $\mathrm{body}(R) \subseteq s$.*

The final program we want to learn should both: (1) match the observations in a complete (all transitions are learned) and correct (no spurious transition) way; (2) represent only minimal necessary interactions (no overly-complex rules). The following definitions formalize these desired properties.

Definition 4 (Rule and program realization). *Let R be a $\mathcal{MVL}$ rule and $(s, s') \in \mathcal{S}^{\mathcal{F}} \times \mathcal{S}^{\mathcal{T}}$. The rule R realizes the transition (s, s') if $R \sqcap s \wedge \mathrm{head}(R) \in s'$. A $\mathcal{DMVLP}$ P realizes (s, s') if $\forall \mathrm{v} \in \mathcal{T}, \exists R \in P, \mathrm{var}(\mathrm{head}(R)) = \mathrm{v} \wedge R$ realizes (s, s'). P realizes a set of transitions $T \subseteq \mathcal{S}^{\mathcal{F}} \times \mathcal{S}^{\mathcal{T}}$ if $\forall (s, s') \in T, P$ realizes (s, s').*

Definition 5 (Conflict and Consistency). *A $\mathcal{MVL}$ rule R conflicts with a set of transitions $T \subseteq \mathcal{S}^{\mathcal{F}} \times \mathcal{S}^{\mathcal{T}}$ when $\exists (s, s') \in T, (R \sqcap s \wedge \forall (s, s'') \in T, \mathrm{head}(R) \notin s'')$. Otherwise, R is said to be consistent with T. A $\mathcal{DMVLP}$ P is consistent with a set of transitions T if P does not contain any rule R conflicting with T.*

Definition 6 (Suitable and optimal program). *Let $T \subseteq \mathcal{S}^{\mathcal{F}} \times \mathcal{S}^{\mathcal{T}}$. A $\mathcal{DMVLP}$ P is suitable for T if: P is consistent with T, P realizes T, and for* any possible $\mathcal{MVL}$ rule R consistent with T, there exists $R' \in P$ s.t. $R' \geq R$. If in addition, for all $R \in P$, all the $\mathcal{MVL}$ rules R' belonging to $\mathcal{DMVLP}$ suitable for T are such that $R' \geq R$ implies $R \geq R'$, then P is called optimal and denoted $P_{\mathcal{O}}(T)$.

In [8], we proposed the General Usage LFIT Algorithm (**GULA**) that guarantees to learn the optimal program of a set of transitions: let $T \subseteq \mathcal{S}^{\mathcal{F}} \times \mathcal{S}^{\mathcal{T}}$, **GULA**$(\mathcal{A}, T, \mathcal{F}, \mathcal{T}) = P_{\mathcal{O}}(T)$ (Theorem 5 of [8]).

The present work builds upon the definitions presented above. The aim is to use GULA to learn about the possible influence of additional properties along the original observations. If those properties respect the following proposition, they can appear in rules learned by **GULA**, encoded as regular $\mathcal{MVL}$ atoms.

Proposition 1 (Properties encoding)

- Let $\mathcal{V} := \mathcal{V}_{\mathcal{F}} \cup \mathcal{V}_{\mathcal{T}}$ a set of $\mathcal{MVL}$ feature and target variables;
- Let $\mathcal{A} := \mathcal{A}_{\mathcal{F}} \cup \mathcal{A}_{\mathcal{T}}$ be the corresponding feature and target atoms;
- Let $\mathcal{S}^{\mathcal{F}} \subseteq \mathcal{A}_{\mathcal{F}}$ be feature states (one atom of $\mathcal{A}_{\mathcal{F}}$ per variable of $\mathcal{V}_{\mathcal{F}}$);
- Let $\mathcal{V}_P$ be a set of variables, $\mathcal{V}_P \cap \mathcal{V} = \emptyset$, and $\mathcal{A}_P$ the corresponding atoms;
- Let $P : \mathcal{S}^{\mathcal{F}} \to \mathcal{S}^{\mathcal{V}_P}$ a function computing a property on feature states;
- Let $T \subseteq \mathcal{S}^{\mathcal{F}} \times \mathcal{S}^{\mathcal{T}}$ be a set of transitions;
- Let $T' := \{(s \cup P(s), s') \mid (s, s') \in T\}$ be the encoding of property P on T;
- Then, **GULA**$(\mathcal{A} \cup \mathcal{A}_P, T', \mathcal{F} \cup \mathcal{V}_P, \mathcal{T}) = P_{\mathcal{O}}(T')$ and the rules of $P_{\mathcal{O}}(T')$ contain atoms of property P only if it is necessary to realize a target.

Proof sketch. By construction from Theorem 1 of [8] and from Definition 6. □

Proposition 1 allows to encode additional properties of the observation as regular **GULA** input. For a given target atom, the atoms corresponding to a property will appear in the rules of the optimal logic program only if the property is a necessary condition to obtain this target atom. One use of such encoding is to obtain more understandable rules as shown in the following sections.

3   Diagnosis of Labelled Event Sequences

Event sequences have the advantages to be considered as raw output data for many dynamical systems while being able to represent the dynamics of a large set of discrete models (Petri nets, logic programs, ...). As such, it is easy to use them to assert the set of desirable (or undesirable) sequences. In this section, we propose a modeling of event sequences and their temporal properties into the LFIT framework. It allows to use **GULA** to learn logic rules that exploit those properties to explain sequences of interest (Fig. 2).

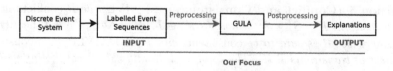

Fig. 2. This paper focuses on the modeling and encoding of labelled event sequence for **GULA** to learn explanation rules exploiting temporal properties.

3.1   Modeling Labelled Event Sequences

Definition 7 (Sequence). *A sequence s is a tuple $s = (s_i)_{i \in [0,|s|]}$. In the rest of the paper, we note s_i the ith element of s.*

An event sequence classification problem (ESCP) is a triple $(E, Seq_{pos}, Seq_{neg})$:

- $E = \{e_0, \ldots, e_m\}$ is a set of elements called *events*;
- $Seq \subseteq E^n$ is a set of sequences of events of size $n \in \mathbb{N}$;
- $Seq_{pos} \subseteq Seq$ is the set of positive examples;
- $Seq_{neg} \subseteq Seq$ is the set of negative examples;
- $Seq_{pos} \cap Seq_{neg} = \emptyset$.

Such classification problem can be encoded into $\mathcal{MVL}$, allowing **GULA** to learn a classifier in the form of a $\mathcal{DMVLP}$. The algorithm takes as input a set of atoms $\mathcal{A}$, a set of transitions T, a set of feature variables $\mathcal{F}$ and a set of target variables $\mathcal{T}$. An ESCP can be encoded as follows.

Proposition 2 ($\mathcal{MVL}$ encoding of ESCP). *Let $(E, Seq_{pos}, Seq_{neg})$ be an ESCP. The encoding of this ESCP is done as follows:*

- $\mathcal{A} := \{ev_i^e \mid 0 \leq i < n, e \in E\} \cup \{label^{pos}, label^{neg}\}$ *the set of $\mathcal{MVL}$ atoms;*
- $\mathcal{F} := \{ev_i \mid 0 \leq i < n\}$ *the set of feature variables;*
- $\mathcal{T} := \{label\}$ *the set of target variables;*
- $f : Seq \rightarrow \mathcal{S}^{\mathcal{F}}$ *with* $s \xmapsto{f} \{ev_i^e \in \mathcal{A} \mid i \in [0,|s|] \wedge s_i = e\}$ *to encode positions;*
- $T := \{(f(s), \{label^{pos}\}) \mid s \in Seq_{pos}\} \cup \{(f(s), \{label^{neg}\}) \mid s \in Seq_{neg}\}$ *the set of transitions.*

Example 1. Let us consider an ESCP with 3 events and sequences of size 4. Consider the following ESCP $(E, Seq_{pos}, Seq_{neg})$ where not all sequences are detailed:

- $E = \{e_0, e_1, e_2\}$
- $Seq_{pos} = \{(e_1, e_1, e_0, e_2), (e_1, e_0, e_1, e_2), (e_1, e_0, e_0, e_2), (e_1, e_0, e_2, e_1), \ldots\}$
- $Seq_{neg} = \{(e_1, e_1, e_1, e_1), (e_1, e_1, e_1, e_0), (e_1, e_1, e_1, e_2), (e_1, e_1, e_0, e_1), \ldots\}$

Now consider the corresponding $\mathcal{MVL}$ encoding: $(\mathcal{A}, T, \mathcal{F}, \mathcal{T})$:

- $\mathcal{A} = \{ev_0^{e_0}, ev_0^{e_1}, ev_0^{e_2}, ev_1^{e_0}, ev_1^{e_1}, \ldots\} \cup \{label^{pos}, label^{neg}\}$
- $\mathcal{F} = \{ev_0, ev_1, ev_2, ev_3\}$
- $\mathcal{T} = \{label\}$
- $T = \{(\{ev_0^{e_0}, ev_1^{e_0}, ev_2^{e_2}\}, \{label^{pos}\}), (\{ev_0^{e_2}, ev_1^{e_0}, ev_2^{e_2}\}, \{label^{pos}\}), \ldots$
  $(\{ev_0^{e_2}, ev_1^{e_2}, ev_2^{e_0}\}, \{label^{neg}\}), (\{ev_0^{e_2}, ev_1^{e_1}, ev_2^{e_0}\}, \{label^{neg}\}), \ldots\}$

Using the encoding of Proposition 2, the call to **GULA**$(\mathcal{A}, T, \mathcal{F}, \mathcal{T})$ will output a set of rules P such that using rule matching (Definition 3) we obtain a correct classifier, as stated by Theorem 1. Indeed, all rules of P that match a positive or negative observation has the correct label as head and there is always at least one rule that matches each observation.

Theorem 1. *Let $(E, Seq_{pos}, Seq_{neg})$ be an ESCP. Let $\mathcal{A}, T, \mathcal{F}, \mathcal{T}, f$ be as in Proposition 2. The following holds:*

$$\forall l \in \{pos, neg\}, \forall s \in Seq_l, \{head(R) \mid R \in \mathbf{GULA}(\mathcal{A}, T, \mathcal{F}, \mathcal{T}), R \sqcap f(s)\} = \{label^l\}$$

Proof sketch. By construction from Theorem 1 of [8], Definition 6 and Proposition 2. □

To ease rule readability in the following examples, atom a^i is written $a(i)$.

Example 2. Let us consider the set of events $E := \{e_0, e_1, e_2\}$ and sequences of size 4. The following set of positive examples $Seq_{pos} = \{$ (e_1, e_1, e_0, e_2), (e_1, e_0, e_1, e_2), (e_1, e_0, e_0, e_2), (e_1, e_0, e_2, e_1), (e_1, e_0, e_2, e_2), (e_0, e_1, e_1, e_2), (e_0, e_1, e_0, e_2), (e_0, e_1, e_2, e_1), (e_0, e_1, e_2, e_2), (e_0, e_0, e_1, e_2), (e_0, e_0, e_0, e_2), (e_0, e_0, e_2, e_1), (e_0, e_0, e_2, e_2), (e_0, e_2, e_1, e_1), (e_0, e_2, e_1, e_2), (e_0, e_2, e_2, e_1), (e_0, e_2, e_2, e_2) $\}$.

All other possible sequences are negative examples: $Seq_{neg} = Seq \setminus Seq_{pos}$, thus: $Seq_{neg} = \{$ (e_1, e_1, e_1, e_1), (e_1, e_1, e_1, e_0), (e_1, e_1, e_1, e_2), (e_1, e_1, e_0, e_1), (e_1, e_1, e_0, e_0), (e_1, e_1, e_2, e_1), (e_1, e_1, e_2, e_0), ..., (e_2, e_2, e_2, e_0), (e_2, e_2, e_2, e_2) $\}$.

Using the encoding of Proposition 2 we obtain the following :
$\mathbf{GULA}(\mathcal{A}, T, \mathcal{F}, \mathcal{T}) =$

label$(pos) \leftarrow$ ev$_0(e_0)$, ev$_1(e_1)$, ev$_3(e_2)$.
label$(pos) \leftarrow$ ev$_0(e_0)$, ev$_2(e_1)$, ev$_3(e_2)$.
label$(pos) \leftarrow$ ev$_0(e_0)$, ev$_2(e_2)$, ev$_3(e_1)$.
label$(pos) \leftarrow$ ev$_0(e_0)$, ev$_2(e_2)$, ev$_3(e_2)$.
label$(pos) \leftarrow$ ev$_0(e_0)$, ev$_1(e_2)$, ev$_2(e_1)$, ev$_3(e_1)$.
label$(pos) \leftarrow$ ev$_0(e_0)$, ev$_1(e_0)$, ev$_3(e_2)$.
label$(pos) \leftarrow$ ev$_0(e_1)$, ev$_1(e_0)$, ev$_3(e_2)$.
label$(pos) \leftarrow$ ev$_0(e_1)$, ev$_1(e_0)$, ev$_2(e_2)$, ev$_3(e_1)$.
label$(pos) \leftarrow$ ev$_0(e_1)$, ev$_1(e_1)$, ev$_2(e_0)$, ev$_3(e_2)$.

label$(neg) \leftarrow$ ev$_0(e_2)$.
label$(neg) \leftarrow$ ev$_3(e_0)$.
label$(neg) \leftarrow$ ev$_2(e_0)$, ev$_3(e_1)$.
label$(neg) \leftarrow$ ev$_1(e_2)$, ev$_2(e_0)$.
label$(neg) \leftarrow$ ev$_1(e_1)$, ev$_2(e_1)$, ev$_3(e_1)$.
label$(neg) \leftarrow$ ev$_1(e_1)$, ev$_2(e_1)$, ev$_3(e_1)$.
label$(neg) \leftarrow$ ev$_0(e_1)$, ev$_1(e_2)$.
label$(neg) \leftarrow$ ev$_0(e_1)$, ev$_2(e_1)$, ev$_3(e_1)$.
label$(neg) \leftarrow$ ev$_0(e_1)$, ev$_1(e_1)$, ev$_2(e_1)$.
label$(neg) \leftarrow$ ev$_0(e_1)$, ev$_1(e_1)$, ev$_2(e_1)$.
label$(neg) \leftarrow$ ev$_0(e_1)$, ev$_1(e_1)$, ev$_3(e_1)$.

This $\mathcal{DMVLP}$ correctly classifies each sequence of Seq_{pos} and Seq_{neg} (see Theorem 1) but position atoms (ev) are not enough to explain simply the whole dynamics.

In Example 2, the encoding of Proposition 2 is arguably not enough for the rules to explicitly explain the real influence of the system. The positive rules (whose head is label(pos)) are very specific and it is not easy to make sense from them individually. But we can see at least that all of them contain both e_0 and e_2, thus their relationship must be of importance. Some negative rules are of interest too: the two first ones tell us that e_2 cannot start the sequence (label$(neg) \leftarrow$ ev$_0(e_2)$.) and e_0 cannot finish it (label$(neg) \leftarrow$ ev$_3(e_0)$.), thus their ordering is also of importance.

With this simple encoding, the learned rules are mere consequences of the real property behind this example, but none of them fully represents the property itself. In order to have more meaningful rules, we could encode some properties of interest as new variables and atoms by following Proposition 1. The idea is to propose an encoding of some simple general temporal property which can be combined to capture and explain the hidden property of the observed system.

3.2 Encoding Elementary LTL Operators

Linear Temporal Logic (LTL) [7] is a modal temporal logic used to characterize the occurrence of properties in a unique linear dynamical path, like the event sequences studied in this paper. It is mainly composed of the following operators:

- $F(\phi)$: ϕ eventually has to hold (Finally);
- $G(\phi)$: ϕ has to hold on the entire subsequent path (Globally);
- $U(\psi, \phi)$: ψ has to hold at least until ϕ becomes true, which must hold at the current or a future position (Until).

These operators over a sequence s can be encoded into a feature state following Proposition 1 and the interpretation given below:

- $Finally(s, e) \equiv e \in s$
- $Globally(s, e) \equiv e' \in s \implies e' = e$
- $Until(s, e_1, e_2) \equiv \exists i \in [1, |s|], s_i = e_2 \wedge \forall j \in [1, i-1], s_j = e_1$

Example 3. Following Proposition 1, we can encode those LTL properties as additional $\mathcal{MVL}$ variables and atoms: $\mathcal{V}_P = \{ F\_e_0, F\_e_1, F\_e_2, G\_e_0, G\_e_1, G\_e_2, U\_e_0\_e_1, U\_e_0\_e_2, U\_e_1\_e_0, U\_e_1\_e_2, U\_e_2\_e_0, U\_e_2\_e_1, \}$, with $\forall v \in \mathcal{V}_P, \text{dom}(v) = \{true, false\}$, where F_e_i encodes $Finally(s, e_i)$, G_e_i encodes $Globally(s, e_i)$, $U\_e_i\_e_j$ encodes $Until(s, e_i, e_j)$.
Using this encoding on the transitions T of Example 2 we obtain:

$$T' = \{(\{ev_0^{e_1}, ev_1^{e_1}, ev_2^{e_0}, ev_3^{e_2}, F\_e_0^{true}, F\_e_1^{true}, F\_e_2^{true}, G\_e_0^{false}, \ldots\}, \{label^{pos}\}),$$

$$(\{ev_0^{e_1}, ev_1^{e_0}, ev_2^{e_1}, ev_3^{e_2}, F\_e_0^{true}, F\_e_1^{true}, F\_e_2^{true}, G\_e_0^{false}, \ldots\}, \{label^{pos}\}),$$

$$\ldots$$

$$(\{ev_0^{e_2}, ev_1^{e_2}, ev_2^{e_2}, ev_3^{e_0}, F\_e_0^{true}, F\_e_1^{false}, F\_e_2^{true}, G\_e_0^{false}, \ldots\}, \{label^{neg}\}),$$

$$(\{ev_0^{e_2}, ev_1^{e_2}, ev_2^{e_2}, ev_3^{e_2}, F\_e_0^{false}, F\_e_1^{false}, F\_e_2^{true}, G\_e_0^{false}, \ldots\}, \{label^{neg}\})\}$$

We can now use **GULA** to learn rules that exploit those encoded properties.
GULA$(\mathcal{A} \cup \mathcal{A}_P, T', \mathcal{F} \cup \mathcal{V}_P, \mathcal{T})$:
label$(pos) \leftarrow ev_3(e_2), F\_e_1(true), U\_e_1\_e_2(false).$ label$(neg) \leftarrow F\_e_2(false).$
label$(pos) \leftarrow ev_3(e_2), F\_e_1(true), U\_e_1\_e_0(true).$ label$(neg) \leftarrow F\_e_0(false).$
$\ldots$ $\ldots$
The resulting $\mathcal{DMVLP}$ $P_{\mathcal{O}}(T')$ contains 824 rules, divided into 735 with label(pos) and 89 with label(neg).

In Example 3, most rules are again obscure consequences of the real property. But some rules are explicit: label$(neg) \leftarrow F\_e_2(false)$ and label$(neg) \leftarrow F\_e_0(false)$, state that both e_0 and e_2 must be present in a positive sequence.

3.3   Encoding Complex LTL Properties

LTL allows to model interesting temporal patterns as shown in [1] where they study infinity sensibility of some specific LTL formula. Table 1 shows some examples of these properties. Encoded as new variables, these properties can be used to enhance the explainability of the rules learned in our running example. Using the encoding of Example 3 and the 18 properties considered in [1] is not enough to construct a rule that explains all positive examples of Example 2. Here, we need to consider an additional property, the "not precedence": $G(b \implies \neg F(a))$, i.e., a cannot appear before b.

Table 1. Examples of sequence properties from [1].

Property	LTL formula	Description
Existence	$F(a)$	a must appear at least once
Absence 2	$\neg F(a \wedge F(a))$	a can appear at most once
Choice	$F(a) \vee F(b)$	a or b must appear
Exclusive choice	$(F(a) \vee F(b)) \wedge \neg(F(a) \wedge F(b))$	Either a or b must appear, but not both
Resp. existence	$F(a) \implies F(b)$	if a appear, then b must appear as well
Coexistence	$(F(a) \implies F(b)) \wedge (F(b) \implies F(a))$	Either a and b both appear, or none of them
Response	$G(a \implies F(b))$	Every time a appears, b must appear afterwards
Precedence	$\neg(U(a,b) \vee G(a))$	b can appear only if a appeared before
Not coexistence	$\neg(F(a) \wedge F(b))$	Only one among a and b can appear, but not both

Example 4. Using these properties and **GULA** as in Example 3, we obtain:

label(pos) $\leftarrow$ $existence\_e_0(True), existence\_e_2(True), not\_precedence\_e_2\_e_0(True)$.

label(pos) $\leftarrow$ $not\_precedence\_e_0\_e_2(False), not\_precedence\_e_2\_e_0(True)$.

label(pos) $\leftarrow$ $existence\_e_2(True), not\_precedence\_e_2\_e_0(True), \mathsf{ev}_0(e_0)$.

label(pos) $\leftarrow$ $existence\_e_0(True), not\_precedence\_e_2\_e_0(True), \mathsf{ev}_3(e_2)$.

. . .

In Example 4, the first rule is the exact representation of the function applied to generate the example, which was: $F(e_0) \wedge F(e_2) \wedge G(e_2 \implies \neg F(e_0))$. The second rule uses $not\_precedence\_e_0\_e_2(False)$ as a divert way to ensure the existence of both e_0 and e_2. The two other rules make use of explicit positions to get the existence of either e_0 or e_2.

3.4   Discussion

In Example 4, we see a few examples of rules that could be discarded. Indeed, **GULA** learns many rules that are redundant when the meaning of the property is known (which **GULA** is oblivious of). Given a subsumption relationship between the encoded properties, a post-processing of the learned rules could be done to simplify or discard rules. Furthermore, in these examples, we guided the rule learning by only giving the property of interest to **GULA** ("existence" and "not precedence") and the optimal program is already almost a thousand rules: 801 label(*pos*) rules and 108 label(*neg*) rules. The rules shown in Example 4 can be found by weighting and ordering rules according to the number of examples they match. The two first rules are the only ones matching all 17 positive sequences of Example 2. If given all 18 properties of [1] and the "not precedence" property, the optimal program will, in theory, still contain the rules shown in Example 4 plus many others. But it would require to handle more than 100 variables to do so, which is too much for **GULA** to handle in reasonable time.

In practice, it is more interesting to use **PRIDE** [9], **GULA**'s polynomial approximated version, to explore the search space in reasonable time. Although **PRIDE** outputs a subset of the optimal program and thus can miss interesting rules, it can be given some guidance in the form of heuristics, such as variable ordering, to find those "best" rules we are interested in here. All the examples of this paper have been generated using the open source python package pylfit[1] and are available as a Jupiter notebook[2] on the pylfit Github repository.

4   Conclusion

In this paper, we proposed an extension of LFIT theory that allows to encode properties of transitions as additional variables, allowing **GULA** to learn rules that exploit them. We proposed a modeling of event sequences and their temporal properties allowing to use **GULA** to learn rules combining properties to explain sequences of interest. Being able to include properties of transitions in the learning process can be useful in a various range of application fields. For instance, in biology, some information on the dynamics of the system to be modelled is expressed as a LTL property by modelers. Inclusion of such knowledge in the global learning process can give more expressive rules about the dynamics and lead to a better understanding of the studied systems by the biologists. We showed through a case study that such encoding can indeed allow to learn more meaningful rules and to capture complex temporal patterns.

However, by encoding properties, we increase the number of variables considered, which leads to a combinatorial explosion of the run time for **GULA**. Its polynomial approximated version **PRIDE** would be preferred in practice, with additional heuristics allowing to guide its search towards comprehensive rules.

References

1. De Giacomo, G., De Masellis, R., Montali, M.: Reasoning on LTL on finite traces: insensitivity to infiniteness. In: Proceedings of the AAAI Conference on Artificial Intelligence, vol. 28 (2014)

---

[1] Package pylfit source code is available at: https://github.com/Tony-sama/pylfit/.

[2] Case study notebook: https://github.com/Tony-sama/pylfit/blob/master/tests/ evaluations/ilp2022/lfit-sequence-patern-learning.ipynb.

2. Inoue, K., Ribeiro, T., Sakama, C.: Learning from interpretation transition. Mach. Learn. **94**(1), 51–79 (2014)
3. Katzouris, N., Artikis, A., Paliouras, G.: Incremental learning of event definitions with inductive logic programming. Mach. Learn. **100**(2), 555–585 (2015)
4. Muggleton, S.: Inductive logic programming: derivations, successes and shortcomings. ACM SIGART Bull. **5**(1), 5–11 (1994)
5. Pencolé, Y., Subias, A.: Diagnosability of event patterns in safe labeled time petri nets: a model-checking approach. IEEE Trans. Autom. Sci. Eng. **19**, 1151–1162 (2021)
6. Petri, C.A.: Kommunikation mit Automaten. Ph.D. thesis, Fakultät für Mathematik und Physik, Technische Hochschule Darmstadt, Darmstadt (Allemagne) (1962)
7. Pnueli, A.: The temporal logic of programs. In: 18th Annual Symposium on Foundations of Computer Science, SFCS 1977, pp. 46–57 (1977)
8. Ribeiro, T., Folschette, M., Magnin, M., Inoue, K.: Learning any memory-less discrete semantics for dynamical systems represented by logic programs. Mach. Learn. **111**, 3593–3670 (2021)
9. Ribeiro, T., Folschette, M., Magnin, M., Inoue, K.: Polynomial algorithm for learning from interpretation transition. In: 1st International Joint Conference on Learning & Reasoning, pp. 1–5 (2021)
10. Sato, S., Watanabe, Y., Seki, H., Ishii, Y., Yuen, S.: Fault diagnosis for distributed cooperative system using inductive logic programming. In: 2020 IEEE International Conference on Prognostics and Health Management (ICPHM), pp. 1–8. IEEE (2020)

Efficient Abductive Learning of Microbial Interactions Using Meta Inverse Entailment

Dany Varghese[1(✉)], Didac Barroso-Bergada[2], David A. Bohan[2], and Alireza Tamaddoni-Nezhad[1]

[1] Department of Computer Science, University of Surrey, Guildford, UK
{dany.varghese,a.tamaddoni-nezhad}@surrey.ac.uk
[2] Agroécologie, AgroSup Dijon, Dijon, France
{didac.barroso-bergada,david.bohan}@inrae.fr

Abstract. Abductive reasoning plays an essential part in day-to-day problem-solving. It has been considered a powerful mechanism for hypothetical reasoning in the presence of incomplete knowledge; a form of "common sense" reasoning. In machine learning, abduction is viewed as a conceptual method in which data and the bond that jointly brings the different types of inference. The traditional Mode-Directed Inverse Entailment (MDIE) based systems such as Progol and Aleph for the abduction were not data-efficient since their execution time with the large dataset was too long. We present a new abductive learning procedure using Meta Inverse Entailment (MIE). MIE is similar to Mode-Directed Inverse Entailment (MDIE) but does not require user-defined mode declarations. In this paper, we use an implementation of MIE in Python called PyGol. We evaluate and compare this approach to reveal the microbial interactions in the ecosystem with state-of-art-of methods for abduction, such as Progol and Aleph. Our results show that PyGol has comparable predictive accuracies but is significantly faster than Progol and Aleph.

Keywords: Abduction · Learning Microbial Interactions · Abductive ILP · Meta Inverse Entailment · PyGol · Bottom Clause of Relevant Literals

1 Introduction

Interactions between microbes are indispensable to successfully establishing and maintaining a population of microbes. For example, microbial communities in the soil significantly protect plants from diseases and abiotic stresses or increase nutrient uptake. This is one of the many ways in which the microbial community plays a vital role in preventing diseases caused by microbes that are themselves infectious. Microbial communities are defined by the interactions that take

ILP 2022, 31st International Conference on Inductive Logic Programming, Cumberland Lodge, Windsor, UK.

S. H. Muggleton and A. Tamaddoni-Nezhad (Eds.): ILP 2022, LNAI 13779, pp. 127–141, 2024.
https://doi.org/10.1007/978-3-031-55630-2_10

place between their members. The most recent mechanisms for meta-barcoding, such as DNA sequencing in conjunction with bio-informatics processes, are able to provide an estimate of the amount of information available on the various microbes present in a community. Machine learning models can infer an interaction network that can generalise the interaction between the microbes by using this information about the abundance and the rules of interactions as background knowledge (please refer to Fig. 1).

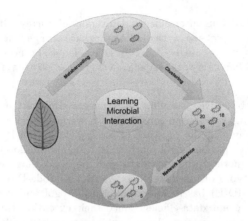

Fig. 1. Different steps involved in Microbial Interaction

Prior studies [2] introduced an Abductive/Inductive Logic Programming (A/ILP) framework to infer microbial interactions from abundance data, and Progol 5.0 [12] was used to infer the interactions in terms of logical rules and presented as a classification problem. This promising study proposes the idea of inferring ecological interaction information from diverse ecosystems, which is currently not possible to study using other methods. However, mode-directed inverse entailment systems such as Progol [12] and Aleph [20] are data-inefficient, emphasising the need for a more efficient approach to abduction.

Inductive logic programming [16] is a machine learning form that induces a hypothesis that generalises examples and can deal with very few amounts of data, even from one-shot data. It can also include background knowledge in the form of logic rules [23,24]. In contrast, most forms of ML use vectors or tensors to represent data. The ILP models are more data-efficient, explainable, and can incorporate human knowledge compared to other forms of machine learning.

Abduction is also counted as a synthetic form of reasoning along with induction. In abductive learning, logic generates new knowledge not directly included in the current theory. This sort of learning can be referred to as knowledge-intensive learning, where the new information generated drives to complete the current knowledge of the problem domain as described in the given theory. Early abduction works by Michalski [10], Ourston and Mooney [18], and Abe et al. [1] consider abductive learning a theory revision operator for specifying where the existing theory could be modified to accommodate the new learning data. Later it was realised that the role of abduction in learning could be strengthened by induction as in Progol 5.0 [12] and HAIL [19].

This paper presents abduction as an inductive approach using a novel method called Meta Inverse Entailment (MIE). In Meta Inverse Entailment (MIE), each hypothesis clause is derived from a bottom clause of relevant literals and meta theory. A bottom clause of relevant literals is a notion that efficiently collects all literals related to an example from the background knowledge and acts as a bound for the hypothesis search while abducing facts. Meta theory is a kind of language bias induced automatically from background knowledge. We implement the new learning framework for abduction using MIE in a system called PyGol[1] and presented as a Python package.

2   Background and Related Work

Abductive learning based on Inverse Entailment (IE) was first introduced in [15] and implemented in Progol 5.0, where the 'start-set' routine is regarded as a form of abduction. The system HAIL [19] also uses Bottom Set, an advanced concept from the bottom clause, and it is presented as a generalisation of Progol. The state-of-the-art system Aleph [20] can also perform abduction using Moyle's ALECTO [11] approach.

Progol 5.0 uses a standard covering algorithm where each example is generalised using a multi-predicate search [14]. This search will be done over all the predicates in the mode declarations. The two-stage process, which includes a "start-set", can be considered as a complex procedure. First, the algorithm generates the bottom clause for a seed example in the start-set and then does a covering test to find the rule covering the given example with maximum compression. Most ILP systems, such as Progol and Aleph, select a positive example and then explore its implied hypothesis space. In all cases, computing the cover set of a hypothesis is a costly process that usually involves sequentially considering all negative and relevant positive examples.

HAIL uses the 'bottom set' routine from Progol 5.0 to compute the body atoms of each Kernel clause, and M-SEARCH performs a recursive specific to general search through the collection subsumption lattices obtained from the given Kernel Set. The high-level operation of the HAIL includes abduce, deduce and search. Like its predecessor, Progol 5.0, HAIL also uses coverage testing. HAIL try to overcome some of the limitations of Progol and can find better-quality hypothesis than Progol. Also, one can consider HAIL as a greedy approach as Progol and Aleph, since HAIL begins by removing the examples covered in each stage.

The basic abductive procedure used by Aleph is a simplified variant of Moyle's ALECTO [11]. The basic workflow of ALECTO is as follows: For each positive example, an "abductive explanation" is generated. This explanation is

---

[1] Available from https://github.com/PyGol.

a set of ground atoms. The union of abductive explanations from all positive examples is formed. These are then generalized to give the final theory. The ground atoms in an abductive explanation are generated using Yamamoto's SOLD resolution or SOLDR [28]. Next, we introduce the fundamental definitions of induction and abduction. We assume the reader to be familiar with the basic concepts of logic programming and inductive logic programming [17]. The goal of an ILP system is to induce a logic program, H, that entails all positive examples and none of the negative examples while some prior knowledge or background knowledge is given. Formally we define the ILP as in Definition 1.

Definition 1 (An ILP learning approach). *Let E^+, E^- be the set of positive and negative examples, and B be the background knowledge. Then ILP system learn hypothesis H and has to satisfy:*

Prior Satisfiability   : $B \wedge E^- \not\models \Box$
Prior Necessity   : $B \not\models E^+$
Posterior Satisfiability : $B \wedge E^- \wedge H \not\models \Box$
Posterior Sufficiency : $B \wedge H \models E^+$

The role of abduction has been demonstrated in various applications [7,21,22]. A/ILP, a high-level knowledge-representation framework, solves problems declaratively based on abductive reasoning. It extends regular logic programming by allowing some predicates to be incompletely defined and declared as abducible predicates. In the context of formal logic, abduction is often defined as follows. Given a logical theory, T represents the expert knowledge, and a formula Q represents an observation on the problem domain, abductive inference searches for an explanation formula $\mathcal{E}$ such that:

- $\mathcal{E}$ is satisfiable w.r.t. T and
- it holds that $T \models \mathcal{E} \to Q$

In general, ε will be subjected to further restrictions, such as the aforementioned minimality criteria and the explanation formula's form (e.g. by restricting the predicates that may appear in it). This view defines an abductive explanation of observation as a rule which logically entails the observation itself. Formally, we can define abduction as in Definition 2. The definitions are taken from [8].

Definition 2. *Given an abductive logic theory (P, A, C), an abductive explanation for a query Q is a set $\Lambda \subseteq A$ of ground abducible atoms such that:*

- $P \vee \Lambda \models Q$
- $P \vee \Lambda \models C$
- $P \vee \Lambda$ *is consistent*

3   Abduction via Meta Inverse Entailment

Abductive learning is a machine learning approach which generates explanation H from a given observation E and background knowledge B. Abduction can be regarded as a form of induction in various ways. Michalski [10] described abduction in terms of induction as follows: "Given a background knowledge Th and observations O, induction hypothesises a premise H, consistent with Th, such as $H \vee Th \models O$ ... Induction is viewed as 'tracing backwards' this relationship". In this section, we introduce a new inductive learning approach called Meta Inverse Entailment (MIE) and present abduction as a form of MIE.

Many ILP methods use the reality that creating hypotheses incrementally as a series of short theories, each covering a few samples at a time, is usually more comfortable than making one large theory covering most of the examples. For this reason, several systems employ a so-called covering-loop [9] that uses one seed example at a time. In an ILP system, the computational cost of the search depends mainly on the cost of subsumption, which is used to evaluate the clause and then on the size of the search space. ILP systems use different kinds of biases to have a tractable search. For example, a language bias restricts the size of an acceptable hypothesis, and a search bias determines the way of the search.

Instead of selecting a random example, MIE generates the hypothesis space from all the examples using a bottom clause of relevant literals (BCRL) and meta theory (MT). MIE takes advantage of IE and MIL by introducing two novel concepts: the bottom clause of relevant literals and meta theory. BCRL bounds the hypothesis space search of MIE, and MT will guide the search. Unlike other metarule-based approaches [4,5,13] in ILP, MIE introduces a higher-order language bias, meta theory, synthesizing automatically from the background knowledge. The complete explanation of MIE is out of this report's scope, so we explain only the major concepts.

Definition 3 (Related literals). *Let $L_1 = P(s_1, s_2, \cdots, s_n)$ and $L_2 = Q(t_1, t_2, \cdots, t_m)$ be two ground literals and $\mathcal{K}$ be a set of constant terms then L_1 and L_2 are related literals if they have any common terms other than terms in $\mathcal{K}$.*

Example 1. Let $L_1 = has\_car(train_1, car_1)$, $L_2 = open(car_1)$, $L_3 = closed(car_2)$ and $\mathcal{K} = \{\}$ then according to Definition 3, L_1 and L_2 are related literals but neither L_1 and L_3 nor L_2 and L_3.

In the Example 1, L_1 and L_2 are connected since they have a common term car_1, but there is no common term between either L_1 and L_3 or L_2 and L_3.

Example 2. Let $L_1 = has\_load(car_1, circle, 2)$, $L_2 = has\_load(car_2, circle, 3)$ and $\mathcal{K} = \{circle\}$ then according to Definition 3, L_1 and L_2 are not related literals because the common term between L_1 and L_2 is present in $\mathcal{K}$.

Ordered clauses will be beneficial for collecting all the related literals of e from B. An ordered clause, denoted by $\overrightarrow{C}$, is a sequence of literals where the order and duplication of literal matter. In ILP, the usage of ordered clauses is not novel. For instance, it may be necessary to duplicate literals when using an upward refinement operator to invert an elementary substitution. Ordered clauses are used since reusing literals is forbidden in the standard encoding of clauses [17].

Definition 4 ($\vec{\mathcal{B}}$). *Let B be the background knowledge. $\vec{\mathcal{B}}$ is an ordered clause of ground literals constructed from B without any repetition of literals.*

Definition 5 (Relevant literals of an example ($\vec{\mathcal{R}_e}$)). *Let B be the background knowledge, $\vec{\mathcal{B}}$ be the ordered clause constructed from B as defined in Definition 4, and e be an example. Then the relevant literals of e is defined as $\vec{\mathcal{R}_e} = L_1 \vee L_2 \vee \cdots \vee L_n$ if and only if $L_i \in \vec{\mathcal{B}}$ and L_i be related literal of either L_j or e such that $1 \leq j < i$.*

Definition 6 (Bottom clause of relevant literals ($\perp_{e,B}$)). *Let B be the background knowledge, e be a definite clause representing an example, $\mathcal{K}$ as defined in Definition 3 and $\vec{\mathcal{R}_e}$ be the relevant literals of example e as defined in the Definition 5. Then bottom clause of relevant literals of e, denoted as $\perp_{e,B}$ is $\vec{\mathcal{R}_e}$ where each unique occurrence of term $t_i \notin \mathcal{K}$ replaced with a new variable.*

The bottom clause of relevant literals introduced in MIE can resemble the bottom clause concept in Progol, but it never uses language bias like mode declaration. The Algorithm 1 sketches a search-based algorithm to generate the bottom clause of relevant literals. Now, we define a language set for a bottom clause of relevant literals, denoted as $\vec{\mathcal{L}_\perp}$, as the set of definite ordered clauses which are sequential generalisations of $\perp_{e,B}$. This chapter focuses on languages such as $\vec{\mathcal{L}_\perp}$, comprised of clauses exhibiting the characteristics of generalisations derived from a flattened bottom clause. Consequently, all the clauses within the language $\vec{\mathcal{L}_\perp}$ can be effectively treated function-free.

Definition 7 ($\vec{\mathcal{L}_\perp}$). *Let $\perp_{e,B}$ be the bottom clause of relevant literals as defined in Definition 6 and $\vec{C}$ a definite ordered clause. $\vec{C}$ is in $\vec{\mathcal{L}_\perp}$ if and only if there exists a substitution θ such that $\vec{C}\theta$ is a subsequence of $\perp_{e,B}$.*

Definition 8 (Meta theory ($\mathcal{M}$)). *A meta theory is a higher-order well-formed-formula*

$$P(s_1, \cdots, s_m) \leftarrow Q_1(t_1, \cdots, t_n), Q_2(u_1, \cdots, u_p), \cdots, Q_N(\cdots) \qquad (1)$$

where P, Q_i are existentially quantified variables and $t_1, u_i, \cdots$ are universally quantified variables and $P \wedge Q_i \wedge \{t_i\} \wedge \{u_i\} \wedge \cdots = \emptyset$. m is the arity of arguments of the target literal, and N is the number of literals in the body of a meta theory. Two kinds of substitution will be involved using meta theory during the learning phase, such as substitution on existentially and universally quantified variables.

Definition 9 (Meta substitution). *A meta substitution Θ is a set $\{v_1/p_1, \cdots, v_n/p_n\}$ where each v_i is a distinct variable, and each p_i is a predicate. Here, t_i represents the value that is substituted for the predicate p_i.*

Algorithm 1. Algorithm to generate $\perp_{e,B}$

Input: Background knowledge (B), pass $= i$, example (e), constant set $(\mathcal{K})$
$HashFn(t)$: A function which uniquely maps terms to variables
$GenerateLiteral(Pred, [Terms])$: A function generates a literal with $Pred$ as predicate
and $[Terms]$ as its arguments.
Output: $\perp_{E,B}$

1: Let $Pred$ be the predicate related to the example
2: $BC = \emptyset$
3: $HeadTerms = \emptyset$
4: $TermSet = \emptyset$
5: $BodyLiterals = \emptyset$
6: **for** each term e_i in e **do**
7:    **if** $e_i \notin \mathcal{K}$ **then**
8:       push $HashFn(e_i)$ to $HeadTerms$
9:       push e_i to $TermSet$
10:   **else**
11:      push e_i to $HeadTerms$
12:   **end if**
13: **end for**
14: Let $h = GenerateLiteral(Pred, HeadTerms)$
15: k=1
16: **while** k $\leq$ pass **do**
17:   **for** each b_i in B **do**
18:      Let P_{b_i} be the predicate related to b_i
19:      **if** any term of b_i in $TermSet$ **then**
20:         $TempTerms = \emptyset$
21:         **for** each term t_i of b_i **do**
22:            **if** $t_i \notin \mathcal{K}$ **then**
23:               push $HashFn(t_i)$ to $TempTerms$
24:               push t_i to $TermSet$
25:            **else**
26:               push t_i $TempTerms$
27:            **end if**
28:         **end for**
29:         **if** $generate\_literal(P_{b_i}, TempTerms) \notin BodyLiterals$ **then**
30:            push $generate\_literal(P_{b_i}, TempTerms)$ to $BodyLiterals$
31:         **end if**
32:      **end if**
33:   **end for**
34:   k = k+1
35: **end while**
36: **return** $BC = h \leftarrow BodyLiterals$

Definition 10 $(\overrightarrow{\mathcal{L_M}})$. *Let* $\perp_{e,B}$ *be the bottom clause of relevant literals as defined in Definition 6 and* $\overrightarrow{C}$ *be a meta theory as defined in Definition 8.* $\overrightarrow{C}$ *is in* $\overrightarrow{\mathcal{L_M}}$ *if and only if there exists a meta substituition* Θ *such that* $\overrightarrow{C}\Theta$ *is a subsequence of* $\perp_{e,B}$.

The definition of meta theory and meta-substitution is motivated by the concept of metarules [3]. The incompleteness of Progol was discussed by Yamamoto [26,27], and one of the incompleteness is due to its inability to generate multiple hypotheses from a single bottom clause. In MIE, we solved the incompleteness of Progol by introducing the concept of the double-bounded hypothesis set.

Definition 11 (Double-bounded hypothesis set $(HS(\perp_{e,B}, \mathcal{M}_e)))$. *Let e be an example, $\perp_{e,B}$ be a bottom clause of relevant literals of e as defined in Definition 6, $\mathcal{M}_e$ be a meta theory as defined in Definition 8. Then*

$$HS(\perp_{e,B}, \mathcal{M}_e) = \{h| \ s.t: \ (1) \ h \in \overrightarrow{\mathcal{L}_\perp}, \ and \ (2) \ h \in \overrightarrow{\mathcal{L}_\mathcal{M}}\}$$

From the Definition 11, it is clear that the double-bounded hypothesis set can be considered as a combination of top-down and bottom-up approaches, and each hypothesis will be generated as sequential subsumption of meta-theory relative to bottom clause of relevant literals. Instead of starting from a seed example, we generate the bottom clause of relevant literals of all the examples. This global-theory generating mechanism is not new to the ILP community, as a similar approach can be seen in the bottom clause propositionalisation [6].

Definition 12 (Abduction using MIE). *Let B be the background knowledge, $HS(\perp_{e,B}, \mathcal{M}_e)$ be the double-bounded hypothesis set as defined in the Definition 11, e be an example, A be the abducible predicate and R be the rule to explain the observable predicates such that $R = R'A$. Let $\perp_{e,B}$ the bottom clause of relevant literals of e, and $\hat{H}$ be the set of inductive hypothesis; $\hat{H} = HS(\perp_{e,B}, R')$. Then the MIE will generate a set of ground abductive hypotheses, $\Lambda = \{a\theta: h\theta \models \perp_{e,B}, h \in \hat{H} \ and \ a \in A\}; \ \hat{H} = \mathcal{HS}(\perp_{B,e}, R')$. Then the MIE will generate a set of ground abductive hypotheses, $\Lambda = \{a\theta: h\theta \models \perp_{B,e}, h \in \hat{H} \ and \ a \in A\};$*

- $R \wedge \Lambda \models E$
- $\Lambda \not\models B$

Example 3. This example illustrates the steps through which we can perform abduction using MIE [22] (please refer the Fig. 2). Let B, e, K, A as formulated in Definition 12. Then the abductive procedure starts by generating the bottom clause of relevant literals, $\perp_{B,e}$ for the example e and later generates the double-bounded hypothesis set $\hat{H} = HS(\perp_{B,e}, R')$. The abductive procedure will keep track of θ for each $h \in \hat{H}$ and generate ground abducible facts.

4 Abduction of Microbial Interaction Using MIE

Microbial interactions refer to the various ways in which microbes interact with each other and with other organisms. Microbial interactions include cooperative and competitive interactions, such as symbiosis, commensalism, parasitism,

B
taxacode(a)., taxacode(b)., taxacode(c)., taxacode(d)., taxacode(e)., taxacode(f)., predator(a)., predator(b)., predator(c)., size_class(a, 4)., size_class(b, 3)., size_class(c, 2)., size_class(d, 1)., size_class(e, 1)., size_class(f, 1)., bigger(a,b)., bigger(a,c)., bigger(a,d)., bigger(a,e)., bigger(a,f)., bigger(b,c)., bigger(b,d)., bigger(b,e)., bigger(b,f)., bigger(c,d)., bigger(c,e)., bigger(c,f)., abundance1(a, s1, down)., abundance1(a, s2, down)., abundance1(a, s3, down)., abundance1(a, s4, down)., abundance1(b, s1, up)., abundance1(b, s2, up)., abundance1(b, s3, down)., abundance1(b, s4, down)., abundance1(c, s1, down)., abundance1(c, s2, down)., abundance1(c, s3, up)., abundance1(c, s4, up)., abundance1(d, s1, up)., abundance1(d, s2, up)., abundance1(d, s3, down)., abundance1(d, s4, down)., abundance1(e, s1, up)., abundance1(e, s2, up)., abundance1(e, s3, down)., abundance1(e, s4, down)., abundance1(f, s1, down)., abundance1(f, s2, down)., abundance1(f, s3, up)., abundance1(f, s4, up).

e	K	A
abundance(a, s1, down).	$\{a,b,c,d,e,f\}$	eats

R	R'
abundance(X,S,D) :- predator(X), bigger(X,Y), abundance1(Y,S,D), eats(X,Y).	abundance(X,S,D) :- predator(X), bigger(X,Y), abundance1(Y,S,D).

$\perp_{e,B}$
abundance(a, B, C):- taxacode(a), predator(a), size_class(a,4), bigger(a,b), bigger(a,c), bigger(a,d), bigger(a,e), bigger(a,f), abundance1(a,B,C), abundance1(a,D,C), abundance1(a,E,C), abundance1(a,F,C), abundance1(b,B,G), abundance1(b,D,G), abundance1(b,E,C), abundance1(b,F,C), abundance1(c,B,C), abundance1(c,D,C), abundance1(c,E,G), abundance1(c,F,G), abundance1(d,B,G), abundance1(d,D,G), abundance1(d,E,C), abundance1(d,F,C), abundance1(e,B,G), abundance1(e,D,G), abundance1(e,E,C), abundance1(e,F,C), abundance1(f,B,C), abundance1(f,D,C), abundance1(f,E,G), abundance1(f,F,G).

$\hat{H}$	θ	Λ
abundance(a,B,C):- predator(a), bigger(a,c), abundance1(c,B,C).	$\{X : a, Y : c\}$	eats(a,b)
abundance(a,B,C):- predator(a), bigger(a,f), abundance1(f,B,C).	$\{X : a, Y : f\}$	eats(a,f)

Fig. 2. (Example 3) Learning abducible explanations using MIE

predation, and competition. Microbes can also interact indirectly by releasing metabolites into their environment, which can affect the growth and development of other microbes. Microbial interactions are essential for the functioning of ecosystems since they contribute to the nutrient and energy cycles and can influence the structure and composition of microbial communities. In a more general way, A microbial interaction can be defined as a conserved effect on the abundance of one microbial species caused by the presence of another. Thus, the abductive procedure aims to infer interactions, following ecological theory to explain the observed changes in the abundance of the species. Barroso-Bergada et al. successfully encoded the microbial interactions into logical clauses and applied A/ILP using Progol in [2].

The abductive procedure aims to infer interactions following ecological theory to explain the observed changes in the abundance of the species. The steps involved in an abductive procedure are shown in Fig. 3.

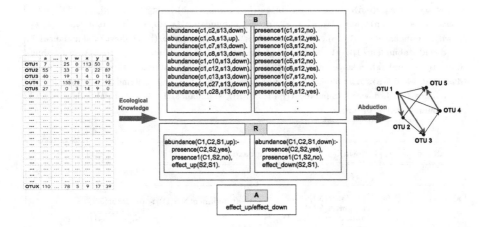

Fig. 3. Abductive learning of microbial interaction

The first step for abducing the inference is to reflect the abundance changes between communities of each species using logical statements. In [2], the 'abundance change' and 'presence' logical statements are used as observations in an abduction process. The observable predicate 'abundance' is defined as 'abundance (C1, C2, S1, Dir)'. Here, C1 and C2 symbolize two different community samples where species S1 is present, and 'Dir' is the change in the direction of abundance. The 'presence' of each species is also converted to a logical statement with the structure: presence(C1, S2, yes/no) where C1 refers to a sample community, S2 to a species and yes/no describes if S2 is present in C1 or not. The second step is to encode the interaction hypothesis using logical statements. The logical statements to define the observations are given in Eq. 2, in which $effect\_up$ and $effect\_down$ are the abducible predicates. These abducibles are used to learn whether two species interact positively (up) or negatively (down) in a community.

$$
\begin{aligned}
\text{abundance(C1, C2, S1, up)} &\leftarrow \text{presence(C2, S2, yes),} \\
&\quad \text{presence(C1, S2, no),} \\
&\quad \text{effect\_up(S2, S1)} \\
\text{abundance(C1, C2, S1, down)} &\leftarrow \text{presence(C2, S2, yes),} \\
&\quad \text{presence(C1, S2, no),} \\
&\quad \text{effect\_down(S2, S1)}
\end{aligned}
\tag{2}
$$

5   Empirical Evaluation

The performance of PyGol was evaluated using artificially generated datasets[2] introduced in [2]. We have mainly considered two criteria for comparison with two state-of-the-art systems, Aleph and Progol: accuracy and execution time.

5.1   Materials and Methods

For the experiment setup, we have chosen nine different datasets of 50 species from 3 different strengths (2, 3 and 5). Table 1 will give you the statistical information of the datasets we are considering. Since the interactions that drive the abundance of the computer-generated tables are known, it is possible to treat interaction inference as a classification problem. Interactions can be classified between existing and non-existing, and the estimator values obtained using the different functions are the classification accuracy. Thus, the area under the curve (AUC) of the true positive rate against the false positive rate (ROC curve) can be used to measure performance.

In all the three systems, we have used the same experimental setup. The search for the best hypotheses is guided by an evaluation function called 'compression', which is defined as $f = p-(c+n)$, where p is the number of observations (training examples) correctly explained by the hypothesis (positive examples), n is the number incorrectly explained (negative examples) and c is the length of the hypothesis (in this study, it always One because the hypothesis is a single fact). The rules to define the observations are shown in the Eq. 2, and atoms $effect\_up$ and $effect\_down$ are the abducible.

Other than Progol, we have also considered Aleph [20], a state-of-the-art ILP algorithm, for the empirical evaluation. Like PyGol, Aleph also uses the advantage of inverse entailment but mode-directed inverse entailment. A novel user-friendly Python/Jupyter interface for Inductive Logic programming, PyILP [25], was used to run the experiments for Aleph and Progol 5.0 was used for progol-related experiments.

6   Results and Discussions

Figure 4, records the area under ROC curves, and Fig. 5 displays the total execution time from different experiments. In Fig. 4, each row represents datasets of different strengths, such as 2, 3 and 5, as in Table 1. PyGol outperforms all other approaches in most of the experiments. The average difference between PyGol and Aleph is 4.3% and 1.7% with Progol. Regarding the execution time, it is evident that PyGol is very fast compared to Progol and Aleph. While considering all the execution time, it is clear that PyGol is 45 to 65 times faster than Aleph and 40 to 60 times faster than Progol.

The primary reason for the speedy execution time for PyGol is its new efficient way of generating the hypothesis space using meta inverse entailment.

---

[2] Available from https://github.com/danyvarghese/IJCLR22-Abduction.

Table 1. Dataset statistics

Dataset	Strength	No. of observations				
		Species	abundance	presence	presence1	Total
S_1	2	40	17690	2000	2000	21690
S_2			25252			29252
S_3			23680			27680
S_4	3		20732			24732
S_5			21774			25774
S_6			28190			32190
S_7	5		20742			24742
S_8			25072			29072
S_9			24708			28708

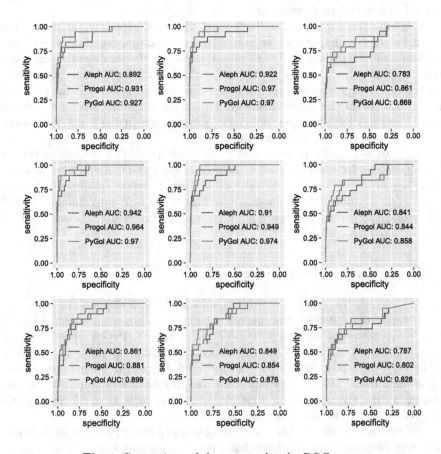

Fig. 4. Comparison of the area under the ROC curve

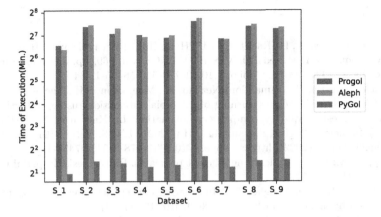

Fig. 5. Comparison on execution time

The theoretical framework for converting the general subsumption to atomic subsumption makes MIE more efficient. While considering the results, the new abductive learning approach using meta inverse entailment is more efficient than Progol and Aleph. MIE could learn all the abducted facts generated by both approaches quickly, showing the system's impact on hypothesis space generation. The abductive framework using MIE will not affect the order of examples as it follows a global-theory-making mechanism, but Progol and Aleph follow the greedy approach.

7   Conclusion

This paper presents an application that uses abductive learning to infer microbial interaction. We presented abduction as a variant of inductive learning in the first part of the paper, using a novel ILP approach called meta inverse entailment. The bottom clause of relevant literals and meta theory is used in meta inverse entailment, generated automatically from background knowledge without any declarative bias of user interaction. In the second part, we presented a novel abductive framework for learning microbial interaction, which we implemented as a Python package in PyGol.

According to empirical evaluations, the MIE is efficient enough for abductive learning regarding execution time and accuracy. The results show that PyGol outperforms other systems by 40 to 60 times. The new learning approach demonstrates the theoretical strength of the system introduced using sequential subsumption of meta-theory relative to the bottom clause of relevant literals, which can be reduced to atomic subsumption and performed without much complexity.

References

1. Adé, H., Malfait, B., De Raedt, L.: RUTH: an ILP theory revision system. In: Raś, Z.W., Zemankova, M. (eds.) ISMIS 1994. LNCS, vol. 869, pp. 336–345. Springer, Heidelberg (1994). https://doi.org/10.1007/3-540-58495-1_34
2. Barroso-Bergada, D., Tamaddoni-Nezhad, A., Muggleton, S.H., Vacher, C., Galic, N., Bohan, D.A.: Machine learning of microbial interactions using abductive ILP and hypothesis frequency/compression estimation. In: Katzouris, N., Artikis, A. (eds.) Inductive Logic Programming, ILP 2021. LNCS, vol. 13191, pp. 26–40. Springer, Cham (2022). https://doi.org/10.1007/978-3-030-97454-1_3
3. Cropper, A.: Efficiently learning efficient programs. Ph.D. thesis. Imperial College London, UK (2017)
4. De Raedt, L., Bruynooghe, M.: Interactive concept-learning and constructive induction by analogy. Mach. Learn. 8(2), 107–150 (1992)
5. Evans, R., Grefenstette, E.: Learning explanatory rules from noisy data. J. Artif. Int. Res. 61(1), 1–64 (2018)
6. França, M.V.M., Zaverucha, G., Garcez, A.: Fast relational learning using bottom clause propositionalization with artificial neural networks. Mach. Learn. 94(1), 81–104 (2014). https://doi.org/10.1007/s10994-013-5392-1. https://openaccess.city.ac.uk/id/eprint/3057/
7. Kakas, A., Tamaddoni, N.A., Muggleton, S., Chaleil, R.: Application of abductive ILP to learning metabolic network inhibition from temporal data. Mach. Learn. 64, 209–230 (2006). https://doi.org/10.1007/s10994-006-8988-x
8. Kakas, A.C., Kowalski, R.A., Toni., F.: Abduction in logic programming. J. Log. Comput. 2, 719–770 (1993)
9. Michalski, R.S.: A theory and methodology of inductive learning. Artif. Intell. 20(2), 111–161 (1983)
10. Michalski, R.S.: Inferential theory of learning as a conceptual basis for multistrategy learning. Mach. Learn. 11(2–3), 111–151 (1993)
11. Moyle, S.: Using theory completion to learn a robot navigation control program. In: Matwin, S., Sammut, C. (eds.) ILP 2002. LNCS (LNAI), vol. 2583, pp. 182–197. Springer, Heidelberg (2003). https://doi.org/10.1007/3-540-36468-4_12
12. Muggleton, S.: Inverse entailment and Progol. N. Gener. Comput. 13, 245–286 (1995)
13. Muggleton, S., Lin, D., Tamaddoni-Nezhad, A.: Meta-interpretive learning of higher-order dyadic datalog: predicate invention revisited. Mach. Learn. 100(1), 49–73 (2015). https://doi.org/10.1007/s10994-014-5471-y
14. Muggleton, S.: Learning from positive data. In: Muggleton, S. (ed.) ILP 1996. LNCS, vol. 1314, pp. 358–376. Springer, Heidelberg (1997). https://doi.org/10.1007/3-540-63494-0_65
15. Muggleton, S.H., Bryant, C.H.: Theory completion using inverse entailment. In: Cussens, J., Frisch, A. (eds.) ILP 2000. LNCS (LNAI), vol. 1866, pp. 130–146. Springer, Heidelberg (2000). https://doi.org/10.1007/3-540-44960-4_8
16. Muggleton, S., de Raedt, L.: Inductive logic programming: Theory and methods. J. Log. Program. 19–20, 629–679 (1994). Special Issue: Ten Years of Logic Programming
17. Nienhuys-Cheng, S.-H., de Wolf, R.: Foundations of Inductive Logic Programming. LNCS, vol. 1228. Springer, Heidelberg (1997). https://doi.org/10.1007/3-540-62927-0

18. Ourston, D., Mooney, R.J.: Theory refinement combining analytical and empirical methods. Artif. Intell. **66**(2), 273–309 (1994)
19. Ray, O., Broda, K., Russo, A.: Hybrid Abductive inductive learning: a generalisation of Progol. In: Horváth, T., Yamamoto, A. (eds.) ILP 2003. LNCS (LNAI), vol. 2835, pp. 311–328. Springer, Heidelberg (2003). https://doi.org/10.1007/978-3-540-39917-9_21
20. Srinivasan, A.: A learning engine for proposing hypotheses (Aleph) (2001). https://www.cs.ox.ac.uk/activities/programinduction/Aleph/aleph.html
21. Tamaddoni-Nezhad, A., Lin, D., Watanabe, H., Chen, J., Muggleton, S.: Machine Learning of Biological Networks Using Abductive ILP, pp. 363–401. Wiley, Hoboken (2014). https://doi.org/10.1002/9781119005223.ch10
22. Tamaddoni-Nezhad, A., Bohan, D., Raybould, A., Muggleton, S.: Towards machine learning of predictive models from ecological data. In: Davis, J., Ramon, J. (eds.) ILP 2014. LNCS (LNAI), vol. 9046, pp. 154–167. Springer, Cham (2015). https://doi.org/10.1007/978-3-319-23708-4_11
23. Varghese, D., Bauer, R., Baxter-Beard, D., Muggleton, S., Tamaddoni-Nezhad, A.: Human-like rule learning from images using one-shot hypothesis derivation. In: Katzouris, N., Artikis, A. (eds.) Inductive Logic Programming, ILP 2021. LNCS, vol. 13191, pp. pp 234–250. Springer, Cham (2022). https://doi.org/10.1007/978-3-030-97454-1_17
24. Varghese, D., Tamaddoni-Nezhad, A.: One-shot rule learning for challenging character recognition. In: Proceedings of the 14th International Rule Challenge, August 2020, Oslo, Norway, vol. 2644, pp. 10–27 (2020)
25. Varghese, D., Tamaddoni-Nezhad, A.: Pyilp (2022). https://github.com/danyvarghese/PyILP/
26. Yamamoto, A.: Revising the logical foundations of inductive logic programming systems with ground reduced programs. New Gener. Comput. **17**, 119–127 (1998). https://cir.nii.ac.jp/crid/1571417125491386240
27. Yamamoto, A.: Which hypotheses can be found with inverse entailment? In: Lavrač, N., Džeroski, S. (eds.) ILP 1997. LNCS, vol. 1297, pp. 296–308. Springer, Heidelberg (1997). https://doi.org/10.1007/3540635149_58
28. Yamamoto, A.: Using abduction for induction based on bottom generalization. In: Flach, P.A., Kakas, A.C. (eds.) Abduction and Induction. Applied Logic Series, vol. 18, pp. 267–280. Springer, Dordrecht (2000). https://doi.org/10.1007/978-94-017-0606-3_17

Functional Lifted Bayesian Networks: Statistical Relational Learning and Reasoning with Relative Frequencies

Felix Weitkämper[(✉)] [iD]

Ludwig-Maximilians-Universität München, Institut für Informatik,
Oettingenstraße 67, 80538 Munich, Germany
felix.weitkaemper@lmu.de

Abstract. Dependencies on the relative frequency of a state in the domain are common when modelling probabilistic dependencies on relational data. For instance, the likelihood of a school closure during an epidemic might depend on the proportion of infected pupils exceeding a threshold. Often, rather than depending on discrete thresholds, dependencies are continuous: for instance, the likelihood of any one mosquito bite transmitting an illness depends on the proportion of carrier mosquitoes. Current approaches usually only consider probabilities over possible worlds rather than over domain elements themselves. We introduce functional lifted Bayesian networks, a formalism that explicitly incorporates relative frequencies into statistical relational artificial intelligence. Incorporating relative frequencies is not only beneficial to modelling; it also provides a more rigorous approach to learning problems where training and test or application domains have different sizes. To this end, we provide a representation of the asymptotic probability distributions induced by functional lifted Bayesian networks on domains of increasing sizes. Since that representation has well-understood scaling behaviour across domain sizes, it can be used to estimate parameters for a large domain consistently from randomly sampled subpopulations.

1 Introduction

Consider the different flavour of the following two statements: "1% of the population are suffering from the disease", which is a statement about the relative frequency of an illness in the population; and "Considering his symptoms, the likelihood that this patient is suffering from the disease is 20%", which is a statement about the degree of confirmation of the assertion that a particular patient has this illness, given the available evidence.

This distinction has first been methodically investigated by Rudolf Carnap [2], who distinguished two concepts of probability, the "degree of confirmation", which he calls "probability$_1$", and the "relative frequency (in the long run)", which he calls "probability$_2$". Carnap goes on to formalise probability$_1$ using a probability measure defined over so-called *state descriptions*, which we can

© The Author(s), under exclusive license to Springer Nature Switzerland AG 2024
S. H. Muggleton and A. Tamaddoni-Nezhad (Eds.): ILP 2022, LNAI 13779, pp. 142–156, 2024.
https://doi.org/10.1007/978-3-031-55630-2_11

identify as *possible worlds* in more modern terminology. Probability$_2$ on the other hand is interpreted by the uniform measure on a given domain set itself.

Forty years later, in his seminal paper on the analysis of first-order logics of probability [5], Joseph Halpern divided approaches to formalising probability in a relational setting along very similar lines. Halpern refers to logics encoding relative frequencies as Type I logics, while referring to logics encoding degrees of belief as Type II logics[1]. As a distinct category, Halpern also considers logics that combine both by expressing a degree of belief in a statement that mentions relative frequencies. He refers to those as Type III logics. Type III logics can express compound statements such as "With a likelihood of at least 10%, more than 60% of the population will have been ill by the end of the year."

In our contribution, we investigate the benefits of a Type III semantics to the context of statistical relational artificial intelligence. They include appropriateness to the intended meaning of queries and a better grasp of extrapolation behaviour, which in turn facilitates transfer learning across domain sizes. We then propose functional lifted Bayesian networks (FLBN) as a Type III formalism. We explore their expressiveness and give a formal account of their extrapolation behaviour. After briefly summarising the learning algorithms that are available or adaptable to FLBN, we give a formal account of their extrapolation behaviour with increasing domain size and explain how this addresses transfer learning between differently sized domains.

The main original contributions of this article are:

1. We introduce and evaluate FLBN as a statistical relational Halpern Type III formalism for continuous dependencies
2. We characterise the asymptotic behaviour of FLBN on domains of increasing sizes.
3. We derive an asymptotically consistent approach to transfer learning across domain sizes from the analysis of asymptotic behaviour.

1.1   Related Work

As Muggleton and Chen [17] and Schulte [20] have noted, the vast majority of statistical relational frameworks in use today are of Halpern Type II—they allocate a probability to each possible world.

This includes Markov Logic Networks (MLN), Probabilistic Logic Programming under the distribution semantics (PLP) and approaches based on lifting Bayesian networks.

As a generalisation of stochastic grammars, Stochastic Logic Programs (SLP) are very different to the approaches above. Rather than providing a probability distribution over possible worlds, they define a distribution over derivations of a goal in a logic programming setting. Since deriving a goal equates to querying a Herbrand base, this can be seen as defining a distribution within that model. Therefore, SLPs can be classified as Type I [17].

---

[1] Somewhat unfortunately, this terminology is reverse to that of Carnap mentioned above.

More explicitly of Type I is the class-based semantics for parametrised Bayesian networks suggested by Schulte et al. [21]. Syntactically, they are similar to the template Bayesian networks mentioned above, but probabilities are defined without grounding to any specified domain. Instead, they are interpreted as arising from a random choice of substitutions that instantiate the template nodes.

Kern-Isberner and Thimm [14] discuss the integration of statistical probabilities into subjective beliefs in a more traditional context, in which different distributions satisfy a probabilistic knowledge base and then a maximum entropy criterion is used to specify a unique distribution. However, Jaeger [8] provides for a 'mean' aggregation function for RBN and Weitkämper [23] investigates scaled Domain-size Aware RLR (DA-RLR) in which parameters are scaled with domain size. Both formalisms induce a dependency on relative frequency (Type I probability) of domain atoms, and we will see in Subsect. 3.1 below how those approaches are subsumed by our Type III framework.

Koponen [16] introduced *conditional probability logic (CPL)* as a language for expressing Type I probabilities, and defined *lifted Bayesian networks (LBN-CPL)* in which the conditional probability tables depend on such CPL formulas. Therefore, LBN-CPL can clearly be indentified as a Type III formalism.

However, unlike the statistical relational approaches mentioned above, LBN-CPL only encode discrete dependencies; rather than specifying an aggregation function, a node in a LBN-CPL is equipped with a finite set of probabilities triggered by CPL-formulas specifying relative frequency thresholds. For instance, one could specify that the probability of a person contracting an illness depends on whether more than 1% of the population are infected, but one cannot specify a continuous dependency on the percentage of people infected.

1.2   Queries Relating to Degrees of Belief vs Relative Frequency

Picking up the thread of disease modelling, we outline how probabilistic models and queries fit into the context of probability types.

Example 1. For a domain of people and a graph of connections between them, consider a model that represents how connected individuals infect each other. A Type II query would ask "what is the likelihood that a given individual is infected at time t (possibly given evidence)".

This is clearly an interesting problem on this domain. However, a main focus of epidemiologic modelling are adaptive interventions. A trigger is set (such as "1% of the population are infected") and then some intervention is performed (such as "schools are closed") as soon as that trigger is reached.

Such trigger conditions that refer to relative frequencies are very common. (see Bisset et al. [1, Table II] for further examples). This naturally also leads to Type III queries, in which the likelihood of a certain frequency event is adressed: "How likely is it that 1% of the population will be infected within the next four weeks?"

1.3   Transfer Learning and Extrapolation

We will see that systematically using Type I probabilities within an outer framework of lifted Bayesian networks also addresses a pertinent problem in parameter learning for statistical relational representations: discrepancies in domain size between training and test or deployment sets. Such a discrepancy could occur in different settings. On one hand, it could be a deliberate choice since learning can be considerably more expensive than inference (which is known to be NP-hard in general [3]). Therefore, sampling small subsets of a complete dataset and then training the parameters on the sampled subsets could be much more efficient than learning the parameters on the entire set. This is recommended by the authors of the MLN system Tuffy [4], for instance. On the other hand, the size of the test set might be variable or unknown at training time.

It is well-known, however, that in general the parameters that are optimal on a randomly sampled subset are not optimal on the larger set itself.

Example 2. Consider the typical example [18] of a relational logistic regression with two unary relations R and Q, and an underlying DAG $R(x) \longrightarrow Q(y)$. For any $b \in D$, the probability of $Q(b)$ is given by sigmoid($w*|a \in D|R(a)|$), where w is a parameter to be learned from data. Now consider a training set of domain size 1000 in which 100 elements each satisfy R and Q. Now assume that we sample a subset of 100 elements in which 10 elements each satisfy R and Q. The optimal parameter on that subset would be a w for which sigmoid($w * 10$) = 10/100, which turns out to be around -0.21. On the original set, however, the optimal parameter satisfies sigmoid($w*100$) = 100/1000, which is around -0.021. Indeed, if we would transfer the original parameter to the larger set, it would predict a probability for $Q(y)$ of less than 10^{-9}!

Jaeger and Schulte [10] showed that for certain projective families of distributions such a sampling approach provides a statistically consistent estimate of the optimal parameters on the larger set. However, projectivity is a very limiting condition; In fact, the projective fragments of common statistical relational frameworks that are isolated by Jaeger and Schulte [10] are essentially propositional and cannot model any interaction between an individual and the population-at-large. For example, to make the relational logistic regression above projective, the probability of $Q(a)$ must only depend on whether $R(a)$ is true, and not on any other elements of the domain. We will show that despite their larger expressivity Type III frameworks can be meaningfully approximated by projective distributions on large domains, allowing us to leverage the statistical consistency results for projective families of distributions.

2   Defining Functional Lifted Bayesian Networks

While LBN-CPL enable us to express Type III conditions, they are intrinsically categorical: They do not allow the probability of $R(\vec{a})$ to vary as a *continuous* function of the Type-I-probabilities of first-order statements. Therefore we introduce FLBN, which are designed to do just that.

By defining the semantics via Bayesian networks, we can use all of the inference methods developed for Bayesian networks. This includes conditioning on given data, and also lets us prescribe the interpretation of root predicates if desired.

Notation. We use the term *relational signature* to mean a (possibly multi-sorted) relational signature (without equality). In other words, a relational signature is a set of relation symbols R, each of which is annotated with a finite list of sorts. A (finite) *domain* for such a relational signature consists of a finite set for every sort. Then a *sort-appropriate tuple* $\vec{a}$ for a relation symbol R is a finite list of elements of the sets for those sorts given in the corresponding sort list of R. Similarly, a sort-appropriate tuple for a finite list of sort vaiables is a list of elements of those sort domains given in the corresponding list of sort variables. A σ-*structure* on a domain is determined by a function that maps each relation symbol $R \in \sigma$ to a set of sort-appropriate tuples. When a first-order formula with free variables $\vec{x}$ is *satisfied* by a sigma-structure with respect to a choice of sort-appropriate tuple for $\vec{x}$ is determined by the usual rules of first-order logic. Given a σ-structure $\mathfrak{X}$ on a domain D, if $\varphi(\vec{x})$ is a first-order formula with free variables $\vec{x}$, we use $\|\varphi(\vec{x})\|_{\vec{x}}$ to denote the fraction of sort-appropriate tuples from D for which $\varphi(\vec{x})$ holds. This is precisely the Type I probability or relative frequency of $\varphi(\vec{x})$ in $\mathfrak{X}$.

Now we can proceed to define functional lifted Bayesian networks, the core formalism investigated here.

Definition 1. *A* functional lifted Bayesian network (FLBN) *over a relational signature σ consists of the following:*

1. *A DAG G with node set σ.*
2. *For each $R \in \sigma$ a finite tuple $(\chi_{R,i}(\vec{x}, \vec{y}))_{i \leq n_R}$ of first-order par(R)-formulas, where $\vec{x}$ is a sort-appropriate tuple whose length is the arity of R.*
3. *For each $R \in \sigma$ a continuous function $f_R : [0, 1]^{n_R} \to [0, 1]$.*

The intuition behind FLBN is that for sort-appropriate ground terms $\vec{a}$, the probability of $R(\vec{a})$ is given by the value of f applied to the tuple $(\|\chi_{R,i}\|_{\vec{y}})$.

Definition 2. *Consider an FLBN $\mathfrak{G}$ and a finite domain D. Then the probability distribution induced by $\mathfrak{G}$ on the set of σ-structures with domain D is given by the following Bayesian network: The nodes are given by $R(\vec{a})$, where R is a relation symbol in σ and $\vec{a}$ is a tuple of elements of D of the right length and the right sorts for R. There is an edge between two nodes $R_1(\vec{b})$ and $R_2(\vec{a})$ if there is an edge between R_1 and R_2 in the DAG G underlying $\mathfrak{G}$. It remains to define a conditional probability table for every node $R(\vec{a})$: Given a choice of values for $P(\vec{b})$ for all $P \in$ par(R) and appropriate tuples $\vec{b}$ from D, the probability of $R(\vec{a})$ is set as $f_R((\|\chi_{R,i}(\vec{a}, \vec{y})\|_{\vec{y}})_{i \leq n_R})$.*

We also draw attention to the degenerate case where the formulas $\chi_{R,i}$ have no free variables beyond $\vec{x}$. Note that in this case the Type I probability can only take the values 1 and 0, depending on whether $\chi_{R,i}$ is true or false. Thus, the only relevant function values of f_R are those of tuples of 0 and 1. In this way, it is possible to specify discrete dependencies on first-order formulas within the model.

Such a situation will always occur at the root nodes R of the network. Since the parent vocabulary is empty, "true" and "false" are the only possible formulas and therefore specifying the function f_R for root nodes is equivalent to specifying a single probability $\mu(R)$.

A special case of degenerate FLBN are *quantifier-free lifted Bayesian networks*, which are those FLBN in which every formula $\chi_{R,i}$ is a quantifier-free formula all of whose variables are contained in the tuple $\vec{x}$. They correspond to Koponen's quantifier-free lifted Bayesian networks [16] or to Jaeger's relational Bayesian networks without aggregation functions [10]. As in the grounding of a quantifier-free lifted Bayesian network the entries of the conditional probability table for $R(\vec{a})$ only depend on $\chi_{R,i}(\vec{a})$, which is a Boolean combination of atomic formulas involving $\vec{a}$, the semantics given above can be simplified in this case by only including edges from $R_1(\vec{b})$ to $R_1(\vec{a})$ if every entry in $\vec{b}$ also occurs in $\vec{a}$.

3   Discussion and Applications

In this section we will discuss how FLBN can be used to express dependencies beyond the existing Type II formalisms, which learning algorithms are supported and how they enable transfer learning across domains of different sizes.

3.1   Expressivity of Functional Lifted Bayesian Networks

Continuous dependencies on relative frequencies are particularly important because they form the basis of the regression models from statistics. From this point of view, one could see FLBN as a general framework for relational regression models contingent on Type I probabilities as data. In particular, consider linear regression and logistic regression, two of the most commonly used regression functions.

A linear regression model with Type-I-probabilities as data corresponds to the following families of functions:

$$f(x_1, \ldots x_n) = \frac{w_1 x_1 + \cdots + w_n x_n}{n} + c \tag{1}$$

where w_1 to w_n and c are coefficients that have to be chosen in such a way that the image of $[0,1]$ under f is contained in $[0,1]$. These families of functions suffice e.g. to express the "arithmetic mean" combination function in the relational Bayesian networks of Jaeger [6].

A logistic regression model can also be implemented; it specialises to the DA-RLR of Weitkämper [23]. Its functions are of the form

$$f(x_1, \ldots x_n) = \text{sigmoid}(w_1 x_1 + \cdots + w_n x_n + c) \tag{2}$$

where "sigmoid" denotes the sigmoidal function

$$f(x) = \frac{\exp(x)}{\exp(x) + 1}$$

By recovering these existing frameworks and combination functions as special cases of FLBN, they are in scope of the rigorous analysis of asymptotic behaviour in Subsect. 3.3.

Beyond those formalisms, functional lifted Bayesian networks can model a variety of other aggregation functions. Consider for instance a unary random variable R that depends on how far the proportion of Qs is from an optimum value p. This can be modelled by a function

$$f(x) = \alpha e^{-\beta(x-p)^2} \tag{3}$$

where $\alpha < 1$ is the probability of R when the proportion of Q is optimal and β determines how quickly the probability of R drops as the proportion of Q deviates from p.

3.2   Learning Functional Lifted Bayesian Networks

We will briefly consider the methods and algorithms that are available for learning FLBN.

When posing the problem of parameter learning for FLBN, we first have to clarify which parameters we are learning in the first place. So rather than just considering functions $f : [0,1]^n \to [0,1]$ we consider a parametrised family of such functions, $f : K \times [0,1]^n \to [0,1]$), where K is the closure of a connected open subset of $\mathbb{R}_\infty^m$ from which the parameters are taken (Here $\mathbb{R}_\infty$ stands for $\mathbb{R} \cup \{-\infty, \infty\}$). For instance, in the cases of linear and logistic regression, Eqs. 1 and 2 define functions taking $m = n + 1$ parameters, $w_1, \ldots, w_n$ and c. In the logistic case, $K = \mathbb{R}^m$, while in the linear case, the parameter space is constrained by the function mapping to $[0,1]$. Jaeger [9] presents a general approach for learning the parameters of aggregation functions using gradient descent whenever the functions are differentiable in the parameters. Clearly both the linear and the logistic regression examples are differentiable in the parameters, and we believe this to be characteristic of a good choice of parameters. Functional gradient boosting has been successfully applied to the structure learning of relational logistic regression by Ramanan et al. [19], and it seems very promising to evaluate this approach with other classes of regression functions expressible by FLBN. We believe structure learning in FLBN to be a promising avenue for further research. Firstly, there is a large bank of work on regression learning in the statistical literature on which relational versions could conceivably be based, and secondly, the scale of the task can be reduced systematically by partly specifying families of functions (recovering e.g. structure learning in relational logistic regression or linear regression as special cases).

3.3   Asymptotic Analysis of the Extrapolation Behaviour

We present a full analysis of the asymptotic behaviour of FLBN. The setting is as follows: On every finite domain D, a functonal lifted Bayesian network $\mathfrak{G}$ over a signature σ induces a probability distribution $\mathbb{P}_{\mathfrak{G},D}$ on the set Ω_D of σ-structures with domain D. The first thing to note is that the names of the elements of D do not matter; all relevant information lies in the cardinalities of the sorts of D. Therefore we will assume from now on that our domain sorts consist of initial segments of the natural numbers, and we will write $\mathbb{P}_{\mathfrak{G},\vec{n}}$ for the probability distribution on the sorts with $\vec{n}$ elements. In an asymptotic analysis, we are interested in the limit of these probability distributions as the domain size of D tend to infinity (If σ is multi-sorted, we require the size of every sort to tend to infinity). A technical difficulty here is that strictly speaking, the probability distributions are defined on different sets $\Omega_{\vec{n}}$, so it is unclear on which measure space a limit would even be defined. To be precise, we consider the measure space Ω_∞ given by all σ-structures with domain sorts $\mathbb{N}$. It is endowed with the σ-algebra generated by *generating sets* of the following form: "Those σ-structures $\mathfrak{X}$ such that the σ-substructure of $\mathfrak{X}$ with domain $a_1, \ldots a_m$ is given by $\mathfrak{Y}$" for a tuple of domain elements $a_1, \ldots a_m$ and a σ-structure $\mathfrak{Y}$. This suffices to give a probability to any query about finite domains that we might possibly be interested in. On such a generating set, all but finitely many $\mathbb{P}_{\mathfrak{G},\vec{n}}$ are defined; indeed, $\mathbb{P}_{\mathfrak{G},\vec{n}}$ gives a probability to any structure with domain $a_1, \ldots, a_m$ as long as every a_i is bounded by the entry of $\vec{n}$ corresponding to its sort. Furthermore, the probability of the generating sets completely determine the probability distribution on the measure space itself. Thus, we can make the following definitions:

Definition 3. *A probability distribution* $\mathbb{P}_\infty$ *on* Ω_∞ *is the* asymptotic limit *of a lifted Bayesian network* $\mathfrak{G}$ *if for any sequence* D_k *of domains which is monotone and unbounded in the cardinality of every sort and any generating set* A *the limit of* $\mathbb{P}_{\mathfrak{G},\vec{n}}(A)$ *equals* $\mathbb{P}_\infty(A)$. *Two functional lifted Bayesian networks* $\mathfrak{G}$ *and* $\mathfrak{G}'$ *are* asymptotically equivalent *if they share the same asymptotic limit* $\mathbb{P}_\infty$.

The discussion above does not imply, of course, that a given functional lifted Bayesian network actually has an asymptotic limit in that sense. However, there is a class of lifted Bayesian networks where the asymptotic limit is clear: those that define *projective families of distributions* in the sense of Jaeger and Schulte [10,11].

Definition 4. *A family of probability distributions* $(\mathbb{P}_{\vec{n}})$ *on* $\Omega_{\vec{n}}$ *is* projective *if for every generating set* A *of* Ω_∞ *the sequence* $(\mathbb{P}_{\vec{n}}(A))$ *is constant whenever it is defined.*

Since clearly every constant sequence converges, every lifted Bayesian network inducing a projective family of distributions has an asymptotic limit. Furthermore, if two families of distributions are asymptotically equivalent and both projective, they must be equal. This leads us to the following observation:

Proposition 1. *If $\mathfrak{G}$ is a* quantifier-free lifted Bayesian network, *then $\mathfrak{G}$ induces a projective family of distributions. In particular, $\mathfrak{G}$ has an asymptotic limit.*

Proof. Let $A \in \Omega_\infty$ be a generating set and let $\mathfrak{Y}$ be the corresponding structure on $a_1, \ldots, a_m$ and let $(\mathbb{P}_{\vec{n}})$ be the sequence of probability distributions induced by $\mathfrak{G}$. Then we need to show that for any $\vec{n}$ for which $\mathbb{P}_{\vec{n}}(A)$ is defined this value is the same. So for any such $\vec{n}$ consider the Bayesian network $G_{\vec{n}}$ induced by $\mathfrak{G}$ on the domain $\vec{n}$. By the analysis at the end of Sect. 2, all incoming edges into $R(\vec{a})$ come from a source node $R'(\vec{b})$ where all entries in $\vec{b}$ also occur in $\vec{a}$. Therefore, the calculation of the unconditional probability of the event A does not involve any node with entries outside of $a_1, \ldots, a_m$. So let $G_{A,\vec{n}}$ be the complete Bayesian subnetwork on the nodes $R(\vec{a})$ for an $\vec{a} \in a_1, \ldots, a_m$. By the discussion above, $G_{A,\vec{n}}$ suffices to calculate the probability of A. $G_{A,\vec{n}}$ has the same underlying DAG for any $\vec{n}$. As the conditional probability tables themselves are also identical for any $\vec{n}$, so is $G_{A,\vec{n}}$ and thus the probability of A.

With these preparations out of the way, we can formulate our main result on the asymptotic behaviour of FLBN.

Theorem 1. *Let $\mathfrak{G}$ be an FLBN such that for all n-ary aggregation functions f_R, $f_R^{-1}\{0,1\} \subseteq \{0,1\}^n$. Then $\mathfrak{G}$ is asymptotically equivalent to a quantifier-free lifted Bayesian network $\mathfrak{G}'$.*

3.4   Proof of Theorem 1

For the proof we will use the classical model-theoretic notion of an *extension axiom* [15].

Definition 5. *A complete atomic diagram in n variables for a signature σ is a quantifier-free formula $\varphi(x_1, \ldots x_n)$ such that for every atom $R(\vec{x})$ of σ with $\vec{x} \subset \{x_1, \ldots x_n\}$ either $\varphi(x_1, \ldots x_n) \models R(\vec{x})$ or $\varphi(x_1, \ldots x_n) \models \neg R(\vec{x})$.*

An r+1-extension-axiom *for a language L is a sentence*

$$\forall_{x_1, \ldots, x_r} \left(\bigwedge_{1 \leq i < j \leq r} x_i \neq x_j \rightarrow \exists_{x_{r+1}} \varphi_\Phi(x_1, \ldots, x_{r+1}) \right)$$

where $r \in \mathbb{N}$,

$$\varphi_\Phi := \left(\bigwedge_{1 \leq i \leq r} x_i \neq x_{r+1} \wedge \bigwedge_{\varphi \in \Phi} \varphi \wedge \bigwedge_{\varphi \in \Delta_{r+1} \setminus \Phi} \neg\varphi \right)$$

and Φ is a subset of

$$\{R(\vec{x}) | R \in \mathcal{R}, \ x_{r+1} \in \vec{x} \ a \ tuple \ from \ \{x_1, \ldots, x_{r+1}\}\}.$$

Fact. As a first-order theory, the set of extension axioms has quantifier elimination [15, Theorem 3.13].

Lemma 1. *Let the distribution* $(\mathbb{P}_{\vec{n}})$ *of* $\{R_1, \ldots, R_l\}$ *be asymptotically equivalent to the reduct of a distribution on* $\{R_1, \ldots, R_l, P_1, \ldots, P_m\}$ *where* $P_1, \ldots, P_m$ *are independently distributed with probabilities* $p_1, \ldots, p_m$ *and* $R_1, \ldots, R_l$ *are defined to be Boolean combinations of* $P_1, \ldots, P_m$ *that are neither contradictory nor tautologies. Furthermore, assume that the following hold for* $(\mathbb{P}_{\vec{n}})$:

1. *For all* $0 \leq q < l$ *and all different tuples* $\vec{a}$ *and* $\vec{b}$, $R_{q+1}(\vec{a})$ *is conditionally* $\mathbb{P}_{\vec{n}}$-*independent of* $R_{q+1}(\vec{b})$ *given the interpretation of* $R_1, \ldots R_q$.
2. *The probabilities* $\mathbb{P}_{\vec{n}}(R_i(\vec{a}))$ *do not depend on* $\vec{a}$.

Then $\{R_1, \ldots, R_l\}$ *satisfies all extension axioms.*

Proof of Lemma 1. For the sake of simplifying notation, we will only consider the single-sorted case. For the multi-sorted case, the calculation is analogous. By induction on l.

$l = 1$: Choose an arbitrary $r + 1$ extension axiom χ corresponding to a set Φ. Let $\vec{a}$ be arbitrarily chosen. Then by asymptotic equivalence, for sufficiently large $\vec{n}$, $\mathbb{P}_n(\varphi_\Phi(\vec{a}, y)) > \delta$ for a $\delta > 0$. By conditions 1 and 2, we can conclude that

$$(\mathbb{P}_n)(\neg\chi) \leq n^r(1 - \delta)^{n-r}$$

which limits to 0 as n approaches ∞.

$l \to l+1$: Choose an arbitrary $r+1$ extension axiom χ corresponding to a set Φ. By the induction hypothesis, all extension axioms hold for $R_1, \ldots, R_l$. Therefore, for any natural number k, there are $(\mathbb{P}_n)$-almost-everywhere more than k witnesses of $\varphi_{\Phi \cap \{R_1, \ldots, R_l\}}(\vec{a}, y)$ for every $\vec{a}$, for arbitrary k. Just as in the base case above, we can now apply asymptotic equivalence and conditions 1 and 2 to conclude that conditioned on there being at least k witnesses $\varphi_{\Phi \cap \{R_1, \ldots, R_l\}}(\vec{a}, y)$,

$$(\mathbb{P}_n)(\neg\chi) \leq k^r(1 - \delta)^{k-r}$$

which limits to 0 as k approaches ∞. □

Lemma 2. *Let* ϕ *be a complete atomic diagram in r variables. Then the relative frequency of* ϕ *with respect to an independent distribution is almost surely convergent to a* $p_\phi \in (0, 1)$. *This also holds when conditioning on a complete atomic diagram in* $m < r$ *variables.*

Proof of Lemma 2. Induction on r.

In the case $r = 1$, $\phi(x)$ is asymptotically equivalent to a sequence of independent random variables, and the strong law of large numbers gives the result.

So assume true for r. Then $\phi(\vec{x}, y)$ is given by $\phi_r(\vec{x}) \wedge \phi'(\vec{x}, y)$, where $\phi'(\vec{x}, y)$ is a sequence of independent random variables and $\phi_r(\vec{x})$ is a complete atomic diagram in r variables. We can conclude with the strong law of large numbers again. □

Proof of Theorem 1. We perform a parallel induction by height on the following statements:

The family of distributions $(\mathbb{P}_{\vec{n},T})$ is asymptotically equivalent to a quantifier-free LBN, in which all aggregation formulas $\varphi_{R,i}$ for which neither $\forall_{\vec{x}}(\varphi_{R,i}(\vec{x}) \rightarrow R(\vec{x}))$ nor $\forall_{\vec{x}}\neg(\varphi_{R,i}(\vec{x}) \wedge R(\vec{x}))$ are true $(\mathbb{P}_{\vec{n},T})$-almost-everywhere, are annotated with a probability in $(0,1)$.

Every extension axiom for the language with those relations that have asymptotic probability $p \in (0,1)$ is valid $(\mathbb{P}_{\vec{n},T})$-almost-everywhere

Let T_h be the fragment of the FLBN of height not exceeding h.

Base step: An FLBN of height 0 is an independent distribution, showing the first statement. The extension axioms are well-known to hold almost everywhere in such an independent distribution [13,15].

Induction step: Since the extension axioms form a complete theory with quantifier elimination, every $\chi_{R,i}$ is $(\mathbb{P}_{\vec{n},T_h})$-almost-everywhere equivalent to a quantifier-free $\chi'_{R,i}$. Since we can replace those relations that are almost everywhere true for all or no elements by $\top$ and $\bot$ respectively, we can assume no such relations to occur in $\chi'_{R,i}$.

Let $\varphi_1,\ldots,\varphi_m$ list the complete atomic diagrams in the variables $x_1,\ldots x_r$ for the signature of T_h, where r is the arity of R. Then by Lemma 2 above, for every φ_j, the relative frequency of $\chi'_{R,i}$ given φ_j is almost surely convergent to a number $p_{\chi'_{R,i},\varphi_j}$, which lies in $(0,1)$ if and only if $\chi'_{R,i}$ is neither logically implied by nor contradictory to φ_j.

Therefore, the family of distributions $(\mathbb{P}_{\vec{n},T})$ is asymptotically equivalent to a quantifier-free LBN, which is obtained by listing $\varphi_1,\ldots,\varphi_m$ and annotating them with the probability $f_R(p_{\chi'_{R,1},\varphi_j},\ldots,p_{\chi'_{R,n},\varphi_j})$.

It remains to show that the additional condition on the annotated probabilities is satisfied.

So assume that $f_R(p_{\chi'_{R,1},\varphi_j},\ldots,p_{\chi'_{R,n},\varphi_j}) \in \{0,1\}$.

By the assumption on f_R, this implies $p_{\chi'_{R,i},\varphi_j} \in \{0,1\}$ for every i. Since each $\chi_{R,i}$ is $(\mathbb{P}_{\vec{n},T})$-almost-everywhere equivalent to $\chi'_{R,i}$, the relative frequency of $\chi_{R,i}$ given φ_j is exactly $p_{\chi'_{R,i},\varphi_j}$ almost everywhere. So almost everywhere the conditional probability of $R(\vec{x})$ given $\varphi_j(\vec{x})$ is 0 or 1. In other words, $\forall_{\vec{x}}(\varphi_j(\vec{x}) \rightarrow R(\vec{x}))$ or $\forall_{\vec{x}}\neg(\varphi_j(\vec{x}) \wedge R(\vec{x}))$ are true $(\mathbb{P}_{\vec{n},T})$-almost-everywhere.

Finally we show that the extension axioms are valid almost surely. We will verify the statement of Lemma 1. By asymptotic equivalence to a quantifier-free LBN and Proposition 1, we can find an independent distribution as required by Lemma 1. The two additional assumptions are clearly satisfied for any FLBN by the Markov condition for the underlying Bayesian network.   □

3.5 Examples

We illustrate the analysis of the last subsection with a sequence of simple examples that serve to highlight the main aspects. Consider the situation of Example 2: The signature σ has two unary relation symbols Q and R, and the underlying DAG G is $Q \longrightarrow R$. We model a relationship between $R(x)$ and those $y \in D$

that satisfy $Q(y)$. In Example 2, we have seen an RLR approach to this problem. Here, the asymptotic behaviour is well-known: as domain size increases, the expected number of $a \in D$ that satisfy $Q(a)$ also does. By the law of large numbers, this increase is almost surely linear with domain size. Therefore the probability of $R(y)$ will limit to 0 if and only if $w < 0$, and limit to 1 if and only if $w > 0$. A similar analysis holds if we consider a noisy-or combination, or the model of a probabilistic logic program.

Example 3. Assume that for every $y \in D$ for which $Q(y)$ holds there is an independent chance $p_1 \in [0, 1]$ of $R(x)$, and that for every $y \in D$ for which $Q(y)$ does not hold there is an independent chance $p_1 \in [0, 1]$ of $R(x)$. Further assume that $\mu(Q) \in (0, 1)$. Then as domain size increases, there will almost surely be at least one $y \in D$ that causes $R(x)$, leading to $R(x)$ being true almost surely—unless two of p_1, p_2 and $\mu(Q)$ are 0. So outside of these boundary cases, p_1, p_2 and $\mu(Q)$ have no influence on the asymptotic probability of $R(x)$ (which is always 1). In the representation of the distribution semantics, there would be additional binary predicates $P_1(x, y)$ and $P_2(x, y)$ with $\mu(P_1) := p_1$ and $\mu(P_2) := p_2$. the definition of $R(x)$ would be $\exists_y(Q(y) \wedge P_1(x, y)) \vee \exists_y(\neg Q(y) \wedge P_2(x, y))$. Asymptotically, when neither of the root probabilities are zero, both existential clauses in that definition will evaluate to "true".

Now consider modelling such a dependency with an FLBN.

Example 4. Let $\mathfrak{G}$ be an FLBN on G with a formula $Q(y)$ and a function $f_R : [0, 1] \rightarrow [0, 1]$. Assume further that Q is annotated with a probability $\mu(Q) \in [0, 1]$. Then by the law of large numbers, $\|Q(y)\|_y$ converges to $\mu(Q)$ almost surely as domain size increases. Since f is continuous, this implies that $f(\|Q(y)\|_y)$ converges to $f(\mu(Q))$ almost surely. So the asymptotically equivalent quantifier-free network will have "true" as its formula for R and then $f(\mu(Q))$ as $\mu(R(\vec{x})|\text{true})$.

3.6   Transfer Learning Across Domain Sizes

As projective families of distributions, quantifier-free lifted Bayesian networks have very desirable properties for learning across domain sizes. More precisely, for the family of distributions induced by any quantifier-free Bayesian network and any structure $\mathfrak{X}$ with $m < n$ elements, $\mathbb{P}_n(\mathfrak{X}) = \mathbb{P}_m(\mathfrak{X})$.

Consider a parametric family of distributions G_θ which are asymptotically equivalent to a parametric projective family of distributions G'_θ. Consider the problem of learning the parameters from interpretations on a structure $\mathfrak{X}$ of large domain size n. Then we could proceed as follows: Sample substructures of domain size $m < n$, where m is larger than the highest arity in σ and the arity of the queries we are typically interested in. Find the parameters of G'_θ that maximise the sum of the log-likelihoods of the samples of size m. Now consider G_θ. By the asymptotic convergence results, if n is sufficiently large, these parameters maximise the likelihood of obtaining the substructures of size m sampled from $\mathfrak{X}$ using G_θ, including realisations of the queries we might be interested in.

For this approach to work, the parametric families G'_θ must actually depend on the parameters, and do so in a regular way; for the learning algorithms discussed above that means that they should be differentiable in the parameters.

Let us evaluate these criteria for the asymptotic approximations in Examples 2–4: In the case of Example 2, G'_θ does not depend on w beyond its sign. Furthermore, there is a discontinuity at $w = 0$. The asymptotic probability of the noisy-or model in Example 3 does not depend at all on p_i as long as $p_i \neq 0$.

In the functional lifted Bayesian network model of Example 4, the parametric family is defined by $f_\theta(\mu_Q)$. If f is linear or logistic, for instance, then $f_\theta(\mu_Q)$ is differentiable in the parameters for any fixed $\mu_Q \in (0, 1)$. Note, that while $f(\mu_Q)$ will vary with every parameter individually, it will take its maximum-likelihood value (which happens to coincide with the true frequency of $R(x)$ in the domain) on an infinite subspace of tuples of parameters. This is not unique to the projective approximation, however, but is a well-known phenomenon when learning the parameters for a relational logistic regression from a single interpretation [12,18]. This can be overcome by learning from several domains, where Q has different frequencies.

In this way, Type III formalisms allow us to leverage the power of projective families of distributions for transfer learning while retaining much more expressive modelling capabilities. While adding either functional or discrete dependencies on the Type I probabilities present in a domain allow us to express rich connections between different domain elements, quantifier-free lifted Bayesian networks themselves do not allow any dependence on the global structure of the model. This is also quite typical of projective families of distributions that can be expressed in statistical relational AI; for instance, any projective LBN-CPL is expressible by a quantifier-free one (as two asymptotically equivalent projective families of distributions are completely equivalent), and every projective probabilistic logic program is determinate [22].

We would like to end this section by remarking how our asymptotic results complement those of Jaeger [7]. There, Jaeger shows that the probability distributions of relational Bayesian networks with *exponentially convergent* combination functions lead to asymptotically convergent probability distributions. However, the exponentially convergent combination are essentially those that given a certain type of input sequence increasing in length converge to a fixed value, regardless of the precise sequence received. The classical combination functions 'noisy-or' and 'maximum' are paradigmal for this behaviour. The central idea of our work here is precisely that the functions converge to a value that depends explicitly on the means of the sequences received, and therefore they are clearly distinguished in their behaviour from Jaeger's exponentially convergent combination functions.

4   Conclusion

FLBN introduce relative frequencies into statistical relational artificial intelligence, making Halpern Type III probabilities available to this field. By supporting discrete and continuous dependencies on relative frequencies, they can express the complex relationships that are required to model application domains such as infectious disease dynamics. FLBN also advance statistical relational learning from large interpretations by supporting learning from randomly sampled subdomains. This is underpinned by a rigorous analysis of their asymptotic behaviour. Furthermore, the transparent relationship of the semantics to Bayesian networks allows the application of well-developed learning and inference approaches.

Acknowledgements. This contribution was supported by LMUexcellent, funded by the Federal Ministry of Education and Research (BMBF) and the Free State of Bavaria under the Excellence Strategy of the Federal Government and the Länder. We would also like to thank Vera Koponen for several insightful conversations, and François Bry and Kailin Sun for their very helpful comments on the manuscript.

References

1. Bisset, K.R., Chen, J., Deodhar, S., Feng, X., Ma, Y., Marathe, M.V.: Indemics: an interactive high-performance computing framework for data-intensive epidemic modeling. ACM Trans. Model. Comput. Simul. **24**(1), 4:1–4:32 (2014). https://doi.org/10.1145/2501602
2. Carnap, R.: Logical Foundations of Probability. University of Chicago Press, Chicago (1950)
3. Dalvi, N.N., Suciu, D.: The dichotomy of probabilistic inference for unions of conjunctive queries. J. ACM **59**(6), 30:1–30:87 (2012). https://doi.org/10.1145/2395116.2395119
4. Doan, A., Niu, F., Ré, C., Shavlik, J., Zhang, C.: User manual of Tuffy 0.3. Stanford University (2011). http://i.stanford.edu/hazy/tuffy/doc/tuffy-manual.pdf
5. Halpern, J.Y.: An analysis of first-order logics of probability. Artif. Intell. **46**(3), 311–350 (1990). https://doi.org/10.1016/0004-3702(90)90019-V
6. Jaeger, M.: Relational Bayesian networks. In: Geiger, D., Shenoy, P.P. (eds.) UAI 1997: Proceedings of the Thirteenth Conference on Uncertainty in Artificial Intelligence, Brown University, Providence, Rhode Island, USA, 1–3 August 1997, pp. 266–273. Morgan Kaufmann (1997)
7. Jaeger, M.: Convergence results for relational Bayesian networks. In: Thirteenth Annual IEEE Symposium on Logic in Computer Science, Indianapolis, Indiana, USA, 21–24 June 1998, pp. 44–55. IEEE Computer Society (1998). https://doi.org/10.1109/LICS.1998.705642
8. Jaeger, M.: Relational Bayesian networks: a survey. Electron. Trans. Artif. Intell. **6**, 1–21 (2002)
9. Jaeger, M.: Parameter learning for relational Bayesian networks. In: Ghahramani, Z. (ed.) Machine Learning, Proceedings of the Twenty-Fourth International Conference (ICML 2007), Corvallis, Oregon, USA, 20–24 June 2007. ACM International Conference Proceeding Series, vol. 227, pp. 369–376. ACM (2007). https://doi.org/10.1145/1273496.1273543
10. Jaeger, M., Schulte, O.: Inference, learning, and population size: projectivity for SRL models. In: Eighth International Workshop on Statistical Relational AI (StarAI) (2018). https://arxiv.org/abs/1807.00564

11. Jaeger, M., Schulte, O.: A complete characterization of projectivity for statistical relational models. In: Bessiere, C. (ed.) Proceedings of the Twenty-Ninth International Joint Conference on Artificial Intelligence, IJCAI 2020, pp. 4283–4290. ijcai.org (2020). https://doi.org/10.24963/ijcai.2020/591

12. Kazemi, S.M., Buchman, D., Kersting, K., Natarajan, S., Poole, D.: Relational logistic regression. In: Baral, C., Giacomo, G.D., Eiter, T. (eds.) Principles of Knowledge Representation and Reasoning: Proceedings of the Fourteenth International Conference, KR 2014, Vienna, Austria, 20–24 July 2014. AAAI Press (2014)

13. Keisler, H.J., Lotfallah, W.B.: Almost everywhere elimination of probability quantifiers. J. Symb. Log. **74**(4), 1121–1142 (2009). https://doi.org/10.2178/jsl/1254748683

14. Kern-Isberner, G., Thimm, M.: Novel semantical approaches to relational probabilistic conditionals. In: Lin, F., Sattler, U., Truszczynski, M. (eds.) Principles of Knowledge Representation and Reasoning: Proceedings of the Twelfth International Conference, KR 2010, Toronto, Ontario, Canada, 9–13 May 2010. AAAI Press (2010)

15. Kolaitis, P.G., Vardi, M.Y.: Infinitary logics and 0–1 laws. Inf. Comput. **98**(2), 258–294 (1992). https://doi.org/10.1016/0890-5401(92)90021-7

16. Koponen, V.: Conditional probability logic, lifted Bayesian networks, and almost sure quantifier elimination. Theor. Comput. Sci. **848**, 1–27 (2020). https://doi.org/10.1016/j.tcs.2020.08.006

17. Muggleton, S., Chen, J.: A behavioral comparison of some probabilistic logic models. In: Raedt, L.D., Frasconi, P., Kersting, K., Muggleton, S. (eds.) Probabilistic Inductive Logic Programming - Theory and Applications. LNCS, vol. 4911, pp. 305–324. Springer, Heidelberg (2008). https://doi.org/10.1007/978-3-540-78652-8_12

18. Poole, D., Buchman, D., Kazemi, S.M., Kersting, K., Natarajan, S.: Population size extrapolation in relational probabilistic modelling. In: Straccia, U., Calì, A. (eds.) SUM 2014. LNCS, vol. 8720, pp. 292–305. Springer, Cham (2014). https://doi.org/10.1007/978-3-319-11508-5_25

19. Ramanan, N., et al.: Structure learning for relational logistic regression: an ensemble approach. In: Thielscher, M., Toni, F., Wolter, F. (eds.) Principles of Knowledge Representation and Reasoning: Proceedings of the Sixteenth International Conference, KR 2018, Tempe, Arizona, 30 October–2 November 2018, pp. 661–662. AAAI Press (2018)

20. Schulte, O.: Challenge paper: marginal probabilities for instances and classes (2012). https://www2.cs.sfu.ca/~oschulte/files/pubs/srl2012.pdf. Presented at the ICML-SRL Workshop on Statistical Relational Learning

21. Schulte, O., Khosravi, H., Kirkpatrick, A.E., Gao, T., Zhu, Y.: Modelling relational statistics with bayes nets. Mach. Learn. **94**(1), 105–125 (2014). https://doi.org/10.1007/s10994-013-5362-7

22. Weitkämper, F.: An asymptotic analysis of probabilistic logic programming, with implications for expressing projective families of distributions. Theory Pract. Log. Program. **21**(6), 802–817 (2021). https://doi.org/10.1017/S1471068421000314

23. Weitkämper, F.: Scaling the weight parameters in Markov logic networks and relational logistic regression models. CoRR abs/2103.15140 (2021). https://arxiv.org/abs/2103.15140

Author Index

S. H. Muggleton and A. Tamaddoni-Nezhad (Eds.): ILP 2022, LNAI 13779, p. 157, 2024.
https://doi.org/10.1007/978-3-031-55630-2

Printed in the United States
by Baker & Taylor Publisher Services